NATHAN HALE

NATHAN
HALE

The Life and Death of
America's First Spy

M. WILLIAM
PHELPS

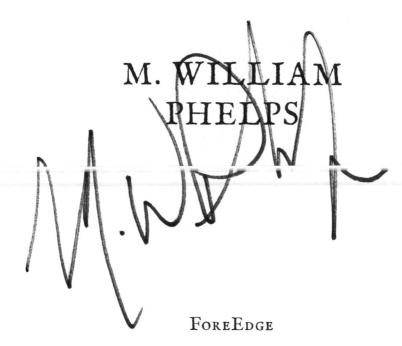

Fo...Edge

ForeEdge
An imprint of University Press of New England
www.upne.com
© 2008 M. William Phelps
Foreword © 2008 Beverly Lucas
First ForeEdge edition 2014
All rights reserved
Manufactured in the United States of America

Paperback ISBN: 978-1-61168-767-5
Ebook ISBN: 978-1-61168-768-2

For permission to reproduce any of the material in this book, contact
Permissions, University Press of New England, One Court Street,
Suite 250, Lebanon NH 03766; or visit www.upne.com

This book was originally published in a cloth edition in 2008 by
Thomas Dunne Books, an imprint of St. Martin's Press.

Library of Congress Control Number: 2014951440

5 4 3 2 1

For Gregg Olsen:
Friend, Mentor, Colleague

CONTENTS

═══════════════════

FOREWORD

ᴛODAY ɴATHAN HALE IS recognized as Connecticut's state hero, known to most for his rumored last words, "I only regret that I have but one life to lose for my country." Although questions and doubts may be raised about his significance in American history, Nathan will always represent the values exemplified by the words *patriotism, loyalty,* and *self-sacrifice.* And these values were not only his, but his family's, his neighbors', and his fellow colonists'.

Nathan's nephew David Hale Jr., cofounder of what is today's *Wall Street Journal,* once wrote: "There is nothing romantic about the life of Nathan Hale. . . . He was a simple-hearted, well-educated, intelligent country youth, always doing what he thought right; and that in those days was nothing singular."

Nathan was considered a hero by many of his fellow patriots and by many authors who wrote about him for history books and novels. In the early twentieth century, George Dudley Seymour was so moved by Nathan's heroism, he had statues made of him, convinced the post office to issue a stamp in his honor, and restored Nathan's family homestead, which is now a museum. By the 1960s, Nathan's significance and authenticity as a hero had been thrown into doubt. He was no longer included in some histories, and the bestselling *Don't Know Much About History* (1990) states that Hale's last words are "most likely an invention that has become part of the Revolution mythology."

Though his mission failed, Nathan Hale's significance never hinged on whether he was an effective spy. As President Dwight Eisenhower explained at the time of the bicentennial of Hale's birth, here was "a supreme example of the willingness of an individual to risk death and sacrifice himself for the common good." With this sacrifice, Nathan Hale became a hero and, as such, represented the colony of Connecticut's significant contribution to the war for independence; he was willing to sacrifice himself for the beliefs that not only he held dear, but that his family, friends, neighbors, and fellow colonists cherished. For this he is a hero and represents others who fought for their beliefs and sacrificed in their own ways for America's independence.

For this reason, Nathan Hale's story should continue to be told.

—BEVERLY LUCAS, CURATOR
Connecticut Landmarks
Hale Homestead Museum

Now, as for me, behold me in your hand!

Do to me according to that which is good—yea,
according to that which is right—in your eyes!

Only ye surely know that, if ye are about to put
me to death, then ye are surely putting innocent
blood upon yourselves. . . .

—JEREMIAH 26: 14–15

NATHAN HALE

PROLOGUE

THUNDER OF HEAVEN

From the western front of the green facing Yale College's Connecticut Hall, a three-story, redbrick building, one could look to the east and manage a squinted glimpse of Long Island Sound and, just over the horizon, the magnificent Atlantic Ocean. Settled in 1638 as Red Mount, New Haven was a thriving colony, steeped in maritime aesthetics and deepseated Christian values, established by its founders on the principles of community, education, economics, and, of course, religion. It was here, in the thick of the city near Chapel Street, that two teenage classmates left the Yale campus on a summer day in 1772 en route to New Haven harbor.[1]

To passersby, the students blended into the milieu of the city as if they had lived in New Haven all their lives. But neither scholar had grown up in town. One of the boys, Nathan Hale, the son of an affluent deacon and farmer, lived sixty miles north in the hills of Connecticut. Having spent the past three years studying at Yale, Nathan held an idealistic view of the city; its tradition of political discourse and fidelity to Christianity fell right into what he—indeed, nearly all colonists—had been raised to believe: that in God all things were possible.[2]

I

Still, beyond a visit to the house of the school's resident physcian, Dr. Eneas Munson, the local tavern, or a shopkeeper nearby, Nathan rarely ventured beyond the surrounding neighborhood, keeping the majority of his socializing confined to campus.[3]

Nathan and his classmate Isaac Gridley were headed to New Haven harbor, a bustling seaport, situated along the jagged coastline between Stamford and Saybrook. There, merchants sold colonial goods—mainly sugar, pewter, nails, timber, fishing gear, compasses, sextants—and coopers and shiphands loitered about the docks in search of work, while businessmen kept tabs on their coastal offices and warehouses. The first Puritans to settle in New Haven 150 years earlier felt there was great value in such a sprawling seaside community and hoped to monopolize what they viewed as a prominent commercial port on the East Coast. The problem became, however, that New York was but a half day's sail south, Boston a day's sail north. Both were larger cities, with much more to offer seafaring merchants and importers. Yet even though their immediate plan for financial success failed, the harbor prospered and sustained a growing economy over the years, providing a viable tract of land and a tenable backdrop for the "neatly painted frame houses of many of the town's influencial families" dotted about the ribboned countryside overlooking the harbor.[4]

It had turned cloudy by the time seventeen-year-old Nathan and his fifteen-year-old classmate reached the shoreline. Undeterred by the gray skies above, they pushed a sloop out into the water and, with their backs to the wind, jumped aboard for what they assumed was going to be an afternoon of leisurely sailing.[5]

But soon after their voyage began, the weather turned volatile and violent. Waves crashed up over the bow of the small sloop as Gridley, certainly worried they wouldn't make it back to shore without being swallowed up by the choppy waters, looked to Nathan for guidance and comfort.

With the confidence he had acquired while becoming one of Yale's top thirteen scholars, Nathan said, "I will never be drowned."[6]

To Gridley, Nathan appeared *too* sure of himself, as if he knew—and firmly believed—that dying in the midst of a storm at sea was not in God's plan for him. Nathan's words did little to suppress Gridley's trepidation; it thundered and lightning cracked in flashing bolts around them.

Maneuvering the vessel back to shore, Nathan explained why he was so certain they would make it in safely. He pointed to a blemish on his neck, beckoning Gridley to have a closer look.

A childhood friend of Nathan's, Asher Wright, who would become his close ally and camp attendant during the Revolutionary War, later described Nathan's pockmark as "a large hair mole on his neck." A mole on one's neck was a sign of bad luck. If one had a hair growing from that mole, it further indicated that death by hanging was in your future.[7] Reflecting back on his life with Nathan, Wright added, "In his boyhood, his playmates sometimes twitted him about [the mole], telling him he would be hanged."[8]

Apparently, Nathan Hale believed it to some extent—because as he and Gridley, surely drenched from the heavy rains, pulled the boat ashore, Nathan spoke of it again. He pointed to the slightly elevated mole on his neck and again said he knew he wasn't going to drown. Gridley wanted to know how his friend could be so certain.

"I am to be hung," Nathan lamented.[9]

Chapter 1

The Righteous and Patriotic Man

THE FIERY COLORS OF leaves burst around New England during the fall of 1769. Fifteen-year-old Enoch and fourteen-year-old Nathan straddled their horses and began what was a sixty-mile journey to New Haven. They had been lectured by their father, Richard Hale, regarding the vices of living in a city far from his supervision. Richard probably told the boys to mind their studies and seek guidance in the word of God while away from home. For Nathan and Enoch, it was the first time they had left home alone, beyond a brief visit to their uncle Strong's in Salmon Brook, or a trip into Hartford, Norwich, or Windham for supplies with their father.

Richard Hale had little to worry about. He had raised well-behaved, mindful, disciplined children. Richard had lofty religious morals and expected no less from members of his family. He could trust that when confronted with the pressures of college life, Nathan and Enoch would make the right choices. The Hale children were said to have been brought up under "the fear of God," drilled by their father on the particulars of right and wrong. In colonial Connecticut, "church and state were not separate." Attending church was not a right—but a requirement of the law. Richard understood that God was the source of *all* life. Without putting the Lord's word first, nothing else was possible; and whatever happened in life, he told the children many times, was God's plan. Never question His Divine Word.

Richard had instilled these ideals in his children at every opportunity. During the Sabbath, for example, the Hales would not have had a fire burning in keeping with Richard's rule of respecting the sacred day (in winter months, a fire would be "banked," the massive granite cooking stone kept warm, but cooking was not allowed on Sundays). As a child, Nathan liked to play the board game morris, which is similar to checkers, with his brothers, but Richard, "thinking the diversion might lead to evil," disallowed it. Once, while reading, Richard fell asleep with a candle burning in his hand. Nathan and his siblings, who had waited for their father to doze off, huddled like campers and played the game in the candlelight around the chair.[1]

Both Enoch and Nathan were prepared for Yale by Dr. Joseph Huntington, who held classes at his home, two miles from the Hale family farm. Huntington was not only a friend and neighbor of Richard Hale's, but a well-respected minister and renowned scholar in the small community of Coventry. "The two boys were fortunate in their preceptor," Hale family expert George Dudley Seymour said of Huntington, "urbanity in an 'Age of Homespun,' a classic scholar."[2]

Nathan became an exceptional student and enjoyed being tutored. His manners were honed by Huntington, who taught Nathan how to truly study the Gospels and also encouraged him to read biographies of Cyrus the Great and Philip of Macedon. Only thirty-three years of age when he tutored Nathan, Huntington, "a man of solid learning and exemplary piety," wrote historian Robert Waln Jr., had received a "liberal education" from a line of distinguished relatives and siblings. His brother Samuel would sign the Declaration of Independence in the coming years and serve in the Continental Congress. Licensed as a reverend on June 20, 1763, Huntington took over the Congregational Church near downtown Coventry a short while later.[3]

"[Reverend Huntington] found his parish," Franklin Bowditch Dexter wrote in 1896, "on his settlement, in a somewhat disorganized state; and was able to unite the people to an unexpected degree, though the entire period of his ministry was one of spiritual declension."[4]

When Huntington's first wife died at twenty-nine after just a brief illness, he married into the Hale family, taking the hand of Elizabeth, a relative of Richard's from Glastonbury. As far as Richard Hale could discern, he could not have found a better scholar to educate his children and prepare them for college. People were attached to Huntington, and Nathan and Enoch, studying with him day in and day out, cared deeply for the man and carried on in his image.[5]

The Yale College Nathan and Enoch came upon after their forty-eight-hour ride was a stunning sight for two kids accustomed to the confines of a farming village such as Coventry. The boys' conception of a large body of water, for instance, had, until then, been Lake Wangumbaug, a 373-acre basin—known as the Great Pond—north of the Hale farm near the center of town. In contrast, the Yale campus was a short walk from the Atlantic Ocean, where the New Haven common housed two Congregational churches alongside one Episcopal, which surely set the tone for Yale's Christian curriculum.

Richard had secured bonds for each of his sons to cover the college's quarterly bills. Tuition was twelve shillings per year for each boy, an amount Richard couldn't come up with immediately in cash, but could certainly afford, based on the earnings of his farm. Enoch and Nathan already had a broad knowledge of Cicero, Virgil, and other classical writers, as well as a complete understanding of the New Testament in Greek. Among the tutors Nathan and Enoch could look forward to studying under were John Trumbull, the painter and son of future Connecticut governor Jonathan Trumbull Sr.; John Davenport, whose father was one of the founders of New Haven; Timothy Dwight, who would become Yale's president; and Dr. Nathan Strong, a Hale relative from their mother's side.[6]

Yale was a fairly modernized school, structured after—albeit in competition with—Harvard. There was room to board sixty students, most of whom had enrolled to study theology, inside thirty-two bedchambers. Connecticut Hall, where Nathan and Enoch would spend the better part of the next four years, was a three-floored building on top of a large, spacious cellar. Several of the floors inside the structure were "devoted almost exclusively to dormitory space," with sixty-two rooms designated for study.[7]

After finding a stable master near campus to put up their horses for the night and return them to Coventry the following day, Nathan and Enoch settled into their rooms inside Connecticut Hall.

Any notion the boys might have had of an easier life at Yale was soon removed. Much to their dismay, the prayer bell rang at 4:30 A.M. the first morning (during winter months, students were afforded an extra hour's sleep). The bell's tolling before sunrise reminded students that, before anything else, scholars were expected to greet the day by dropping to their knees and connecting with God. After a brief time of private prayer, it was off to the chapel next door for daily service. Then they marched in rows into the courtyard and down to the College Commons for breakfast. Many students routinely complained the food there was overpriced and bland.[8]

A day's studies consisted of courses in Greek, Latin, and, occasionally, Hebrew. "Some attention was given to logic and rhetoric," Charles Swain Hall wrote in his biography of Benjamin Tallmadge, one of Nathan and Enoch's close friends and classmates, "but many of the subjects were oriented to provide a preliminary training for the ministry."

That goal inspired Enoch to endure the often strict guidelines of the school's religious policies and class structure. Nathan, however, was thinking of tutoring as a profession, but had left the door open to anything—that is, except the ministry. In a world of males bred to be involved in church leadership, his turning his back on religion as a vocation gave him a reputation, whether he wanted it or not. Yale College was organized under a rigid rule of discipline, Henry Sheldon wrote in his study of colonial student life and customs, "particularly the relation between professor and student, [which] likewise made for some strong form of association. . . . Like its English prototype, the colonial college was pervaded with a strong ecclesiastical flavour."

On Mondays, students were expected to summarize sermons from Sunday. Tutors and Yale's president, Naphtali Daggett, dressed in customary gownlike black robes and powder-white wigs. The wigs were not at all that shocking to Nathan or Enoch. Back home, Richard would don his familiar gray hairpiece on special occasions.[9]

For the next four years, aside from a few brief visits back home to Coventry, Yale would be Nathan's home. Unbeknownst to him, he would never return to Coventry to live again, but would leave Yale a distinguished scholar. Before then, temptations of mischief during his formative years of college life would ultimately get the best of him.

Two years after settling in Coventry in 1744, twenty-nine-year-old Richard Hale married seventeen-year-old Elizabeth Strong. If Richard had wanted to marry into a respected, wealthy, and established family, the Strongs were certainly one of the more affluent. Elizabeth's father, Captain Joseph Strong, had been a justice of the peace, leading townsman and treasurer, and represented Coventry in Connecticut's General Assembly for sixty-five sessions. He displayed a lively outlook even at an advanced age, chairing town meetings well into his nineties.[10]

Richard's great-grandfather, Robert, had set sail with family members from Kent, England, to America during the early 1600s, shortly after the *Mayflower* landed. Robert Hale settled in Charlestown, Massachusetts. Both he and his wife, née Joanna Cutler, were "among the original members of the First Church of Boston." Robert held many jobs throughout his life, which his descendants, as they began to journey into Connecticut and northern New England, carried on through generations: blacksmith, deacon, carpenter, and surveyor of the many new "plantations" being bought up throughout the Northeast.[11]

The earliest Hale most often highlighted by his contemporaries in literature, although often misrepresented, was Richard's grandfather, who established his family in Beverly, Massachusetts. The Reverend John Hale, at fifty-four, served as a chaplain, "despite the protests of his congregation," during an "ill-fated New England expedition into Canada in 1690," during which time he was captured in a roundup of suspected rabble-rousers one day and thrown in prison. Released two years later, John returned to Salem,

Massachusetts, to find the town embroiled in a witchhunt. John was in attendance for many of the trials, "participated in the religious exercises," and sanctioned—at least during the early days—many of the executions. At first, John believed he was doing the work of God and his community. But as the trials continued, it seemed some women in town were pulling people they didn't favor out of their homes and accusing them of witchcraft. The Reverend John's sentiment changed for good when his wife, Sarah Noyes, was herself dragged in and charged as a witch. The accusations in town were unrelenting, and although her case never came to trial, Sarah's reputation took an enormous blow.

Before his death on May 15, 1700, the Harvard-educated reverend wrote a book about his Salem witch-trial experiences, *A Modest Inquiry into the Nature of Witchcraft*, published a year after his death. In it, he noted, "The object sought unto is the devil, or another God . . . some of the Heathen did not [s]eek to the devil, as a devil, that is, as a malicious, wicked, and unclean spirit; but as to their God whom they thought ought to be worshipped by them." Reading John's various papers on the Salem witch trials, one gets a sense that he was speaking from a rather progressive standpoint for the time. He believed the "possessed" victim was influenced by the devil, not that the witch had impregnated these specters in the victim by casting spells.

The subject of Sarah's part in witchcraft was a "terrifying but fascinating topic in Deacon [Richard] Hale's own household," Hale family expert George Dudley Seymour wrote in his 1933 history of Nathan Hale and Major John Palsgrave Wyllys. In Seymour's opinion, Nathan and his siblings "thought it something of a distinction to have had a great-grandmother accused of being a witch." Today's historians, with a clearer understanding of the Hale household, would disagree with Seymour, however. "I don't think the Hale family would have wanted it discussed," Linda Pagliuco later noted. "They were *very* religious—and many of those who believed in witches were religious. I think they would not have wanted to discuss Sarah *outside* of the family, and doubt that they even knew the facts [of her case] as they are known today."[12]

Nathan's eldest sister was Elizabeth Rose Taylor. Her second husband,

John, had studied to become a minister, but was never able to find a parish that would accept him. Thus, John opened a tavern in downtown Coventry. Elizabeth ended up spending a majority of her time at the tavern and may have worked as a barmaid. "Richard Hale is said to have hated it," Pagliuco added. "Thus, if Richard was *that* bothered by his daughter working in a *tavern*, they probably weren't going to brag about having a great-grandmother . . . accused of being a witch."[13]

A branch of the Hale family tree was closely connected to the founding of Yale. Sarah Noyes's brother, the Reverend James Noyes, was one of Yale's original trustees, along with his brother Moses, both Harvard men who were "influential in the founding of Yale College."[14]

Nathan's mother, Elizabeth, was a fifth-generation Strong, born in Coventry in 1727. Many viewed Elizabeth as a woman of "high moral worth, with strong Puritan faith and devoted to the religious culture of her children." She was by all accounts beautiful and had an "uncommon strength of character." For Nathan and the other Hale boys to head off to Yale would be no surprise to Elizabeth, who had been born into a family with over a dozen Yale graduates. When Nathan grew up in Coventry, there would have been no shortage of Strongs around to instill in the boy the Christian moral values expected of him as he grew into manhood. The Reverend Nathan Strong, Elizabeth's second cousin, presided over the meetinghouse in Coventry for five decades as first minister. From his early sermons, a respect for the colonies and the Puritan way of life emerges. Nathan Strong, a man of "solid judgment" and "acute penetration of mind," was widely viewed as an innovator within the growing structure of local churches joining together pre-Revolution. He often "quiet[ed] disturbances in sister churches" before they became public nuisances. As a child, Nathan listened as the minister "espoused the cause of his country, in the War of the Revolution." Even before war broke out, the reverend spoke harshly of the king's mandates, not to mention the attempts to put a stranglehold on colonial businesses with taxes. He let his congregation know God's will included standing up and speaking openly about what they believed.[15]

The Strongs and Hales were joined in marriage at the turn of the eighteenth century. The Strong family name carried authority throughout New

England. Like the Hales, their ancestors had landed on colonial soil after sailing from Kent, England, and were among the first Puritans to incorporate outer Boston. Soon after crossing the Atlantic in 1630 aboard the *Mary-John,* John Strong settled south of Boston and helped found the town of Dorchester. From there, the family spread throughout Connecticut and Massachusetts. In 1659, John helped to establish Northampton, a neighboring town in the mountains of western Massachusetts that Enoch would one day call home. Elizabeth's brother Elnathan Strong settled in Coventry some years later, while Joseph established his family northwest in Salmon Brook.[16]

As soon as they were married, Richard and Elizabeth Hale got busy right away building what would be a sizable home on an initial 240 acres of fertile land in South Coventry, a few miles from where Elizabeth had been born. Within a few years, Elizabeth gave birth to the first of what would be a total of nine sons and three daughters. A son, Jonathon, and one of the daughters, Susannah, died at birth, leaving her with only two daughters to help with the cooking, cleaning, and tailoring.[17]

A large section of the Hale farm was devoted to harvesting feed corn and grain for Richard's cattle business. He also set aside plenty of acreage for flax, used for making cloth. During the French and Indian War, colonial New England lived under a law that mandated farmers to reserve a certain amount of acreage for the production of flax in order to help outfit the army. For the Hales, however, it was also essential to the family. Though each of the boys owned three outfits (at best), because they spent sunup to sundown playing in and working the fields, they went through clothes quickly. Hemp was another important commodity. As far back as the mid-1600s, early colonial governments legislated colonies to grow as much hemp and flax as they could, putting "servants and children to work spinning yarn in their idle hours," historian Margaret Ellen Newell wrote, and offering "bounties for finished linen and cloth." Later, when the Revolution drew closer, England made it clear that it did not want colonists to make their own cloth; Americans were supposed to buy English products. The Hales supported any colonial effort to break from England and did their part by harvesting extra crops of flax to sustain the colonial army's needs.[18]

The sixth child in the Hale family, Nathan was born on June 6, 1755, while Richard was out working with his men. While they tilled the fields, the anxiety over his baby got the best of Richard as he periodically dropped his tools and snapped orders. Throughout the morning he had been taking "frequent trips" back to the house as Nathan's mother, Elizabeth, lay on her back struggling through the birth. But when it at last happened, Richard was said to be "bending over a furrow." A woman servant helping Elizabeth inside the house suddenly "ran . . . from the kitchen down the long slope" in the back of the house and reported to Richard. With the news, he addressed his men, "The Lord be praised for the mother and the child. Let him be a worthy servant," before cutting them loose for the day to "do as you will with your time." As Richard and the servant rushed back to the house, the servant asked him if he was going to name the child a junior. "He shall be called after that righteous and patriotic man, my kinsman Nathan, and I shall be well pleased if he have as high a sense of duty," answered Nathan's proud father.[19]

Nathan "was feeble in body at the beginning of his life," Benson Lossing wrote. Despite being born underweight and, in subsequent days, given "very little promise of surviving the period," he surprised everyone and grew into a brawny, muscular child. During that "critical second year," Lossing noted, Elizabeth's fifth son rebounded into a "robust child, physically and mentally."[20]

Two months before Nathan turned twelve, the first of many tragedies struck the Hale household. The Hale's twelfth child, Susannah, was born in February 1767, but died a few weeks later. Then, on April 27, 1767, Nathan's mother, Elizabeth, lost her life due to the complications from giving birth to Susannah. Although the family "revered the Bible as the voice of God" and perhaps viewed Elizabeth's and Susannah's deaths as part of the Lord's plan, Nathan was overwhelmed by both losses, his mother's probably more so than that of a sister he had never really known. He and Elizabeth had been close. She had sat and told Nathan many stories about Yale, from her many family members that attended the school. Because Nathan had struggled with life early on, he and Elizabeth had, by merely spending so much time together, bonded. But now she was gone. And just like that, Nathan and his siblings were motherless.[21]

At the time of Elizabeth's death, Richard Hale had eight small children to raise (two were grown) and a farm to manage. Nathan's slightly older sister, Elizabeth, picked up several of her mother's duties and helped where she could, but Richard needed a woman to run the household. He couldn't do it alone. It was customary in colonial New England to mourn the loss of a spouse for two months, then quickly find another, more out of necessity than love. But Richard had cherished Elizabeth's company deeply, and their relationship was unlike most Puritan marriages; it would take him several years to recover.

Abigail Adams (not to be confused with President John Adams's wife of the same name) had grown up in Canterbury, a twenty-mile trip east of Coventry. After meeting through mutual acquaintances, within a few months of courtship Abigail and Richard Hale married a week after Nathan's fourteenth birthday on June 13, 1769, about eight weeks before Enoch and Nathan left for Yale. Abigail was the widow of Captain Samuel Adams, with whom she'd had two daughters. Daughter Sarah moved into the Hale house with Abigail; while Alice, who had gone to live with her uncle in Canterbury, visited when she could. With hazel eyes and "jet-black hair," Alice was a beautiful, diminutive girl, who would become known in her elder years as "one of the brightest ornaments of [her] society." She and Nathan became close almost immediately as she began to visit. As friends, they adored each other's company.

Contemporary historians and writers, and even Abigail's family, have indicated that Nathan and Alice corresponded regularly while he was away at school, building on a friendship (and many suspected romance) they had started before he left. Yet none of those letters between them—if they ever existed to begin with—remain. Alice moved into the Hale house *after* both Enoch and Nathan had left. At fifteen, she became linked romantically with Elijah Ripley, a respected, wealthy Coventry merchant ten years her senior. A year later, on February 8, 1773, sixteen-year-old Alice married Elijah.

From a journal Alice kept later in life, a portrait of her thoughts emerge. She did not want to be married to Elijah, but in spite of what some nineteenth-century biographers of Nathan might have hoped, it had little to do with a quixotic love she had for Nathan. Instead, her melancholy demeanor developed after her father passed: "How oft have I wished," Alice wrote, "and even prayed that this mighty affair [she was speaking then about her third marriage to a Hartford man] might be wholly left to ye will of providence?—and 'tis certainly by the divine institution that this change had been wrought—heaven only is my witness of the doubts & fears struggles & anxieties of mind which I have suffered."[22]

Throughout her life, Alice Adams would struggle with depression. Soon after she married Elijah, she bore him a child. Both offspring and father would die inside the next few years. Within several years, Alice had lost her father, child, and first husband. "A heavy gloom hangs upon my mind—O the pilgrimage of this life is infinitely troublesome & perplexed by all trials & afflictions that I meet with here . . . may I be brought nearer to god and divine things & whenever the blessed redeemer shall resume that life he gave me I shall resign it into his hands without sorrow and without fear."[23]

Unlike Alice with her unfortunate future marriage, Richard Hale and his new bride were quite happy in Coventry. They were building a life for themselves after early deaths had taken each of their spouses. By then, Richard had been elected to the General Assembly of the state. As Enoch and Nathan prepared for a life at Yale, Richard and his new family were getting along well and keeping the farm running without difficulty.[24]

In the years following the American Revolution, the Hale family would refer to an acre-sized lot out in front of the north side of the family mansion, where roadways intersected to form a triangular plot of land, as Holy Grove. David Hale Jr., the son of Nathan's younger brother David, planted a large formation of rock maple trees in between the dirt roadways and South Street, the main thoroughfare leading up to the farm. The trees had been sowed like rows of corn, standing perpendicular to one another like a line of fence posts. The area was said to be named Holy Grove after neighborhood open-air prayer meetings were held underneath the canopy of trees.

Generations earlier, during Nathan's days on the farm, one would be lucky to find a small throng of trees anywhere in town. When Coventry was incorporated in the early eighteenth century, its settlers cleared large tracts of land, stripping away much of the town's natural forest for fuel, building materials, and cropland. Standing on the second floor of the Hale mansion, one could see twenty miles on a clear day in any direction.

Before and during the Revolution, the Hales raised beef cattle. When it was time for the cattle to go to market, Richard and the kids drove the herds into Norwich, a port town twenty-three miles southeast of Coventry. In Norwich, the cattle boarded a riverboat two by two, arklike, and set sail for New London, where they were grouped onto schooners and merchant ships headed to the West Indies and England. In the late 1760s, as the tensions between the British and the American colonies rose and a rebellion seemed imminent, Richard Hale's farming business was partially disrupted. Many of his customers were English. Part of the colonial drive for independence was based on American opposition to British taxation laws, but also to the export to England of goods manufactured and farmed in the colonies. As it seemed more and more likely war was the only option the colonists had left, Richard was appointed to head a provisions committee in Coventry that would eventually sell beef cattle and other items to American forces. So while talk of war seemed to put a damper on the Hales' business at first, the Hale farm—like thousands of others throughout New England—prospered.[25]

In 1769 colonial New England, it was unusual for a household to send even one child to college. Hardworking Richard Hale was able to send three. So he was sure to check in on his latest investments from time to time and let Enoch and Nathan know what he expected from them. As a dedicated Christian, Richard hardly ever talked or wrote to Nathan without encouraging him to continue studying God's word. He was likely upset that his son wasn't following in the family tradition by joining the ministry. Instead, Nathan leaned toward following one of his uncles into education and becoming a tutor and schoolmaster. Although Nathan was devoutly religious, he realized that teaching future scholars was his passion. Still, his father took advantage of every opportunity to make sure Nathan understood that without God he could expect nothing out of life.

A few months after Nathan and Enoch settled in New Haven, Richard sent a letter addressed to both. It was a day after Christmas 1769. Richard had received a letter from one of the boys on December 7, in which they noted how "well suited with living in college" they had become. Richard responded clearly:

> I . . . would let you know that we are all well through the Divine goodness, as I hope these lines will find you. I hope you will carefully mind your studies that your time be not Lost and that you will mind all the orders of College with care and be sure above all forget not to Learn Christ while you are busy in other studies.

Richard explained that he wanted to send the boys money, but he had been waiting to entrust it to a neighbor who was heading into New Haven as soon as he returned from a tenure on the circuit court. Richard obviously missed his sons immensely. He expressed a desire for the boys to visit home, noting, "If you can hire Horses at New Haven . . . without too much trouble and cost, I don't know, but it is best and should be glad to know how you can hire there and send me word."

At the end of the letter, he explained that if he had not heard from them by May 6 the following year, 1770, he would send horses for a trip home— that is, if their Yale tutors allowed them a leave. "Your friends are all well," he concluded, ". . . from your kind and Loving Father, Rich Hale."[26]

During his years at Yale, Nathan grew into an insightful and outspoken contributor to the college culture. As he and Enoch entered their sophomore year, Enoch was chosen for membership in Linonia, a secret fraternity founded in 1753. Nathan became a member two weeks later on November 20, along with his new friend James Hillhouse. Labeling Linonia a "secret society" makes membership sound more romantic than it actually was. Primarily, it was a literary organization, a group of scholars who met once or twice a week to discuss, in no specific order, slavery, astronomy, literature, women's rights, and other important social and academic issues. Yale scholars worked themselves to the bone. Linonia was one way, certainly, for some to further their studies, while enjoying a bit of social intercourse among future leaders and members of the communities they were headed for. Late nights and weekends at Yale were not a time for frat parties, heavy drinking, and promiscuous sex. According to Benjamin Tallmadge, Fridays and Saturdays were devoted to students—"in small groups"—appearing "before their tutors to recite in the three classical languages." Saturday afternoons were built around supplementary study of theology.[27]

Nathan held several positions within Linonia, including the office of chancellor, and became one of its primary members, choosing many of the books for its growing library. Inside that tight-knit group Nathan developed a commitment not only to education as a career, but to debating politics and popular issues of his day. For the first time, his opinions were put before a group of his peers and discussed. He began to see the benefits of a democratic system, if only on a small scale.[28]

As fellow students James Hillhouse and Nathan became closer through their membership in Linonia, it was obvious to both that they viewed American politics and colonial life similarly. Six months older than Nathan, Hillhouse had an academic look about him, with his dark hair, sharp features, and serious eyes. Born into a long line of Northern Irish immigrants, Hillhouse grew up in Montville, Connecticut, just outside New London, a town Nathan would eventually call home. He and Nathan saw a common bond between them in their views on contentious issues of the day. A revered candidate for Nathan's friendly affections, Hillhouse was sent from his home as a boy to live with his uncle in New Haven, who promptly adopted him, so he could be closer to his studies. He grew up an only child, which afforded his parents the opportunity to help him focus his studies on law. Hillhouse would go on to spend fifty years as Yale's treasurer and, as one historian later said, "did more for New Haven than any one else of his generation."[29]

Linonia was primarily a debating society, "exalted and warmed by friendship and nourished by books," George Dudley Seymour later wrote. It was, for Nathan, one of the first times in his life where his remarkable skills as a leader began to stand out.

As Nathan's class took over the society, members tailored its structure to fit the political community and scientific needs of the day. It was decided that instead of a member giving a closing speech after each session, "a Dissertation on some branch of the Sciences" would be more appropriate. Books were collected and Linonia started its own library, which Nathan, if he didn't suggest its inception, immediately began to manage. Members were allowed to "take out Books on Saturday at two o-clock in the after Noon, that no one might keep a Book longer than a Week without returning it."[30]

Enoch was mentioned in the society's minutes first, on October 31, 1770, along with Stephen Keyes, Ebenezer Williams, and Noah Merwin, all of whom would befriend Nathan, look up to him, and correspond with him in the coming years. Nathan was admitted into the society along with nine other scholars. With Nathan's input, debate topics changed from meeting to meeting. One question would be "What is the Reason that the Moon is not always Eclipsed every Opposition of the Sun and Moon?" And then a day later, "How do you solve Questions, when the unknown quantity has several Powers in one Equation, and only the first Power in the other Equation?"

Nathan kept detailed minutes and asked questions that would later mesh with his character as a humorist and patriot. In one, he wrote, "What thing is the most delightful to Man in the World?" Answering his own question, a bit of irony leapt from Nathan's quill: "It is much as the Parson is, if he . . . delights most in what he ought most to be ashamed of—Virtuous Men will take the greatest Delight in Virtuous Actions, but what is most delightful to most Men, is getting Money."

Athletics were prescribed, in part, to relieve Yale scholars from a stressful seven-day study week. Wrestling, a sport Nathan would excel in, was a common way for scholars to bond and, as with youth of every era, assert an aspect of their masculinity. Because of his size, Nathan surpassed most others in the sport. In a testament to his athletic ability, honed while at home working long days in the fields, legend says that no other student among his class could best Nathan in the long jump—and a record Nathan set on the green of New Haven was "pointed out" and "preserved" well into the nineteenth century. However successful he might have been, whenever kicking a ball around or wrestling with peers became dull, Nathan passed what little free time he had by getting involved in another traditional Yale pastime: mischief.

On a clear and cool night in March 1771, Nathan, Enoch, Benjamin Tallmadge, and a few fellow classmates roamed around campus looking for something to keep themselves occupied. Fueled by the tedium of such a structured curriculum and possibly also by an evening at the local tavern, the boys went out and broke several windows around campus. Later, Tallmadge excused his misbehavior by writing, "Being so well versed in the Latin and Greek languages, I had not much occasion to study during the first two years of my collegiate life, which I have always thought had a tendency to make me idle."

Nathan would never make valedictorian or any other distinction at Yale beyond honors. Jared Sparks, who was friends with many of the scholars Nathan mingled with, summed up perfectly, perhaps, Nathan's early years in New Haven: "Possessing genius, taste, and order, he became distinguished as a scholar; and endowed in an eminent degree with those graces and gifts of Nature which add charm to youthful excellence, he gained universal esteem and confidence."

Sparks further explained that the habits Nathan picked up at Yale developed in him a "high moral worth," which lent to a remarkable "gentleness of manner [and] . . . ingenious disposition."

As he immersed himself in college life, Nathan began to realize how serving the needs of his fellows was possibly more important to him than his own selfish needs. "No young man of his years," Sparks wrote, "put forth a fairer promise of future usefulness and celebrity; the fortunes of none were fostered more sincerely by the generous good wishes of his superiors."[31]

Richard Hale knew his sons' characters as well as he knew the contours of the land of his farm. He was well aware that Nathan, who was inherently more outgoing than Enoch, tended to succumb to the temptations of peer pressure. Nathan's classmates would later say he adored card playing and drinking, not to mention window breaking and chasing the young maidens around town. In that respect, when Richard wrote to the boys as they headed into their second full year, he advocated once again his firm belief that if they needed answers while away and found letter writing too fleeting, a good place to turn was the Scriptures:

> I have nothing special to write but would by all means desire you to mind your Studies and carefully attend to orders of College. Attend not only Prayers in the chapel but Secret Prayer carefully. Shun all vice, especially card playing. Read your Bibles a chapter a night and morning. I cannot now send you much money but hope when Sr Strong comes to Coventry to be able to send by him what you want.[32]

What Richard would find out later was that part of the money Nathan and Enoch demanded was for the fines they had to pay the school for the broken windows.

Nathan wasn't about to question his father's words; he cherished Richard's dutiful advice and certainly had no trouble seeking comfort in the Bible. A passage he made note of in his personal Bible: "In my father's house are many mansions, and I go to prepare a place for you."

On August 13, 1771, Richard wrote again. Both Enoch and Nathan had come down with a terrible case of the measles, which had spread throughout their class of thirty-six. They had been bedridden and horribly lethargic for weeks. Through "Divine Goodness," Richard wrote, he first let them know the family was doing well. "I have heard that you are better of the measles. The Cloth for your Coat is not Done. But will be Done next week[,] I hope the furthest."

To save on materials and money, Richard had the boys take one common measurement between them and send it home. Instead of sister Elizabeth Rose making two suits, she tailored only one, which they were asked to share. "I know of no opportunity we shall have to send it to Newhaven and have Laid in with Mr. Strong for his Horse, which if he can get Leave and have your clothes made at home. . . . I am told that it is not good to study hard after the measles—hope you will use Prudence in that fare."

Richard sent the boys eight pounds in cash and said he hoped they could do without new clothes until after commencement. The garments would have to be quite durable—commencement was two years away.[33]

Chapter 2

Most Intimate Friends

I N LATE J ULY 1773, as the afternoon sun fell behind the horizon of Long Island Sound, an imposing figure on horseback emerged from the crest of a hill near College and Chapel streets in downtown New Haven. As the young man, surely exhausted from his difficult and dusty trip, came upon the west side of Yale's green, before him stood the college's two main buildings, Connecticut Hall and the school's chapel, its steeple and clock towering above the New Haven skyline.[1]

Tucked inside the rider's leather saddlebag was a letter addressed to Nathan. He and Enoch were scheduled to graduate that fall. Nathan had just turned eighteen in June. After nearly four years at one of New England's most celebrated colleges, he was weighing whether to take a position as schoolmaster in Moodus (Haddam Landing), Connecticut, or return home to Coventry to work the land with his father and siblings.

The letter was from Nathan's friend Benjamin Tallmadge, who had left Yale a few months earlier and settled in Wethersfield. Tallmadge, who had roomed with Nathan and Enoch in Connecticut Hall, signed the letter "Damon." When Nathan returned Tallmadge's correspondences, he generally signed off as "Pythias." In Greek legend Damon and Pythias exemplify true friendship because of their loyalty to each other. Pythias was sentenced to death for his plot against the tyrant Dionysius I of Syracuse. Once caught, he was allowed a leave to take care of his affairs. In turn, Damon pledged to hand over his own life if Pythias failed to return. When Pythias came back as promised, Dionysius was so enamored with their loyalty to each other, he released them. Like many Yale students, Nathan and Tallmadge had chosen the fourth century B.C. Greek names as nicknames while studying together and thought it endearing, if not comforting, to continue exchanging letters in the same manner.

Tallmadge was born on February 25, 1754, the second son of a Setauket, Long Island, reverend of the same name. He was a little more than a year older than Nathan, and the two had become close friends soon after meeting at Yale. A chubby boy with a baby face, Tallmadge had been a model student all his life, and his father had made it clear that his future was to include a stint at Yale. "As [my father] was preparing a number of boys for college," Tallmadge wrote later, "he placed me as a student among them, and when I was twelve . . . I had acquired such a knowledge in classical learning, that [Yale] President Daggett, on a visit to my father, examined and admitted me as qualified to enter college."

Tallmadge and Nathan wound up in the same class because Tallmadge's father had held his son back a few years, deeming "it improper for [him] to go to college so young," and thus enrolled him in 1769, the same year as Nathan. Together Nathan and Tallmadge had stocked the Linonian library with books such as Homer's *Iliad,* Andrew Michael Ramsay's *Travels of Cyrus,* and an early edition of *The History of Philip's War,* a book about the armed conflict between early colonists and Native American Indians— works that introduced Nathan to combat strategy and gave him a taste for studying the history of warfare.

Because he had advanced in his studies faster than his peers, Tallmadge was afforded the opportunity to graduate several months earlier. After leaving school, he went directly into a teaching assignment in Wethersfield, Connecticut, with the intention of earning some money while furthering his studies in law.[2]

The letters Tallmadge wrote to Nathan articulate the profound appreciation the two men shared for each other. Here were two Yale friends eager to get out into the world and experience life as adults, expressing feelings of affection and concern for one another as they knew their Yale days would soon be behind them.

"The Reception of your Epistle," Tallmadge wrote, ". . . has sensibly increased my happiness, as perhaps any one accidental Circumstance which hath happened to me since my first arrival."[3]

For the first time in his life, Tallmadge was alone in an unfamiliar place. It would be the same for Nathan once he took a schoolmaster's tenure. This situation caused a great deal of impatience, detachment from family, and mild depression for Tallmadge. He missed being around the people he knew—especially his Yale friends. Further into the same letter, he mused, "Although my Company & present Condition is far from tending to Melancholy & Dullness; yet in a place where few intimate friends, or even acquaintance are at first to be found; that absolute Contentedness of Mind, which is so necessary to true Happiness, is not so readily obtained. But perhaps I am more than commonly delighted with the Perusal of such friendly Epistles."[4]

Tallmadge found that in Wethersfield he was becoming overwhelmed by boredom, living thirty miles from New Haven in a place where he knew no one. And it was clear he missed Nathan:

> Indeed I know of no one Circumstance which would tend more directly, to make me contented in any particular Place than the Correspondence which I should hope to maintain with some of my most intimate Friends. THAT which has for some time subsisted between you & myself, I desire may never have an End. . . . Yet I hope you will by no means suffer your pen to be in doleness . . . so long as you can both be contributory to my advantage & happiness.[5]

On the one hand, the society and culture of Wethersfield had come as an immediate shock to Tallmadge. Yet, on the other, the town seemed quite "agreeable" once he got settled and started meeting people. It was the company he kept that he found so intellectually fascinating. "Perhaps in a Place is there more distinction with regard to Company," he wrote to Nathan, pointing out that he was among some of Wethersfield's most respected citizens. Wethersfield was a short ride on horseback from Hartford. Near the school where Tallmadge taught was a large cove, in which ships frequently unloaded goods and docked. "One of the oldest of the Connecticut Valley towns," Charles Swain Hall wrote in his biography of Tallmadge, "[Wethersfield] had achieved a prominent place among New England shipping centers."[6]

The community in which Tallmadge now lived was incredibly studious. Nearby Hartford, for example, was made up of many wealthy families whose children Tallmadge was now in charge of preparing for college. On any given night in Wethersfield, however, it wasn't unlikely for the Yale scholar to run into Silas Deane, who would become America's first foreign diplomat, or Jeremiah Wadsworth, a member of the Connecticut state legislature and soon-to-be close confidant of General Washington's. Downtown Wethersfield consisted of a rather spacious main street where the James Lockwood house stood. Lockwood had been Wethersfield's most important and admired vicar and had died the previous year. Tallmadge was proud to pay for room and board at the Lockwood house. South of downtown, he would spend his nights at what was known as Hospitality Hall, where he spent the evenings "dancing and flirting with the attractive daughters of the town's best families."[7]

Tallmadge considered himself quite a humorist and often wrote to Nathan describing the many young ladies he'd had the opportunity to entertain. Writing to Nathan about the girls of Wethersfield stirred Tallmadge's spirit, whereas his professional life of teaching hardly tested the boundaries of his intellect. The letters he and Nathan exchanged were a way to infuse a bit of vitality into what had become, essentially, a mundane life, quite different from their invigorating academic days together: drinking, playing cards, causing mischief, courting the young ladies of New Haven, and, most important, studying complex languages and sacred texts.

Mainly because of his looks, but perhaps more so because he went wooing at every opportunity, Nathan had a reputation at Yale as a flirt. For that, Tallmadge often teased him. In that same letter already quoted, he explained, "In such Company [the ladies of Wethersfield] we have not only the advantages of friendly Intercourse . . . but it may also be rendered very useful & instructive—the Female part of this place, you have often heard, is very agreeable."

Reading this, Nathan must have had a good chuckle. His old classmate was out and about, carrying on the tradition they had begun while at Yale. Nathan was so enamored with Tallmadge and so valued their friendship he later wrote a poem to him that outlined how close they had become and how central humor was to their otherwise solemn and pious colonial lives:

> *Reviv'd a little by your letter,*
> *With hopes of speeding better,*
> *At length I venture forth once more,*
> *But fearing soon to run ashore.*
>
> *My thoughts had once convey'd you home,*
> *In safety to your wonted dome;*
> *But gladly went a second time,*
> *Attended by your muse and rhyme.*
>
> *That you are there, the single proof,*
> *You bring, to me, is quite enough.*
> *But here, I think you're wrong, to blame, Your gen'rous*
> *muse, and call her lame.*

The poem went on for several more verses in Nathan's rather light-hearted writing style. Clearly, the time the two shared at Yale would forever be etched in Nathan's mind and heart.[8]

From several composite sketches later drafted of him, in addition to numerous written and oral descriptions, we know that Nathan had the well-defined features and chiseled physique of the accomplished athlete he had become during his days at Yale College. His rather powerful build—fortified by his days of wrestling—had been founded on the hard physical labor of the family farm. Quite imposing at six feet,* in an era when the average height was much shorter, Nathan drew attention wherever he went, from both his size and stunning good looks. According to recollections, he had flawless "light blue" eyes, sparkling with a natural contentment and confidence, set below a full shock of blondish brown hair that, in keeping with the times, was pony-tailed halfway down his back. On an average day, Nathan would have worn a white-bordered, black wool tricorn, waistcoat, trousers, hip coat or frock, and large-buckled shoes. "In dress, he was always neat," recollected Dr. Eneas Munson, a Yale physician who had become Nathan's mentor during his years in New Haven. "He was quick to lend a helping hand to a being in distress, brute or human: was overflowing with good humor, and was the idol of all his acquaintances." Munson described Nathan's frame as "perfectly proportioned . . . the most manly man I had ever met"; he was "broad-chested," with "firm muscles" and skin of a "roseate complexion." His voice, moreover, tingled with a "low, sweet and musical" affect. "His face wore a most benign expression. . . . His personal beauty and grace of manner were most charming. Why, all the girls in New Haven were in love with him."[9]

Nathan visited Munson on many occasions. In 1836, Munson's son spoke of Nathan's visits as having had an "indelible impression on my mind." The boy was captivated by his father's Yale friend, looking up to him as some sort of heroic figure. On one such afternoon, Nathan had just walked out of the Munson house after a long visit when the elder Munson turned to his son and stated firmly, "That man is a diamond of the first water, calculated to excel in any situation he assumes. He is a gentleman and scholar—and last though not least of his qualifications, a Christian."[10]

As Nathan matured, many regarded him as an educator. Although the normal path for a young man of his caliber would have been farming, law, or clergy, Nathan never imagined himself in any of those roles. He had a natural urge to travel and meet new people, who might in turn value his company and admire him.

---

* I found one description of Nathan at five feet seven inches; however, all of the other descriptions we have put him at six feet tall. With so many sources describing his appearance as larger-than-life and big in stature, he was almost certainly taller than many of his contemporaries.

"People were exceedingly attached to him," wrote a former student. General opinion held that he had the soft and elegant demeanor of an aged academic, yet, when the situation warranted it, the earnestness of a boy eager to prove himself.

"He had a face & appearance," a former pupil said, "that would strike any one anywhere—a face indicative of good sense & good feeling—warm & ardent—captivating to all who saw him. . . . Children all loved him for his tact and amiability."[11]

As Nathan looked ahead to what he was going to do after graduation, he took on mature social and political positions—one of which was a desire to educate females in a colonial society that rarely did. England prohibited females from attending school, and not a schoolmaster in New England ignored this law. Most of the schools set up for females centered on sewing and stitch marking, among other feminine duties of the household. Nathan didn't know it then, but he would soon change that standard even if his primary motivation in teaching females was at first simply to earn extra money.[12]

Chapter 3

From Boys to Men

COMMENCEMENT WAS A DAY for Nathan's class of thirty-six to celebrate their accomplishments of the past four years and absorb a few parting words of wisdom from their tutors. Benjamin Tallmadge had made the trip from Wethersfield to be there on September 8, 1773; he, too, was officially graduating, even though he had left Yale to begin teaching months before.[1]

It was a glorious morning. Forty-six-year-old Yale president Naphtali Daggett, the school's first professor of divinity, had been with Nathan's class throughout their tenure. He stood proudly on the podium erected in front of Connecticut Hall as the crowd, said to be full of young ladies there to bid adieu to their favorite scholar, Nathan Hale, waited eagerly for Daggett's opening words.[2]

He began the service with a prayer, followed by several moments of silent reflection and a few heartening words of wisdom based on the Scriptures. Then the valedictorian of the class of '73, James Palsgrave Wyllys, walked to the center of the stage and gave the Latin salutatory oration. This honor was bestowed upon the student whose work stood out most during the three years leading up to graduation. There's no denying Wyllys was, hands down, academically smarter than Nathan and most of the rest of the '73 class. As a classmate and friend, Nathan viewed Wyllys as an astute scholar and potential eminent statesman. Nathan and his friend James Hillhouse, who often held similar views, were never more in agreement than in their shared envy of Wyllys. In a letter Hillhouse later wrote to Nathan, he noted, "Wyllys is a man of Pleasure, and applies himself entirely to the acquirement of knowledge, for which . . . he has an Insatiable Thirst." According to George Dudley Seymour, the word *pleasure,* as Hillhouse used it here, was likely a substitute for *leisure.* Wyllys came from a wealthy family of status and position; after graduation, he didn't immediately pick a vocation—as Nathan and Hillhouse soon would—but instead hung around his childhood home deciding what to do. In a way, Hillhouse was poking a little fun at his friend, while at the same time honoring his accomplishments at Yale.[3]

As commencement morning continued, four of Nathan's classmates participated in a debate titled "Whether a large Metropolis would be of public advantage to this Colony?" After that, three students and one of their tutors broke into a more serious English oration regarding the disadvantages and problems of prejudice. And when the noon bell struck, the morning's services concluded with a rather enthusiastic anthem.[4]

After lunch, John Davenport, a young tutor Nathan had studied under, warmed the crowd with a lecture on the state of private schools in the colonies surrounding New Haven, a talk that was of great interest to Nathan, as he was considering a career in education.[5]

As Nathan stood alongside Enoch and his fellow graduates, he relished the work he and his classmates had accomplished. To say that the Hale brothers had become men since that first ride to New Haven in 1769 would be to understate the nature of leaving home as fourteen- and fifteen-year-old boys for the first time and heading into an unfamiliar city where they would remain for several years. They had left as children and been turned into two well-educated men, ready to begin adult life, no less than what Richard Hale had wanted.

The debate that afternoon carried great weight with Nathan. "Whether the Education of Daughters be not without any just reason, more neglected than that of Sons?"[6]

Beyond earning extra money by providing classes for females, Nathan may well have believed in the need to edify the women of the colonies. George Dudley Seymour would later suggest Nathan had a calling to educate females, although not much definitive evidence exists to prove this notion. "By nature," Seymour wrote, Nathan "was a progressive." As the world changed around him and the colonies seemed more at odds with England, the time seemed appropriate to give women the skills to do whatever they wanted—which began in the classroom. As long as the British ruled, however, the idea of allowing female students into classrooms to learn the basics—reading and writing—would never be legally accepted. Women were meant to be home, working the land, hovering in front of the kitchen hearth preparing meals, tending to the children, spinning flax into linen thread or yarn, sewing clothes and doing other household chores. Nathan's mother, Elizabeth Hale, may have been an example for him: She'd died while giving birth, and Elizabeth's struggle as the head female in the household, which Nathan witnessed personally, may, as Seymour later suggested, have fueled a passion in him to educate females.[7]

With his diploma in hand, Nathan left New Haven on what would be a four-day journey to Portsmouth, New Hampshire, to seek advice from his uncle Samuel Hale. A job was waiting for Nathan at Haddam Landing, in Moodus, Connecticut, but the eighteen-year-old Yale graduate wasn't so sure he wanted it. He knew Samuel, a schoolmaster himself for decades, could offer a bit of germane advice.[8]

For the wary eighteenth-century rider, the dirt roads of New England provided several stopovers as he galloped through the small towns and villages, particularly taverns.[9]

At Yale, Nathan was said to have participated in his share of drinking. The taverns en route to Portsmouth were not only a place to scratch that itch, but also to fraternize among other men, mail letters, and debate the politics of the day with fellow colonists. The political atmosphere around

Nathan was thick with tension; American politicians and colonists were standing toe-to-toe with British leaders over English taxation and Britain's hard-line position. Anxiety mounted as Boston became the epicenter of rebellion against King George. The Committee of Correspondence, a secret society that exchanged intelligence information and planned revolts against British law, was gaining momentum. Most of the colonies were incapable of resisting British control, and preparations were being made to stage more concerted, military efforts to repel taxes.[10]

The seaside community of Portsmouth was the center of a flourishing maritime economy—"a mecca for a varied multitude of craftsmen," historian Eleanor Spiller called it. No other seaport like Portsmouth existed in the region. Shipwrights and sailmakers contributed greatly to a trade market in town, a place filled with rope makers and blacksmiths, sawyers, candlemakers, pewterers, potters, wigmakers, tailors, shoemakers, and farmers.[11]

For Nathan's uncle Samuel Hale, who began his career running classes twenty miles north of Portsmouth in Dover, teaching was his passion. His students later marked him as a strict mentor and disciplinarian, but respected his classroom ethos. In 1741, when Samuel had opened his first classroom, a common punitive action, known as cuffing, was to slap an unruly student on both ears at the same time. Although it was a common Christian punishment then, not one student of Samuel's ever reported him using it.[12]

Nathan wasn't just traveling two hundred miles north to hear war stories from Samuel's days of teaching, or to learn how to control his future students; he was also paying a visit to his uncle and cousins, which he had likely never done, to discuss the pros and cons of life in the classroom. Was it the right profession for him?

Although he only spent approximately three days in New Hampshire, a letter Nathan sent to Samuel a few weeks after the visit made it quite clear that he enjoyed himself immensely. "My visit to Portsmouth . . . served only to increase the nearness of your family and make me the more desirous of seeing them again."[13]

Samuel's sons, William, Thomas, and Samuel Jr., were products of their father. They obeyed the major's rules and lived by his stern voice. Shaking hands with each before he saddled for his ride back to Coventry, Nathan could not have guessed that Samuel Jr.'s name would become synonymous with treason in the years to come.[14]

There's no doubt that Uncle Samuel had given Nathan an earful of sage advice regarding a life in the classroom as a pedagogue. Whatever Samuel said must have solidified Nathan's decision, because several days after he rode out of Portsmouth, preparations were made for him to move to Moodus to teach.[15]

Chapter 4

SCHOOLMASTER

IN AMERICAN LEGEND, HADDAM Landing and the village of Moodus in particular—or "*Machemoodus,* the place of noises"—was considered a town with evil spirits lurking underneath the soil and in the slate rock cliffs that seemed to fence in the entire town. The noises reported throughout the decades turned out to be, however, earthquakes, a common natural occurrence in New England during the eighteenth century.[1]

Nathan chose to begin his teaching career in Moodus, thirty miles south of his Coventry home. On the outskirts of town, the red, one-story Cape-style schoolhouse Nathan took over sat on a hill where the Salmon River emptied into the busy Connecticut River. The magnificent view was unlike anything Nathan had seen before. Around the school were sharp, steep cliffs dotted with immense pine trees for as far as the eye could see. According to I. W. Stuart, Moodus was a town of "much wealth and business activity" when Nathan began teaching at what was a select school, "where he was required to instruct both in English and the Classical Tongues." In 1662, the town had been purchased for "30 coats" (a total of one hundred colonial dollars' worth of garments) from four Native American kings by a group of twenty-eight European men from a town outside Hartford. With its stone fences, high cliffs, waterways, and close proximity to Long Island Sound—sixteen miles down the Connecticut River—Moodus proved to be a settlement where generations of Puritans would later live and prosper. Yet, during the time Nathan began his teaching career, the town was just beginning to become well populated.[2]

For Nathan the scholar, who felt he could have chosen any number of jobs within what was a broad field of education, Moodus didn't turn out to be quite what he had expected. It was so secluded from any major city in the state, Nathan felt as if he were living on an island. His disappointment is clear from the letters he wrote during his first days in town. Nathan dreaded waking up in the morning to face another day in what he saw as such a remote community. As he later wrote to his classmate Thomas Mead, reflecting on his time there, "I was, at the receipt of your letter, in East-Haddam (alias Moodus), a place, which I at first, for a long time, concluded inaccessible, either by friends, acquaintances or letters." Nathan would also receive letters from John Alden and James Palsgrave Wyllys, though, he told Mead, "It was equally or more difficult to convey anything from Moodus."[3]

Nathan had become used to large groups of people: mainly his former Yalies and, before that, his rather large family. He craved the company of his fellows who could stimulate his intellect the way his tutors and peers had at Yale. Becoming a prominent member of Linonia, he had built his life around comradeship, academic deliberations, and a deep appreciation for theology, the classics, and discussions within a social circle he felt comfortable in. Save for a few families who lived miles from his schoolhouse, it seemed nobody was around for Nathan to converse with regularly. He had spent the past four formative years in one of the most progressive, dynamic cities in New England. Now Nathan was living in the country. For him to be cooped up alone at night in a schoolhouse no bigger than a tool shack, spending his days with young children from eight to fourteen years of age, was a culture shock.[4]

Still, those few people in town he came in contact with adored Nathan's company and certainly viewed themselves lucky to have such a well-educated tutor for their children. "Everybody . . . loved him," Mrs. Hannah

Pierson, an elderly townswoman, said years after Nathan's departure. "He was so sprightly, intelligent, and kind—*so* handsome."[5]

With nothing but time on his hands as the days passed in Moodus, Nathan wrote often to his former classmates; their responses kept him company during what was proving to be the loneliest period of his life. Fellow classmate Elihu Marvin had turned twenty-one that December. Raised in nearby Lyme, the future lieutenant, adjutant general, and physician was himself teaching in Norwich. Nathan had written to Marvin that November 1773. What's clear in Marvin's response to that letter (Nathan's doesn't exist) is that Nathan had discussed the state of the colonies and begun to express his passionate feelings regarding patriotism and liberty. Nathan also chided his friend for an earlier letter, scolding Marvin for what seemed to be Tory sentiment. A spirited dislike for the king's rule had recently sparked violence on many fronts throughout the colonies. In Rhode Island, for example, protesters had burned a British sloop left unguarded in the waters off Providence harbor.[6]

For two old friends such as Nathan and Marvin, which side one took could result in a college friendship being destroyed. As the boys of his class were outside playing, Marvin wrote back. After two paragraphs, in which he referred to several sentences in Nathan's previous letter he wanted to clarify, he added, "Well I must call in the Boys & set them to work, for you know we must not neglect our main business—then I'll endeavor to go on with the explanation."[7]

When Marvin returned to his letter, he let Nathan know that he "did not mean thereby to express any thoughts or inclinations of my mind tending to enslave my country or any way to assist or abet the enemies of my Country."[8]

Nathan supported the mounting rebel effort. In Boston, the Sons of Liberty and other rebel factions were staging meetings and sit-ins at various public places around town to show their unity and support for liberation from England. Pamphlets with pleas to repeal taxes were distributed. Many merchants were refusing to trade with England. Nathan's suspicion of Marvin's disassociation with the effort could not have been more accurate. For Marvin would resign from the army only a year into his tenure after spending the winter of 1777–78 at Valley Forge, during which time he was said to have "in some way felt slighted" by America and her efforts to break free from British rule.[9]

Nathan and Marvin represented two different sides that colonists were taking in response to the growing problems between England and America. Brothers and cousins and friends alike faced off against one another as tensions mounted in Boston. One side supported British rule and had little trouble accepting the laws and restrictions of rights England had set forth; while the other wanted the liberty and freedom that a break from the motherland could provide.[10]

In a previous letter, Nathan seems to have accused Marvin of using texts in his classroom that were considered a slight on God's word. "To be brief," Marvin shot back, "In the 2nd sentence is contained no witchcraft—nor any thing which inevitably proves & demonstrates that the writer [Marvin] had any thing to do with evil spirits—in any way means or manner whatsoever."[11]

Nathan's strict stance on all things political and his responses to Marvin made it clear that Nathan would not be swayed by public opinion or even friends—that he was a man of his own mind, beliefs, and thoughts. No one was going to tell Nathan Hale what to think or how to react to Britain's rapidly increasing hatred for the colonies' growing idea of freedom.[12]

As the wind howled through the slats of the schoolhouse Nathan now called home, he huddled by the fieldstone fireplace, trying to keep warm as the Christmas of 1773 approached. Around that time, he decided he'd had enough of Moodus and came up with an idea for escape. He had heard there was a school in New London, a port town much like New Haven and just south of Moodus, looking for a schoolmaster. New London would suit him. It was a progressive, blossoming, liberal city, a place where he could earn more money and prestige, not to mention be around more people.[13]

Nathan's former tutor from Coventry, the Reverend Joseph Huntington, had connections in New London, as did Nathan's uncle the Reverend Joseph Strong. That winter, Nathan wrote Huntington a letter describing his unhappiness with his situation in Moodus and want of a job in New London, sending along several writing samples, urging the preacher to use any contact he could to help Nathan apply for a new teaching position.[14]

Near Christmas, Nathan received an answer. It was a letter from Timothy Green, the editor and proprietor of the *New London Gazette,* who also happened to be one of twenty-four administrators on the board of New London's Union School. Nathan must have taken great delight in the letter, though it included no guarantee of employment. Green seemed optimistic, but not altogether certain he could get Nathan a job. "I have [showed] Mr. Huntington's Letter and the Sample of your writing enclosed in it, to several of the proprietors of the School in this Town; who have desired me to inform you that there is a Probability of their agreeing with you to keep the School; and for that Reason desire that you would not engage yourself elsewhere till you hear further from them." Green promised to get back to Nathan inside the next week, but then crossed out the sentence in favor of some prudent advice: "But should you think proper to ride to this Place immediately upon the Receipt of my Letter, the matter might be sooner determined; and in which Case I will see that you are at no Charge while here."[15]

If Green had ended his letter there, Nathan might have saddled and rode, even in the bracing New England temperatures of the season. But Green added a postscript, dated two days later, December 23, that had surely disappointed Nathan. "P.S. Since writing the above Mr. Phineas Tracy of Norwich has took our School."

Another teacher had beaten Nathan to the job.[16]

Tracy wasn't planning on staying in New London, however, Green said he would likely spend three months and then return to Norwich. "Should you take a ride here," Green encouraged once again, "it might be to your advantage."[17]

The political atmosphere in the colonies was tense at this time. After the French and Indian War, Britain began taxing the colonies to pay off the debt from that military effort. This caused resentment among colonists, who were beginning to take sides. The Quartering Act was soon passed, which required Boston colonists to house and feed British troops. Many in Boston reacted by having the Sons of Liberty attack and burn Chief Justice of Massachusetts Thomas Hutchinson's home. The Boston Massacre, in which British troops patrolling the city shot and killed five civilians, had taken place in the spring of 1770. Since then colonists were thirsty for revenge. In several other colonies, such as New York and Virginia, meetings were held to protest the treatment of colonists by Britain. Nathan knew that New London, much like New Haven, was a hotbed of political discourse. Nathan wanted to be in the thick of it, speaking out and standing up for what he believed.[18]

While in Moodus, Nathan was not quite as lonely—at least as far as female companionship went—as he might have led his close friends to believe in the letters he wrote. From a poem he penned while in town, Nathan appears to have kept up his reputation for romantic interests:

A Line or two can give no great Offence, 'Tho' void
every thing that looks like Sense:
For if you're not inclin'd, you need not read them,
But have my leave to burn them, with all Freedom.

You thought, no doubt, I took my leave last Night,
But 'tis not so; you ha'n't come off so bright. It's true, I
said good By; But Notwithstanding, I only took my leave of
Haddam Landing.

Good by is not enough; it needs more words than
two, When friends do bid a long Adieu.

I trust, our Friendship, 'though begun of late, Hath
been no less sincere, than intimate.

Of this I'm sure; I've not as yet regretted, That to
your Company I've been admitted.

The untitled poem was later called "The Tryst at Haddam's Landing" by those scholars who discovered it. Historians believe Nathan wrote it for a woman he had met and possibly fallen for while in Moodus, yet had bid farewell once he got word that a position had opened at the Union School in New London. If Nathan had wanted to, he could have continued the relationship; New London was less than a half day's ride from Moodus, but there is no indication in any of his correspondences or evidence to prove he ever returned.[19]

In January 1774, Nathan rode into New London to meet with Timothy Green. Nathan was not about to pass up an opportunity for a more promising position in such a liberal-minded city. Before Nathan left Moodus, Green had sent ahead word that a decision was forthcoming: "Soon after the rising of the [General] Assembly," Green promised, "you should receive a definitive answer from the Proprietors of the School."[20]

When Nathan didn't hear from Green inside the two-week window he had mentioned, he sent a short note, asking about the status of his future employment. In response, Green apologized for not writing sooner. But nonetheless, said he was "glad . . . to receive a Line from you as it may serve to quicken the Proprietors of the School to act upon the matter."[21]

By February 4, the proprietors still hadn't met to discuss Nathan. One thing or another had taken up their time, and they hadn't had a chance to sit down and decide if Nathan was qualified. In a letter dated that day, Green said he was sorry, but he still didn't have an answer.[22]

Six days later, the answer Nathan had been waiting for finally arrived. "Since my last to you," Green wrote on February 10, "the Proprietors of the New School House in this Town have had a meeting, and agreed that you should take the School for one Quarter."[23]

Green wasn't sure of an exact date, or when the current schoolmaster, Mr. Tracy of Norwich, would be leaving. He didn't want to give Nathan a date to start until he was "acquainted by a Line from you whether we may depend on your taking the School, which you will please write to me at [your first opportunity]."[24]

If Nathan wanted the job, Green encouraged him to arrive in town three days before the date on which he was to start teaching, so the proprietors could be certain he wasn't going to accept the job only to leave soon after, as

Tracy had. "In which Case it is agreed that your Wages shall commence from the Time of your arriving here."[25]

Green ended the latest note saying that he had recently found out that "Mr. Tracy's Time will be up about the middle of March."[26]

In a month's time Nathan would be living in New London, continuing his teaching career. What he didn't know was that events taking place in Philadelphia and Boston during this period, as the First Continental Congress prepared to convene, would change the course of his life and set him on an entirely new path, one that he would embrace with the tenacity and commitment of a natural-born leader. In and around Boston, British troops were arriving in large numbers. Besides soldiers and government, the streets of Boston were "deserted," one local said, while Congress was putting together a plan to respond to any brutality by the British military. In the "Address of the First Continental Congress to the People of Great Britain," Congress made clear where it stood in its relations with the king: "When a nation, led to greatness by the hand of liberty, and possessed of all the glory that heroism, munificence, and humanity can bestow, descends to the ungrateful task of forging chains for her friends, and children, and instead of giving support to freedom, turns advocate for slavery and oppression, there is reason to suspect she has ceased to be virtuous, or been extremely negligent in the appointment of her rulers."[27]

Chapter 5

A BORN PATRIOT

As the spring of 1774 ended, Nathan looked forward to setting up a home and teaching school in a wonderfully liberal town by the sea. Meanwhile, the proprietors of the Union School, not to mention the people of New London, had awaited the arrival of their new schoolmaster with great anticipation. A Yale grad, a top scholar, had come not only to teach the classics, theology, Greek, Hebrew, and Latin, but hopefully to take charge of the school for an extended period. The children needed a permanent schoolmaster, a mentor who could inspire them to go on and become great leaders, thinkers, and, with the threat of confrontation with England mounting, dedicated patriots.

During that spring, Thomas Gage, a British general, was sailing to Boston with thousands of troops as colonists rebelling against the king's strong-arm tactics collected powder and ball and prepared for a standoff. Samuel Adams began organizing the Sons of Liberty and Committees of Correspondence, legislative groups formed in response to Britain's taxation laws and military action. The possibility of conflict was already being considered, although it was nearly a year away. Colonists would no longer accept the king's every order.

The clapboard schoolhouse, called Union because "twenty gentlemen united and built" it, had been dressed with a fresh coat of red paint shortly before Nathan rode into town. The building had four windows (each as tall as a man) on each side, with three in the front, four in the back. It sat squarely on a rock foundation near the edge of a small rise at the end of State Street, but was soon made into a corner lot by the construction of Union Street, a dirt road cutting several yards into the plot of land in back of the schoolhouse, leading the way into New London's thriving business district.[1]

The building was what we would call a colonial home today, fitted with a stone wall running along the eastern property line at eye level. The schoolyard was dotted with maple trees, their branches hanging over the roof. The facility was so new when Nathan took over, it wouldn't be incorporated and established by the Connecticut General Assembly until October 1774, months after Nathan's arrival, when twelve proprietors signed a petition, stating they had "built a commodious [new] school-house, and for several years past hired and supported a schoolmaster."[2]

The curriculum the proprietors set was "intended to furnish facilities for a thorough English education and the classical preparation necessary for entering college." Union, known as a "post of honor," was much larger than an average colonial school and could accommodate up to forty students at once. Parents lined up to enroll their children.[3]

Soon after Nathan got settled, he celebrated his nineteenth birthday. He had graduated from Yale, already taught in Moodus, and was now looking at a prosperous career in New London, all while still a teenager. Enoch wrote to Nathan not long after he arrived in town, mentioning a visit that Nathan had made to the Hale farm before relocating to New London. Enoch was in Lyme, a coastal town not too far south of New London, but would soon head to Coventry. He apologized for not stopping for a visit on his way, but explained there was trouble at home. "Mother [Abigail Adams] and Sally [Noyes, their great-grandmother, were] in a poor way," Enoch wrote, explaining that both women were sick. "I fear not so well."[4]

On his return to Lyme to hone his preaching skills, Enoch had left Billey, their youngest brother, "with Mr. Huntington to learn the Blacksmith's trade."[5]

Enoch had earlier told Nathan that he was going to drop off a cache of books Nathan had requested during his visit home, but "had no conveniency" to make the trip anytime soon. Because of that, he said, he "left word to have" the books ("*Pope's Iliad* & the 5th Vol. of the late war [an unnamed book] . . . which I found . . . and placed in my chest") "sent to you if opportunity presented."[6]

Enoch also said he was "in need of a pair of breaches" and knew of "no better place to purchase cloth than at New London." He wanted Nathan to visit a local merchant in town and "get as good & fashionable as you can but not too costly: for it is every day, therefore cheaper the better, & likewise trimmings."[7]

And so, within just a short time of being in New London, Nathan was back in the swing of life: conversing with family, taking nightly strolls through a bustling city, and preparing to educate the children of the most esteemed members of New London's society—everything he had been waiting for.

As soon as Nathan began holding classes, townspeople were enthralled by his charm and dedication to education. Frances Caulkins, who lived in New London all her life, would later interview former students of Nathan's and speak to other people in town who remembered him. During those early months when Nathan was still proving himself worthy of his position, he was said to be "frank and independent in his bearing." Others described him as "a man of many agreeable qualities . . . social, animated . . . a lover of the society of ladies, and a favorite among them."[8]

Nathan's teaching habits impressed the parents of his pupils. When the situation called for it, he could be a ruthless disciplinarian, lecturing the students if they failed to adhere to the classroom's strict rules. Nathan expected the children to dedicate themselves to the curriculum the same way he had, and they respected his love of literature and his ability to explain lessons in a way the children could easily grasp.[9]

During the summer and fall of 1774, as Nathan began to spend more time in the classroom, student Samuel Green got to know him well and became impressed by his charm and impartiality. Nathan was only a few years older than some of his students, including Green, who would later become one of Washington's colonels. Nathan and the children shared the same values and morals. But as Green later pointed out, how Nathan celebrated and taught those principles made the difference. Many of Nathan's students, if not all, were from affluent families. Religion had an integral part in the students' understanding of what it meant to be a colonist. Every school day began with Nathan leading the class in prayer. Only after the day had been given to the Lord would the hours of education commence.[10]

In Nathan, Samuel Green saw a role model. Nathan wasn't simply a tutor, as Union's previous schoolmaster had been; Green found him a magnetic presence. "Everyone who knew Hale," he later said, "was attached to him—that's the fact."[11]

This charisma struck Green as unusual, mostly because it came without hubris. Nathan had a "good sense & good feeling—warm . . . captivating to all who saw him. . . . Hale was a man particularly engaging in his manners— scholars young & old exceedingly attached to him—respected him highly by all his acquaintance—fine moral character."[12]

While in the classroom, Nathan kept the focus—"without severity"—on academics and theology; however, after school, when he headed out the door with the students trailing behind, he made sure to interact with them in a more relaxed way. Several times, Green reported, when the children were playing what we would call tag today or other games, Nathan joined in, displaying his athleticism. He could "jump from the bottom of one hogshead up and down into a second and from the second up and down into a third like a cat." On other occasions, he would place his hand on a wooden fence "high as his head" and, with the ease and grace of a gymnast, fling himself over in a one quick move.[13]

As the boys of Union came to know their teacher, they looked forward to heading off to school. They found in their new tutor a mentor and role model the likes of which they had never known and were excited to think that they had many years to soak up what this talented, delightful man was willing to share.

While Nathan was settling in New London, getting used to his new surroundings, rebel support for the Revolution was building. Because of its proximity to the Atlantic Ocean along the southern shore of Connecticut, the port of New London was vulnerable to British attack during the days leading up to war (and after), as England and America began a slow promenade into battle.[14] With rebels all across New England taking public stances against the British, staging meetings and displays of outrage over England's taxations, the king was determined to prove the British were still in charge. Tensions between the colonies and England began to escalate when what would become known as the Boston Tea Party erupted one night as Bostonians protested the taxes and economic policies of England. Word of what was referred to as the "destruction" that took place in Boston harbor didn't reach King George's desk until March 1774. When the message of what was considered an open act of rebellion by colonists reached the throne, details of the colonial revolt were immediately sent to Parliament, under orders to come up with a course of action for the British to take to keep the colonies under control.[15]

King George viewed the behavior in Boston as unwarranted, "obstructing the commerce of his kingdom." The Boston Tea Party seemed a violent and outrageous act that could not be brushed off with a single regiment filing into town to restore public order. Drastic action had to be taken. Parliament talked about what measures it should take to "put an immediate stop to those disorders," along with what "further regulations and permanent provisions might be necessary to establish, for better securing of the execution of the laws, and the just dependence of the colonies upon the Crown and Parliament of Great Britain."[16]

First, Parliament suggested sanctions. It demanded the British withdraw from the city and port and asked that all its officers begin to shut down the port to the shipping of any goods, which would greatly disrupt commerce for colonists. In addition, Parliament stressed the need to get a better handle on its American leaders in Massachusetts Bay, regulating the colonial government. Finally, they decided to strip executive power from the Democratic party, which consisted of local legislatures elected by the people.[17]

Smaller acts of rebellion by colonists prior to the Boston Tea Party were viewed by Parliament as excusable growing pains. The king had ignored colonists' complaints about laws and their holding public meetings to complain. But the Tea Party was a congregated, well-planned act of defiance; it was not a mere spur-of-the-moment act of rebellion. To quell any future acts of disobedience, a show of military might was the only way Britain could deal with this new situation. On the colonial side, rebels were privately meeting to discuss the various ways they could stage protests.

A bell had been rung, and the call to take up arms against England would soon hit the streets of Boston and branch out into New England and the rest of the colonies. If colonists couldn't trade goods with other countries or sell their products without British approval, what, essentially, did they have left? Americans needed to import and export products and goods. What jarred many was that the charter governments throughout America beginning in Massachusetts were "by an act intended to alter the constitution" stripped of their basic rights.[18] It was a change "so radical," Boston lawyer and writer George Ticknor Curtis wrote in 1860, "in the constitution of a people long accustomed to regard their charter as a compact between themselves and the crown" that it "could not but lead to the most serious consequences."[19]

With frustration increasing on both sides, on May 13, 1774, General Thomas Gage stepped off a ship from England at Long Wharf in Boston and was welcomed by a momentous parade. Gage was in town to take back control of Boston, which had, from Britain's point of view, turned toward anarchy over the past several months. To the dismay of Bostonians, just weeks before Gage's arrival, the Earl of Dartmouth, speaking on behalf of the king, had appointed Gage royal governor of Massachusetts, replacing Royal Governor Thomas Hutchinson, who was on his way to England to report to the king. Royal Lieutenant Governor Andrew Oliver, too sick to govern, was considered to be at death's door.

Gage not only had great leadership skills but years of military experience, having fought in the French and Indian War. Fearing violence could break out at any moment, he declared martial law immediately. Colonists had given the sanctions Britain had placed on them after the Tea Party a name: the Intolerable Acts. Gage knew Bostonians were angry and prepared to revolt. Within a few days after his arrival, he reached out to Connecticut governor Jonathan Trumbull, expressing a "readiness to cooperate" with him "for the good of his Majesty's service," with the hope Trumbull could help the situation in Boston. Trumbull was well respected and well known in Connecticut. A lawyer, he had been chief justice of the superior court and deputy governor—someone, in other words, who knew the ins and outs of negotiations.[20]

The "sovereignty of the king . . . over the colonies" required America's "full and absolute submission," the Earl of Dartmouth wrote. The earl, William Legge, was a devout Methodist and respected by the religious leaders of America. At one time, Legge had been the president of the Board of Trade and Foreign Plantations, which supervised colonial affairs. During this pivotal period of the conflict, however, Legge was the British secretary of state for the colonies, thus wielding great power over policy (though he would soon resign when war became inevitable).

The king wanted to punish those responsible for the uprising in Boston to send a message to the other colonies. He considered the penalties for such behavior "a very necessary and essential example," the earl continued, "to others of the ill consequences that must follow from such open and arbitrary usurpations as tend to the subversion of all government."[21]

In the meantime, England positioned a fleet of warships and schooners in Boston harbor to block trade as well as to remind Bostonians that superior firepower could claim dominance.

For the most part, Boston patriots sat back and made it appear as if the uprising they had staged was an anomaly, not the beginning of a more concerted revolt, which was coming together on its own. Britain felt confident that Gage had succeeded: Order was seemingly in place. Near the end of May, Gage wrote to his superiors describing how his presence had altered the unruly situation: "I am told that people will then speak and act openly, which they now dare not do."[22]

Still, the king sent several supporting divisions to Boston as the month of June passed. By August, British troops from Quebec, Halifax, the Jerseys, New York, and other regions along the coast were rallying in Salem, Danvers, Boston, Lexington, and Concord, not quite putting the brakes on the rebel effort, but certainly sending groups of rebels deeper underground. "Your Lordship will observe," Gage wrote, "that there [is] now an open opposition [to the rebels] . . . carried on with a warmth and spirit unknown before, which it is highly proper and necessary to cherish and support by every means; and I hope it will not be very long before it produces very salutary effects."[23]

Unbeknownst to the king, however, this show of might, along with the Boston Port Bill, which closed the port, thus taking the legs out from underneath the small businessmen, created poverty in Boston by not allowing merchants to sell their products. Unemployment skyrocketed and people starved. Soon, one local reported, "gloom pervaded the streets."[24]

Now, what did colonists have to lose if they rebelled? They had lost everything already. The one thing the king had not intended to inspire was exactly what took root: a belief that colonists had nothing left to lose.[25] After all, Puritans were not going to lie down and become slaves to Britain; it was time to unite and take a position of power against the king and his laws. After Parliament made its decision to amend the constitution, the First Continental Congress basically formed itself, with John Adams and cousin Samuel leading the way. Twelve of the thirteen colonies (Georgia opted out) sent delegates to Philadelphia's Carpenters Hall. George Washington and John Jay, Richard Henry Lee and Patrick Henry, were among the fifty-five delegates not necessarily ready to break entirely from Britain, but to make England fix taxation problems the Tea Party had pointed out in Boston that had led to such resentment against the king. Still, with word spreading of such a dramatic change in the political landscape taking place, young men such as Nathan Hale knew the next step might just be war with England, which many were now willing to drop everything for and participate in without question.[26]

The salty afternoon air blowing in off New London harbor was as thick and dense as the mist that hung over the town on most mornings. On clear days, the sky reaching out into the Atlantic turned an aquatic bluish purple, like that of ripened plums. As Nathan continued his new life as New London's teacher, he embraced the city and its citizens. He began to sense that he had not only found a job with a good salary and enthusiastic, obedient students, but a home for himself. In addition, many of Nathan's former Yale classmates, as they began to send him letters, viewed his move to New London as a step toward a more prestigious life. Ebenezer Williams, a Yale friend, wrote to Nathan on June 7. Williams already had his own teaching position in Wethersfield and opened the letter with a bit of congratulatory humor: "'What you too Brutus!' said Caesar when he saw his naked sword. What you too Nathan! Says Ebenezer when he finds you engaged the amorous pursuit."[27]

Williams wondered how Nathan had landed such an admirable job in a town that was viewed as an ideal home for a boy just out of college and hoping to court several young ladies. "What is there in your *London* air," Williams asked, "that so powerfully instigates the young People to such Business, which we are destitute of here in the little Village of Wethersfield? In the air I say, because I am positive it can be nothing else."[28]

Like most young men their age, both Nathan and Williams were preoccupied with another sort of "amorous pursuit." In a previous letter, now lost, Nathan seems to have told Williams he had set his sights on a few New London ladies who visited him at Union. Now Williams wanted more details. "What is there in your *London* air," he asked again. ". . . You whose pursuits, I am sure, were once far different. At Yale Your Character was that of a Scholar, & not of a Buck!"[29]

Nathan's predecessor may have gotten into a bit of trouble with a girl in town, as Williams referenced his exploits as a cautionary tale, writing, "You will not, however, carry matters to so great a length as he did I hope & trust. For a Wife without an Employment is not the most desirable acquisition. I will therefore do more honor to your Judgment than to suppose you entertain designs of marrying at present. . . . We are apt to gaze with pleasure on anything Beautiful. We are too little able to withstand any Evil that comes in the form of a beautiful female.[30]

"But will for once suppose you mean only to endeavor to fix the affec-

tions of the young Lady, that you may be in danger of losing her while engaged in different Parts."[31]

Smallpox had recently taken its toll on the tiny village where Williams
lived. Most of the girls in town, he said, had been sent away to a hospital on
Duck-Island, near New London, a few miles out into Long Island Sound.
He also talked about riding into Coventry in search of Nathan's brother
Enoch the week before. But Enoch had already left for Lyme. "As I would
tell you, your Mother and Sister-in-Law were unwell."[32]

Several of Nathan's nineteenth- and early-twentieth-century biographers, as well as members of the Adams family, claimed that by this point
Nathan had his heart set on his stepsister Alice Adams, and that the two of
them had carried on a romance in secret since Richard Hale had married
Alice's mother, Abigail, and brought the child into the Hale household.
Some even claimed that a poem allegedly written by Nathan during this
period was for Alice, or, as the poem states, "Alicia." One problem with this
theory, however, is that Nathan never mentioned Alice by name in *any* of
his letters to friends or relatives. On the contrary, he wrote often about *other*
girls during this period. If Alice had taken up such a large portion of
Nathan's heart, one would think he (or Alice) would at least have mentioned
it. Marrying or courting among stepchildren in eighteenth-century New
England was not frowned upon—it was often encouraged. As for the poem,
it's difficult to claim this poem was written for Alice Adams, or that it was
even written by Nathan. No one in the family referred to Alice by the name
Alicia. The poem cannot positively be attributed to Nathan because the
handwriting was vastly different from his known penmanship. So we are
left with a poem addressed to a woman named Alicia by a writer who might
not have been Nathan Hale. George Dudley Seymour, in his book *Documentary Life of Nathan Hale*, addresses this issue. According to oral tradition, Seymour noted, "The manuscript, as [I] understand it, is that from
Hale's stepsister, Mrs. Alice (Adams) (Ripley) Lawrence, [and was] passed
to her granddaughter, Miss Alicia Sheldon, and from her hands into those
of the late Mr. George E. Hoadley of Hartford, who afterwards furnished
a copy of it to Johnston [one of Hale's early biographers], who accepted it
and used it as authentic."

The debate over whether Nathan and Alice had a romantic affair has gone on now for over a century. Some claim that Richard, Nathan's father, actually tried to keep them apart by marrying Alice off to an affluent, local Coventry man, Elijah Ripley. But this, too, seems highly unlikely, seeing that one of Nathan's brothers married another of Abigail Adams's daughters near the same time. Why would Richard disallow Nathan to marry Alice but allow another son to make a similar bond?

Then there are Alice's supposed deathbed words of devotion to Nathan. As she lay dying, the octogenarian supposedly said, "Write to Nathan," as she slipped away. This, too, is fodder for the romantic legend, seeing that Nathan had long been dead.

It seems possible that Nathan felt an affection for Alice, who was, by many accounts, beautiful, well-spoken, and close in age. But there is not sufficient evidence to say they were romantically attached in *any* manner. Furthermore, Nathan was nowhere near Coventry when Alice began living with the Hale family. He was already at Yale, then Moodus, and later at New London.

Nathan wrote often to his peers and family members about his job, the people around him, and the politics of the day. "I love my employment [and] find many friends among strangers," he wrote shortly after settling in New London. "I will have time for scientific study," he explained to Dr. Eneas Munson, his mentor and friend from Yale. "My school is by no means difficult to take care of. It consists of about thirty scholars; ten of whom are . . . college bound and all but six of the rest are writers" (boys interested in learning only reading and writing, which was a normal course of study for a Puritan child with the means to attend school, but not college).[33]

Occasionally, his recipients would find vague references regarding the formation of Congress and the talk of war. On September 8, 1774, for instance, Nathan sat down at his desk inside the Union School and wrote a brief note to Enoch. In it he promised to buy his brother the cloth he had so desired and deliver it home as soon as he could. But the main theme of the letter centered on the escalating political situation:

No liberty-pole is erected or erecting here: but the people seem much
more inspired than they were before the alarm. Parson Peters of Hebron,
I hear, has had a second visit paid to him by the sons of liberty in Windham. . . . I have not heard from home.[34]

The Sons of Liberty was the name given to any colonial group of men
who opposed taxation laws set in place by Parliament. Towns and villages
throughout New England, and many in New York, had erected "liberty"
poles around which colonists rallied in support of America and to protest
British law and taxes. To stand under a liberty pole was to say, *Enough is
enough.* The British authorities would tear down the poles whenever they
could, but as soon as the British left the area, a new pole was erected. New
England was changing. Connecticut colonists were beginning to speak their
minds about Britain's latest attempts to take away some of their basic rights.
Enoch and Nathan had discussed the situation throughout the summer and
vowed to support the colonies in any way they could, probably under the influence of their father, who later talked about his devotion to the rebel effort.

In the meantime Nathan continued his role as schoolmaster, and his letters reveal a young man looking forward to a life of reading, teaching, and
studying science. New London was a wondrous place for a man of Nathan's
age, full of political opportunities, high-paying jobs, and wealthy intellectuals. In addition to the day's classes, Nathan was overjoyed, he wrote, at
having "a morning class of young ladies—about a score—from five to seven
o'clock" in the morning to teach.[35]

As September drew to a close, the absence of family or friends around
him began to put a damper on the novelty and thrill of living in such a
thriving community. Nathan was lonely once again. The freshness of the
place and the people had been lost. He had been in New London for seven
months; and he began to miss being around people he knew. Though he
filled his time teaching and dining among New London's elite, the boredom
Nathan had suffered in Moodus returned. He wrote to his uncle Samuel on
September 24, expressing his unhappiness. Describing his prior visit north
to Portsmouth, New Hampshire, he noted how much he missed everyone

and wanted to make a second trip, but added, "This is a happiness, which at present, I have but little prospect of enjoying."[36]

He then explained how he felt he had lost touch with his "Father and family." Richard was busy with the farm. Nathan hadn't seen or heard from anyone for at least three months. The last letter he'd received from Enoch was in May, who mentioned that Elizabeth Rose, their sister, had married a doctor and "has, as I suppose, the prospect of very comfortable living."[37]

Next, he explained to Samuel that his salary would be seventy pounds, supplemented by earnings from his morning class for girls. "The people with whom I live are free and generous," he continued, "many of them gentlemen of sense and merit." He said he didn't mind settling down, but it would take "a considerable increase in wage" by the proprietors, who had already made an offer of a slight increase Nathan wasn't sure he wanted to take.[38]

Then Nathan asked his uncle for his advice regarding a more permanent position at the school the proprietors were pressuring him to take, knowing that the best guidance was from someone "who has spent his life in the business." Nathan's current agreement had run out, and the school wanted him to sign a contract for an extended period. For Nathan, money wasn't the issue; he just wasn't sure he wanted to stay in New London and continue teaching. "Your advice in the matter . . . would, I think, be the best I could possibly receive." Ending the letter with a postscript, he asked Samuel to "please present my duty to my aunt, and my fondest regards to all my Cousins."[39]

The ambition Nathan displayed was part of whom he had grown into since leaving Yale just a year earlier. Whenever he achieved a chosen goal, he immediately set higher standards for himself. He was rarely ever satisfied with an accomplishment for long and put considerable pressure on himself to continually seek bigger and better things, always searching for a new opportunity to prove himself—and the conflict on the horizon would soon provide the chance he had been looking for.

Chapter 6

TALK OF WAR

THE FALL OF 1774 came to New London with cool temperatures and, on more days than not, a hard, slanting rain. Yet despite the dreary conditions, it was the absence of Nathan's peers that brought on his spells of melancholy. Nathan was anxious to hear what was going on in their lives. By this point, it had been more than a year since he had seen many of them. New Haven was only a two-hour ride west, and yet he did not make a trip into the city. "I want much to receive a letter from you," Nathan wrote to Thomas Mead, one of five members of the Quintumviri, a group of Yale alumni Nathan belonged to, "and a full history of the transactions of the winter [1773–74]. I have heard many flying reports, but know not what to conclude as to the truth of them."[1]

Each of Nathan's closest friends from college had gone his separate way after graduation, though they had made detailed plans to keep in touch. The Quintumviri had been formed by Nathan, Thomas Mead, James Hillhouse, John Alden, and James Wyllys. The members planned to meet in the years after graduation for discourse regarding matters of public importance: politics, commerce, the state of the colonies, and social ideals the members held deeply. The Quintumviri was mainly designed to continue and fortify their companionship. Nathan and his Yale friends wanted something to keep them connected for life and believed the Quintumviri could do that. Not hearing from the other members bothered Nathan. He felt the promise to keep in touch slipping away. "Upon the whole I take it for certain," Nathan continued to Mead, "that the *Quintumviri* have been massacred, but in what manner I have not been sufficiently informed.—From what I can collect, I think probable you have had some *high doings* this winter, but expect a more full account of these matters in your next [letter]."[2]

Nathan was at ease in New London, certainly, but he couldn't help trying to figure out what had gone so wrong back in Moodus. Was it teaching in general or the school that had let him down? Was there something *he* could have done to better his circumstances or supplement his work? It seemed as if constant change and challenge were the only means to keep life interesting for him.[3]

Nathan explained to Mead that the Union School he was overseeing was "somewhat preferable to" where he was "last winter," adding, "My school is by no means difficult to take care of." And this was the crux of the problem: In New London, there was little for Nathan to fix. Settling into a post that carried on so smoothly, without much complication, he feared life would soon turn boring; if there was nothing to strive for, the repetition of waking up and working would eventually wear him down.[4]

Ending the letter, Nathan showed his resolve and determination to stay in touch with Mead, acknowledging:

> For the greater part of last year, we were good neighbours, and I always thought, very good friends. Surely so good on my part, that it would be [a] matter of real grief to me, should our friendship cease.—The only means for maintaining it is constant writing: in the practice of which I am ready most heartily to concur with you; and do hope ever to remain, as at present.[5]

In practice, Nathan was not always so dedicated a correspondent. His friend Benjamin Tallmadge had written twice that summer, chiding him for not holding up his end of their planned correspondence. Tallmadge, a sprightly young man enjoying the single life, liked to poke fun at his friend from time to time. In just a few short years, war would change Tallmadge from that boisterous teenager, full of life, into a hardened, serious soldier. But for now he was full of the vigor of life. In one letter, Tallmadge teased Nathan about the maiden he had left behind in Moodus. "Friend Hale," he wrote, ". . . I should be very glad to have some direct news from you, I do assure you: for by the last accounts you was all over (head and heels) in love." Some later speculated that this "love" Tallmadge was referring to was Alice Adams. This is highly unlikely: Alice was married by this time to Elijah Ripley and raising their child.[6]

In that same succinct letter during the summer of 1774, Tallmadge joyfully ended by making light of the situation he believed Nathan had fallen into with a local lass, saying, "Now if you do not get shifted in the *scrape*, I should be very glad to know of it. I can say, as an Irishman has said before me, 'I know you are not dead, for if you was you would have sent me word before now.'"[7]

In August, Silas Deane, a prominent Hartford lawyer and Yale grad, made the trip to Philadelphia in a private coach with Roger Sherman and Eliphalet Dyer, two additional delegates selected for the Continental Congress from Connecticut. Deane would soon become America's father of foreign diplomacy, before being kicked out of Congress, but along the trail to Philadelphia, he met up with John Adams and soon befriended George Washington. The First Continental Congress convened on September 5, 1774; by the end of October, it had taken several assertive positions against the British. For one, a "Declaration of Rights and Resolves" was approved, claiming the rights of assembly, petition, and trial by peers, as opposed to trial in England, and also proposed was an "Association," or small governing body, inside each colony, to object to trade and consumption of British goods. With that, war was no longer a possibility, but an imminent reality.

As Nathan ruminated about his time in New London and talk of war dominated public discourse, he struggled between contentment and what he thought he was missing in the world beyond New London. He was frequently looking around the next corner, wondering what life was going to bring his way. And sure enough, something new finally arrived. Days after Tallmadge wrote, Nathan received a letter from another of his Quintumviri mates, James Hillhouse, who also jabbed Nathan for not being more productive with his quill, writing, "How to account for your long silence I know not. It can't be you did not know the place of my abode; or that your Letters would not be acceptable."[8]

Hillhouse said he had at first thought Nathan was in Windsor, Connecticut, or Providence, Rhode Island, and because of that confusion, it had been tough to find him. Flattering Nathan with a bit of ornamented jealousy, he added, "Thus you post about the world, & nobody is able to find you, forming to yourself new Friends and acquaintance, who in length of time may Root out old ones."[9]

Studying law in New Haven, Hillhouse reported, was not turning out the way he had thought it might. The laziness he had fallen into while at Yale was coming back to hurt him. Apparently, after graduating, he had expected any subsequent lessons would be a breeze. But that hadn't been the case: "The study of Law I find to be very Intricate and difficult study, that Requires much Labor & Patience—I now wish I had improved my time [to a] better advantage when at College."[10]

In the same letter, Hillhouse urged Nathan to take a look at where his life was headed and the call that was waiting for him: "Liberty is our reigning Topic, which loudly calls upon every one to Exert his Talents & abilities to the utmost in defending of it—now is the time for heroes—now is the time for great men to immortalize their names in the deliverance of their Country, and grace the annals of America with their Glorious deeds."[11]

Hillhouse's words were a call to take a stand. For the first time since Nathan had been in New London, one of his peers had written to push Nathan to take an active role in the colonial struggle. As the days progressed and tensions between colonists and the British mounted, however, the question for Nathan became, how would he respond to such a call?

Harvard-educated Connecticut governor Jonathan Trumbull viewed it as his duty as an American statesman to further the colonies' standing in the world, rather than to think only of his immediate community. George Washington would become so impressed with Trumbull's sense of dignity, he would one day brand Trumbull "the first of the patriots" and refer to him as "Brother Jonathan."[12]

As the colonies squared off politically with the throne through the fall of 1774, sixty-four-year-old Trumbull was putting in place an infrastructure of officials to assist the Continental Congress in Philadelphia with what appeared to be an impending split with the king. Trumbull was no longer concerned only with Connecticut's fate.

Another staunch opponent of the British who generally agreed with Trumbull was Samuel Adams. With talks between American and English leaders breaking down, and colonists staging public acts against the king's orders in Boston, Adams took charge of putting together a more concerted political party to provide leadership if talks between the two powers ended and bloodshed began.[13]

As Adams worked to set up committees in towns throughout the Boston region, supporting efforts to form local governments, in Connecticut Trumbull made public his state's part in the new America. That previous May, before the General Assembly, it had been decided that liberty and freedom were now at stake and something political needed to be done about it. The colonies had to step away from Britain on their own.[14]

The colonies were preparing in case England decided to take military action in response to the Tea Party, or against the mass gatherings of rebels throughout New England. Congress agreed that it would convene, on a moment's notice, should a threatening situation arise. After Trumbull declared his state's willingness to participate in a full-scale rebellion, an "order to all the towns [throughout New England and Virginia] to double the quantity of their powder, balls, and flints" was issued by Congress. "Also by a series of Resolutions," Trumbull urged, "on the part of Connecticut . . . America denounced [Britain's laws] as usurpations that placed life, liberty, and property, in every English Colony, at utter hazard." In no way were the British going to be able to strip Americans of their rights through force.[15]

As this political and social disorder went on around Nathan, tragedy struck the Hale family. While Nathan was in New London during the winter of 1774–75, sleet and rain keeping him indoors, word came of a death in the family. Alice Adams's husband, Elijah Ripley, died of consumption a day after Christmas. He was twenty-eight years old. Alice was eighteen, a widow and mother already. And although she had been unhappy with the marriage from the start, Elijah's death sent her into pure misery. They had been married for nearly two years. Alice had recently given birth to their first child. But now she was alone and caring for a child by herself, though their child would also succumb to disease and die within the next six months.[16] Surely Nathan felt for his stepsister's loss; however, no record of his reaction exists.

During this period, the world around Nathan was in a constant transformation. He had decided to stay in New London and was asking the proprietors of the Union School for a raise, while also juggling several different romances. His friend Ebenezer Williams, writing over the summer, believed his friend was in love with Betsy Adams, the daughter of Pygan Adams, a New London socialite Nathan had boarded with for a time. Other letters Nathan received during this period indicate he was also courting two other ladies.[17]

As 1775 dawned, Nathan's fellow Yale alumni continued to complain about his lack of correspondence. He still wasn't writing with any consistency, and seemed only to write when he needed a favor or wanted to scold someone for saying something about him or getting too involved in his personal life. On January 11, 1775, Ebenezer Williams wrote a letter accusing Nathan of abandoning his former classmates and peers. Williams was in New Haven and scolded his old friend for not visiting. He said he would likely spend the winter in town, "to which no son of Adam would be more heartily welcome than a quondam [former] friend vulgarly call'd Nathan Hale."[18]

Williams said he was suffering from bouts of melancholy and "I doubt not but you have yours also. . . . I am peculiarly subject to these turns" of depression, he partly joked, "when employed in writing Letters to absent Friends."[19] He wanted Nathan to write back to him at once and tell him if he felt the same. Nathan had friends who were there for him, people who cared about him, if only he could swallow his pride and reach out.

Nathan had spent nearly a year in New London, and despite his students and romances with the neighborhood lasses, the letters his friends wrote to him make it clear that he felt something was missing. He decided to stay at the Union School, but he never mentioned that he was happy about it and seemed to keep asking himself, "Is this all there is?"

Following the situation in Boston throughout that winter, Nathan began thinking more about his duty as a colonist in the dispute with Britain than about the affairs of New London's faithful scholars. In February, Nathan wrote to Richard Sill, a fellow student he had met while in New Haven. Nathan was two years older than Sill, who was in his final semester at Yale. Sill was pleasantly surprised to hear from Nathan, knowing of course how sporadic he had been with his correspondence. Nathan told Sill he was going to begin the year on a high note, making sure to reform his lackadaisical letter-writing habits. "I trust it will be to my great satisfaction as well as your other friends," Sill wrote in return.[20]

Sill painted a fairly dreary picture of Yale, letting Nathan know that Sill's studies were now structured more around military training than texts, which he would have preferred. Yale was staging drills in the College Yard in support of the rebel effort. The campus, Sill said, "constantly sounds with, *poise your firelock, Cock your firelock.*" The military presence at Yale seemed like "great evidence that war will be proclaimed soon."

New Haven was predominantly for the rebel effort; however, as in many of the larger cities throughout New England, Tories were not hard to find. There were two "Regular Soldiers," Sill explained, training students, getting them ready in case of a surprise attack by the British. He talked about the "shortness of time" they had to prepare, as the officers running the training program said fighting could break out at any moment. "You know New Haven hath had the name of entertaining a great number of Tories, take this in some measure of their Justification—It was reported in Town that [two deputies in the rebel movement] were Tories."[21]

Getting word from back home in Coventry, Nathan heard that a terrible throat ailment had been working its way through town, already having taken a number of lives, including those of many infants. Nathan's brother Richard was "very sick" with the same infection, wrote Nathan's brother John, his throat "very much Swelled so that he can't Swallow but a very Little."[22] Ending the letter, John asked Nathan to place an ad in the New London newspaper announcing, "All persons having Accounts against the Estate of Mr. Elijah Ripley . . . are desired to" make a claim in Coventry. John was clearing up Elijah's debts, so he could set Alice up with a home and fewer worries.[23]

All around Nathan were the signs of coming war. He watched as cannons were moved into the port in New London, pointed outward into the harbor, and took note as the legislature in Hartford began assembling military divisions. For Nathan, like many young men his age, life was about to change considerably. In weeks, Nathan would fill that void that had clearly consumed him over the past six months, while encouraging many of his fellow Americans to follow him. Although a majority of New Londoners weren't thrilled about the prospect of fighting a war, and the town was made up of mostly intellectuals and the wealthy elite, Nathan would inspire many to see that the issues at hand were far-reaching.

Chapter 7

Free from the Shadow of Guile

W HEN SAM ADAMS HEARD shots had been fired between American minutemen and British soldiers near Lexington Common and Concord on April 19, 1775, he was so overjoyed by what had finally occurred, he was said to have exclaimed, "Oh, what a glorious morning is this."[1]

The fighting near Lexington and Concord that followed was intermittent. These were common men engaged in a small skirmish resulting in bloodshed. As one soldier later put it, those defending America's honor did mostly surveillance. They moved stealthily about the countryside, watching the British and their activities rather than actually fighting. "We marched from Roxbury . . . to Concord and there they were Defeated and Drove Back fighting as they went they gat to Charlestown hill that night." After arriving outside Roxbury later on, "We stayed there some time and refreshed our Selves and then marched to Roxbury parade and there we had as much Liquor as we wanted and every man drawed three Biscuit which were taken from the regulars the day before which were hard enough for flints."[2]

The following day, April 20, plants were rising from the ground already, and passing soldiers were surprised to see flower buds poking through the soft crust of the earth. Although the conflict at Lexington wouldn't last long, and each side blamed the other for firing first, men had died and blood had soiled the ground. Thus, with the start of spring, the Revolution had begun.[3]

At about 9:00 A.M. on that same April morning, a committee from Watertown, Massachusetts, ushered express postrider Israel Bissell, a young colonist who had proclaimed a desire to help the rebel effort any way he could, into its office and gave him specific instructions to ride through the country spreading the news of what had occurred in Lexington and Concord. As Bissell entered the town of Worcester at noon, about thirty miles west of Boston, heading for the meetinghouse, he barely pulled back on the bridle of his horse before shouting, "To arms, to arms . . . the war is begun."

After he stopped, Bissell fell from his white horse, whose hind legs, from his violent spurring, had been bloodied, and watched the horse fall to the ground, exhausted from the nonstop trip.[4]

Rather than finding another horse, Bissell rested for the night. He had much ground to cover inside the next twenty-four hours. He would be meeting a fellow postrider near New York to hand off the news and continue on into Westchester County, the Bronx, and, finally, the City of New York. Saddled on a new horse given to him by the people of Worcester, Bissell reached Brooklyn, Connecticut, a farming community in the northeastern part of the state, by 11:00 A.M. on the morning of April 21. According to one story, Israel Putnam, set to become one of Washington's adjutant generals and a central figure in Nathan's early military life, was working in the fields on a stone wall when Bissell rode into town. After waiting for word of war to come any day, Putnam dropped what he was doing upon hearing the news and immediately left for Boston.[5]

The Root family of Coventry was one of the more affluent in town, with a lineage dating back to the township's earliest settlers. Eighteen-year-old Nathaniel Root, a hardworking, devoted son who spent his spring and summer days under the scorching sun in the fields just down the road from the Hale farm, was plowing an acre by himself that afternoon when the news reached Coventry. Walking steadily behind his oxen, guiding the jumpy plow, Nathaniel looked off into the distance and saw a man waving his arms and hat, running toward him.[6]

Nathaniel stopped his plow upon seeing the man and, within a few moments of learning the news, abandoned his plow and oxen where they stood, ran inside the Roots' farmhouse, and "quickly said goodbye to his mother," who no doubt stood in utter shock that the boy was leaving town so suddenly to join the rebellion.[7]

Meanwhile, Bissell made it thirteen additional miles to Norwich by 7:00 P.M. The town newspaper, the Norwich *Packet*, would detail the patriotic zeal sweeping across middle New England as Bissell rode into each town and shared the news: America was now engaged in war with England— there was no turning back. And even at this early stage, a bit of reality for the colonists was interjected into the discourse as the *Packet* noted what stood before the rebel army and freedom from England:

> Boston is now reduced to an alarming crisis, big with important events. Like a new piece of ordnance, deeply charged for the trial of its strength; we listen with attention to hear its convulsed explosion, suspending ourselves in mysterious doubt, whether it will burst with dreadful havoc, or recoil upon the engineers to their great confusion. The blocking up of Boston is like turning the tide of a murmuring river upon the whole land, and thereby spreading a dangerous inundation through the continent, for resentment already flows high ... and if it join with the flux of Boston, it may occasion a sea of troubles.[8]

Governor Trumbull was in Norwich when Bissell arrived. As the news made its way through each village by town crier, different scenarios played out, different versions of the truth were repeated, and different stories of what was going on in Boston were made more dire and dramatic. By one account, the British were said to have "landed two brigades, have already killed 6 men, and wounded 4 others, and are on their march into the country." When Nathan's friend Ebenezer Williams got word in Pomfret, a small village just outside Norwich, where he had been living, he heard that

"50 of our people are killed and 150 of the regulars [British soldiers]—that is, as near as they could determine when the express came away."

In a letter home, Israel Putnam, having ridden over sixty miles in eighteen hours to reach Boston, called for "immediate supplies of troops and provisions" to be sent. Putnam described the British as barbaric. He claimed the "invading enemy" had burned down houses, "killing children, and putting the muzzle of the gun into the mouths of sick people not able to move, and blowing their heads to pieces."[9]

In Coventry, 116 men and children, among them Richard Hale's sons John, Joseph, Richard Jr., Samuel, and David, dropped everything in the days that followed and traveled to Boston, where military leaders were preparing an army. In towns throughout northeastern Connecticut, as well as in the seashore communities along Long Island Sound, including New Haven, New London, and Saybrook, men and children deserted civilian life on a moment's notice and rode east without question. Thousands of able-bodied Americans from all over New England, some as young as ten years old, assembled in Boston to take up arms against the British.[10]

Late in the afternoon of April 22, a breathless, fatigued messenger, possibly Israel Bissell on his way to meet his New York rider (although the messenger was never identified), stopped in New London. At the time it was considered a village, more laid-back, tranquil, and academic than martial. Sea trade was New London's main source of commerce. With the new sanctions Britain was proposing for America, however, the city had a lot to lose.[11]

Curious about the commotion in town, Nathan walked out of his school-house and joined the growing crowd. The news had motivated and mobilized the people of New London, and many around him cheered at the sound of the alarm. For Nathan, a new opportunity had arrived: a call to serve. He just didn't know it until it was there in front of him. Many colonists saw the call as God's will more than simply a question of politics; there could be no other explanation for it. Later, author Charles Dudley Warner reflected on this moment, speculating on what Nathan and men like him felt as the news reached town: "American faith, invincible, American love of country, unquenchable, a new democratic manhood in the world, visible there for all men to take note of, crowned already with the halo of victory in the Revolutionary dawn."[12]

As people talked, some bewildered by the thought of war, some unquestionably relieved, a man stepped forward and announced there would be a town meeting at twilight inside the courthouse. Everyone was expected to attend. New London, as a community, would decide on a strategy and devise a way to respond to what had taken place in Boston. Nathan returned to his classroom and pondered what he was going to do.[13]

Around 7:00 P.M. on that same day, thirty-nine-year-old Judge Richard Law banged his gavel to begin the town meeting, once most of his fellow New Londoners joined him at the meeting's new location, Miner's Tavern on Bank Street. The boisterous crowd of people, jockeying for elbow space, were excited to decide how New London was going to respond to the call for men and arms.[14]

Among the many patriotic resolutions Judge Law addressed was whether Captain William Coit's independent military company, which had been formed during the winter of 1775 as hostilities between the nations developed, would be sent to Boston. Coit was a native New Londoner, a Yale graduate, and "prominent in the patriotic cause before the beginning of hostilities," historian Frances Caulkins wrote. Described as a "blunt, jovial, eccentric" man, quite strange in composure, Coit stood tall and "very large in frame." His presence alone turned heads. Around town, Coit was known never to leave his house without first donning a scarlet and black cloak, which earned him the nickname the Great Red Dragon. His company, made up of volunteers, was well trained and equipped, proclaiming itself ready for any emergency. Standing and looking out at the crowd, Coit suggested now was as good a time as any for them to saddle and ride to Boston. This was the moment they had been training for all along, he said.[15]

After it was settled that Coit's company would leave at the break of dawn, Nathan stood and walked toward Judge Law's makeshift bench, motioning for an opportunity to be heard. Law asked for order, as the town's schoolmaster stood before the crowd, waiting to speak.[16]

After everyone settled down, Nathan explained that he wanted to march as a volunteer to Boston with Coit's company. It was the least he could do. Others, he added, should follow him. As he spoke, Judge Law's son, Richard, one of Nathan's youngest students at approximately ten, stood by his schoolmaster's side, wondering what he meant.[17]

Nathan finished his speech with a powerful, heartening message: "Let us march immediately and never lay down our arms until we obtain our independence."[18]

This was, many nineteenth- and twentieth-century scholars and historians later argued, probably the first time a colonist had publicly announced that the colonies desired independence from Britain—that they weren't only protesting sanctions and taxation. But as Nathan suggested, bloodshed near the Lexington green had turned a political fight into a greater matter. Independence was a calling. God's will. And Nathan Hale may well have been the first to say in public what most were thinking: Drop your life and give it up to our God and country.

For some, the word was not at all familiar. "It is worth noting," Nathan's great-grandnephew E. E. Hale, a prolific writer and Unitarian clergyman, would say many years later, "in this connection that the word 'independence' was at the time a new word. It was a word which does not appear in Shakespeare; it came into existence as a theological term to represent the position of . . . extreme Puritans." The word originated between 1630 and 1640.[19]

Richard Law tugged at his father's cloak upon hearing Nathan utter the word, eager to know what he meant. Richard, who would himself soon become a captain, later said that "he was very young at the time, but partaking to the general excitement . . . [of the meeting, he was] struck by the noble demeanor of [his teacher], and the emphasis with which he addressed the assembly."[20]

One reason why Nathan made such an impression on many that night, thus gaining standing among the townspeople as a military leader, was that his reputation in the community was then, as one citizen later put it, unsurpassed. Though not even twenty, he spoke with the passion and wisdom of a cleric or tutor ten years his senior. There was something different about him, a magnetism that drew people to him in ways others, even elders who had lived in town all their lives, could not explain. "His Capacity as a Teacher," wrote Elizabeth Poole, who boarded in the same New London house as Nathan for a time, "and the mildness of his mode of instruction, was highly appreciated by Parents & Pupils; his appearance, manners, & temper secured the purest affections of those to whom he was known." Poole noted that in public settings Nathan's character truly outshone that of those around him, as if the words he spoke off-the-cuff were prepared beforehand. "As a Companion in a social, particularly in the domestic circle, his simple unostentatious manner of imparting right views & feelings to less cultivated understandings [was unrivaled] by any individual who then, or since, has fallen under my observation." Furthermore, Poole explained, Nathan was "free from the shadow of guile." When he spoke to a group outside the classroom, which wasn't often, it was because he had something important to share. Not only was he able to talk of England's oppression over America, he did it in an understandable manner; he was speaking from his heart, articulating what he honestly believed. "No species of deception had any lurking place in his frank, open meek & pious mind; his soul disdained disguise."[21]

As much as Nathan wanted to pack and ride with Coit and his men the next morning, he had obligations to tend to beforehand. He wasn't running a farm or striking metals for a local blacksmith; he was a highly regarded schoolmaster who needed to conduct himself with professionalism. After all, when the war was over, Nathan expected to return to civilian life and continue working.

The next morning, Nathan addressed his pupils. He wanted to put their minds at ease. He explained that he was indeed leaving. But not right away. After thinking it over, he decided that it was best to enlist in the army, instead of dropping everything and running to Boston, as many colonists had been doing in joining the militia units popping up all over.[22]

Joining hands with them, Nathan knelt and prayed alongside his students. When they finished, he addressed each one personally, consoling each student separately before extending a firm handshake good-bye.[23]

This was one of the most pivotal moments in Nathan's short life. Overnight, it seemed, he had been commissioned a lieutenant in Colonel Charles Webb's Connecticut Seventh Regiment, given that high position of authority mainly because he was well educated and could read and write. In the months to come, seemingly speaking of the day when he gave up his studious, untroubled life of teaching, in a way that was both professional and of great value to the community, Nathan would write, "A man ought never to lose a moment's time. If he put off a thing for one minute to the next, his reluctance is but increased."

For the past few months Nathan had wrestled with the idea of leaving New London; now it was utterly clear to him that his first instinct to go to Boston was the right decision.[24]

Chapter 8

A Sense of Duty

O N J UNE 15, 1775, one month and five days after the Second Continental Congress had convened in response to the ongoing conflict in
and around Boston, it unanimously chose General George Washington to
act as commander in chief of the Continental Army. A delegate from Virginia, Washington reluctantly took on the leadership role that was essentially thrust upon him.[1] In keeping with his often reserved sense of self,
which many viewed as stubbornness, Washington would not take the position without expressing a hint of indecision.[2]

In his acceptance speech, Washington said he was "truly sensible of the
high honor done me, in this appointment, yet I feel great distress, from a
consciousness that my abilities and military experience may not be equal to
the extensive and important trust."[3]

It had originally been John Adams's idea to form a Continental Army
and select Washington as its leader. When Washington, who was sitting in
Congress listening to the discussion, heard Adams's proposal, he was said to
have retired from his seat and withdrawn from the state room. In the days
that followed, Washington continued to hesitate, making his feelings clear

in a letter to his wife, Martha: "You may believe me, when I assure you, in the most solemn manner, that, so far from seeking this appointment, I have used every endeavor in my power to avoid it, not only from my unwillingness to part with you and the family, but from a consciousness of its being a trust too great for my capacity."[4]

Because of his heroic actions and the leadership he displayed in the French and Indian War, delegates viewed Washington, despite what he thought of himself, as the only man for the job. After Washington grudgingly accepted, Congress quickly chose his supporting staff. Horatio Gates was later added to the faction as an adjutant general, soon to be riding side by side with Washington into the hazardous grove of the battlefield.[5] From Philadelphia, Cambridge was a three-hundred-mile hike. Washington and his team left Philadelphia on June 21. After an extraordinary reception in the City of New York, including a parade, they rode into Cambridge on July 2 just as a torrential rainstorm pounded the region.

By now, towns and cities throughout New England were meeting to discuss the basic structure of the army and how each colony would supply Washington with stores and troops. In Hartford, the General Assembly met and, as in many other towns throughout Connecticut, began to govern themselves by voting to send regiments of troops to the Boston region. Connecticut secretary of state Royal R. Hinman wrote in 1842 describing the nominal transition from *colonies*, each "subject to the crown of Great Britain," into one united *colony*. The colonies understood that during a time of war the objective was to join together and support one another.[6]

While Washington and his team set up camp in Cambridge, anticipating a full assault by the British, who were sending fleets of warships toward Boston harbor and other points along the eastern shoreline, in New London Nathan worked on finding his place in the new army. Wherever he went, the patriot cause dominated conversation, and Nathan took a spirited interest in the political rhetoric and exchange of patriotic ideas. "Politicks," a former Yale classmate wrote to Nathan near this time, "engross so much of the attention of people of all ages & denominations among us that little else is heard of or thought of."[7]

Nathan held a similarly loyal outlook, which would soon become obvious as he began to document his life in an army journal. Confidence in the rebel effort was growing across New England as the call to take up arms was broadcast from Maine to Virginia. Determined to defend the honor of their colonies, galvanized by the idea of freedom, men were showing up in cities and towns throughout the Northeast, often with every male member—including children as young as ten—of their families in tow. Nathan heard that all "publick exercises and exhibitions" at Yale had been "discontinued" as its students answered the call for troops. In good fun, Nathan's friend Ebenezer Williams wrote to him, saying, "It would I suppose be nothing new to inform you that the best military Company on the Colony consists of the Members of Yale College who appear stately under arms 3 times per day."[8]

In contrast to just a few short months ago, the tone of the letters Nathan now received and wrote was sobering. No longer was Nathan's love life, or his idle quill, the main theme of the discourse. He and his fellow Yalies were now totally focused on—if not already absorbed in—the oncoming conflict and how each could do his small part to back Washington and America.

While Nathan was still in New London, the war in Boston had already begun, and his friends were already seeing its effects firsthand. Ezra Selden, another Yale classmate, was in Roxbury already, serving just outside Boston. In a rushed letter, Selden described for Nathan the carnage and death around him, which was something he had not expected to see so soon. "We came into Roxbury on Sunday . . . they have been firing upon Roxbury a great Part of Saturday, killed one Man June 24 . . . and killed two men with small arms which through presumption attempted to set on fire their guard house supposing that they had quitted their house but they ran in great numbers." Selden described watching shingles fly as the redcoats bombarded houses and spoke of a battle between a regiment of rebel Israel Putnam's and Britain's Thomas Gage's in which casualties were so numerous the dead and wounded had not yet been counted. The mere size of the British regiment impressed Selden. As the fighting continued and men dropped dead or left the battlefield injured, another sixteen hundred troops appeared from seemingly nowhere, Selden wrote. Putnam's regiment had lost "150 men," many of whom had been taken prisoner by Gage, in what was only the second battle Selden had observed since entering camp.[9]

The situation in Boston appeared to be chaotic. But that had little to do with the fighting. Even this early on, soldiers were scurrying to get their hands on simple provisions such as tents and eating utensils. Finding land to set camp was not a problem, Selden wrote, but feeding and arming what was a massive influx of soldiers from all points south and west was beginning to take its toll on everyone.[10]

Selden's letter inspired Nathan. A later letter Selden would write made it clear that Nathan was anxious to ride to Boston himself and engage the enemy with his fellows. Yet, a letter from Benjamin Tallmadge three days after Selden's truly stirred Nathan to act. At this time, it was fairly common knowledge in New Haven and New London that Nathan had been commissioned a lieutenant in Colonel Charles Webb's Connecticut Seventh Regiment, but had remained idle since the instatement. John Richards, Nathan's landlord, Tallmadge said, had informed Tallmadge of Nathan's assignment. Like hundreds of soldiers commissioned by the Hartford General Assembly, Nathan was now waiting for orders to ride east while trying his best to recruit as many men as he could find in and around New London.[11]

Like Nathan, Tallmadge had also been commissioned a lieutenant. With all the downtime he'd had in Wethersfield while teaching, Tallmadge had attended assembly meetings in nearby Hartford and built a broad base of military knowledge from those meetings. In his letter, Tallmadge didn't feel compelled to congratulate his friend on his commission; instead he wanted to provide Nathan with a bit of advice regarding how to handle himself in public now that he was an official member of Washington's army. "You must already be considered as acting in a publick capacity, and in a sphere which no one can say is [demeaning to] the Publick."

Tallmadge's main point, however, was more serious: "When I consider our country, a Land flowing as it were with milk & honey, holding open her arms, & demanding Assistance from all who can assist in her sore distress, Me thinks a Christian's counsel must favour the latter." Tallmadge understood that before a commanding officer could deploy him and Nathan and bestow upon them orders, they were subject first to God's will, bound by the Lord's word. Without that guidance, neither could expect to serve the cause to the best of his abilities. "Our holy Religion, the honour of our God, a glorious country, & happy constitution is what we have to defend. . . . We should all be ready to step forth in the common cause."[12]

Nathan and Tallmadge were among those for whom nothing, save for God, outweighed their commitment to duty. After reading Tallmadge's letter, Nathan realized there was a loose end to tie up, something he should perhaps have done weeks ago. Three days later, Nathan sat down at his desk inside the Union schoolhouse and put quill to paper: "Having received information that a place is allotted me in the army, and being inclined, as I hope for good reasons to accept it, I am constrained to ask as a favour that which scarce anything else would have induced me to: which is, to be excused from keeping your school any longer."[13]

Nathan was still hanging around New London because his regiment hadn't been given official orders to march into Boston. The last thing Washington needed was thousands of soldiers showing up at the same time. In light of this, regiments such as Nathan's were told to wait while they assembled more men and supplies.

Obviously most members of the proprietary committee would not be surprised to learn that he was planning on leaving, and more than a few suggested a meeting at Union for six o'clock that evening—Friday, July 7— to discuss how they might go about finding a replacement. "The year for which I engaged will expire," Nathan continued, "within a fortnight, so that my quitting a few days sooner I hope will subject you to no great inconvenience."[14]

He went on to explain that he had always been "fond" of "school keeping," and "since my residence in this Town, every thing has conspired to render it more agreeable." Nathan had valued teaching as an important service to the community, not just a job. "I have thought much of never quitting it . . . but at present there seems an opportunity for more extensive public service."[15]

Near the end of July, Nathan heard from another lieutenant in his company, John Belcher, who was living in the neighboring town of Stonington. Nathan had seen Belcher, who had been commissioned a second lieutenant under Nathan, just weeks before. He and Belcher were in charge of employing a brigade in the southern part of the state and preparing them for a march into Boston. They knew orders to leave could come any day. Belcher had enlisted twenty-two men. Talking good men into joining the rebel effort was not a problem for either lieutenant. What was becoming increasingly difficult, on the other hand, Belcher noted, was paying them, as he explained their cash was "pretty much exhausted, should be glad of a Supply as soon as possible."[16]

Belcher said he had heard that marching orders were coming within the next week. He wanted to know how many recruits Nathan could guarantee on his end, as "I . . . should be glad if our Company is not near completed."[17]

In what would become a common theme in the coming months with Washington's army, Belcher pointed out his biggest worry: "The greatest part of the Men I have enlisted are destitute of Guns, suitable to carry, which we ought to make timely provision for."[18]

Throughout that summer, Nathan spent his days guarding the coastline of New London, training recruits to watch out for the enemy, as the British might send a warship or two into the New London port.[19] During this period Nathan wrote a short note to his father, explaining in part the reason for his decision to leave his post as schoolmaster and join the rebellion. By then Richard Hale had sent five other of his eight sons to Boston. He had raised a small troop of deeply patriotic young men who were more than glad to defend the honor of God, Coventry, and their colony. After explaining to his father his decision to enter the army, Nathan summed up his feelings rather pointedly: "A sense of duty urged me to sacrifice everything for my country."[20]

Stationed at Cambridge in the early days of the war, General Washington had high expectations for his troops. Within days of being at camp, he began sending out daily orders to his growing team of commanders. He was trying to set an example early on that could be followed throughout the war. The general informed his commanders in early July that their men were now considered "Troops of the United Provinces of North America," made official by an order of Congress. The word *colony* (or *colonies*), Washington added, was no longer part of the American military lexicon. Without delay, Artemas Ward, Charles Lee, Philip Schuyler, and Israel Putnam were appointed "major generals of the American Army," Washington said, "and due obedience is to be paid them as such."[21]

Washington took control immediately, doing his best to command with an iron fist. He was firm in his desire to see that soldiers acted properly now that every rebel with a gun in his hand represented America. The Great Cause was not a militia's effort or an unscripted clash with the Indians. "It is required and expected," the commanding general wrote, "that exact discipline be observed, and due Subordination prevail thro' the whole Army, as a Failure in these most essential points must necessarily produce extreme Hazard, Disorder and Confusion; and end in shameful disappointment and disgrace."[22]

Although Washington understood that he was dealing with a band of largely ragtag soldiers, some of whom were overweight, sick, untrained, and prepared to drop arms and run at the first sight of bloodshed, he demanded respect, not so much for him, but the cause:

> The General most earnestly requires, and expects, a due observance of those articles of war, established for the Government of the army, which forbid profane cursing, swearing and drunkenness; And in like manner requires and expects, of all Officers, and Soldiers, not engaged on actual duty, a punctual attendance on divine Service, to implore the blessings of heaven upon the means used for our safety and defence.[23]

At this point, the fighting consisted of small skirmishes: troops conducting brief assaults that kept tensions high for soldiers on both sides. In one instance, Samuel Haws, who was part of a regiment guarding and surveying Roxbury, watched as soldiers from his brigade taunted a British unit, to prove they wouldn't back down. Haws and his unit were considered true minutemen, a term derived from the fact that rebels throughout Massachusetts, busy manufacturing gunpowder and arms, "enrolled in companies and prepared to take up arms at a moment's warning." On July 7, Haws's company, early in the morning, came upon a house that was engulfed in fire, flames quickly swallowing up the entire structure. "These were Set on fire by some of our brave Americans," Haws wrote. The house had been occupied by British redcoats. When a rebel company supporting Haws's saw the British run away from the burning building, they stood by and waited for the flames to subside before plundering the house of its provisions and arms.[24]

As fall approached, this was the way of the war, or siege, as it has commonly been referred to: The American army was building up its defenses and supporting divisions with all the arms and provisions it could muster, some sent from colonies and Congress, others stolen. With cold weather on the way, warm clothing and shelter became as scarce and valuable as gunpowder and bayonets. Still, Washington demanded his commanders "pay diligent Attention to keep their Men neat and clean; to visit them often at their quarters, and inculcate upon them the necessity of cleanliness, as essential to their health and service."[25]

In addition, he made it clear that with winter swiftly moving in, all units were to collect enough hay to make beds and to use as insulation to keep the cold out of their tents. Even more important to the health of the army as a whole, anyone that fell sick should immediately be removed from camp and placed in a restricted area so as not to spread infection.[26]

As he made his way around Cambridge assessing his army and planning his next move, one of the essential assets Washington quickly realized he needed turned out to be well within his reach. As he prepared his men for the large number of British soldiers sailing toward Boston harbor from England, the general was aware that the more men he had, the better his chances. Experience had taught him that he could only compete with an army as well equipped, well trained, and immense as the British if he, too, had a large group of men standing by his side willing to lay down their lives. Colonies throughout America had sent word that as the bone-chilling cold of the winter of 1775–76 settled in, divisions from Maryland, Virginia, Connecticut, and New York would be heading north. It was a race now between Washington and Gage to equip each of their armies as best they could, dig in, and see who moved first. But as the army grew, the already scarce provisions became a source of growing worry.[27]

Chapter 9

BAND OF BROTHERS

UNDER COLONEL CHARLES WEBB'S command, Connecticut's Seventh Regiment gathered in New London on or about September 21, 1775, in preparation to march north and join the main body of some thirty thousand troops amassing near Roxbury and Cambridge. Nathan had been promoted to first lieutenant, as was an old friend of his, William Hull. Besides Hull and Webb, there were nine commanders in Nathan's division—ranging from lieutenants down to ensigns and captains—and by the time they had completed recruiting in late August, the Seventh could add seventy-four men to Washington's Continental Army.[1]

After whipping the group of mostly merchants, farmers, tailors, tutors, and common men and children into fighting soldiers over the past two months, on September 1, Nathan was promoted to captain of the Seventh Regiment's Third Company, which placed him second-in-command of the company under Major Jonathon Lattimore. To Nathan's delight, a rather large allotment of ammunition arrived: a consignment of 242 pounds of musket balls and 66 pounds of powder. Suddenly, things did not appear to be as dismal as they might have seemed just a week prior. With that, Nathan wrote to Colonel Stephen Moylan, who was stationed in New York and in charge of every Connecticut division heading to Cambridge. In his brief note, Nathan asked for "fifty-five Canteens or Runlets [barrels]," which would supply his company as they traveled and settled near Boston, he noted, and once he had them, he and his men could leave New London.[2]

Moylan, soon to be named an aide-de-camp to Washington, was an admired commander in his own right, someone Nathan could look up to and learn from in the coming months. As the Connecticut General Assembly gave orders to its commanders to keep their men "exercised, instructed . . . clean, and free from idleness and bad practices," the scarcity of armaments became a chief complaint among officers in the field. A story later surfaced about Moylan that revealed how he injected humor into his commanding tactics. He and Israel Putnam were together that winter, and Moylan wrote home explaining that, although the cold season had enveloped them, the weather had been "mild," adding, "The bay is open. Everything thaws here except 'Old Put.' He is still as hard as ever, crying out for powder—powder—ye gods, give us powder!"[3]

In late September, Nathan was ordered by the Connecticut Council of Safety to be ready to leave New London at a moment's notice. While he and his regiment waited, he was instructed to "make such entrenchments and works of defense as should be directed by the civil authority and field officers." Word was that several British men-of-war were spotted "hovering on the adjacent coasts."[4]

By the end of the month, Washington had given an order to the Connecticut General Assembly "requiring peremptorily" that Major Lattimore's Company be "immediately ordered to march to the camp near Boston."[5]

In his later recollection, Elisha Bostwick, an officer who had befriended Nathan while in New London, saw him as a captain who could figure prominently in Washington's war. "His mental powers seemed to be above the common sort, his mind of a sedate and sober cast, & he was undoubtedly pious." When Nathan took on his role as leader, he put his entire self into it. If one of his men—or several at the same time, for that matter—had taken ill, Nathan would visit with them routinely and sit by their side. Many later said it was not unusual to see Nathan with a Bible in one hand, the hand of an ill soldier in the other, praying aloud for recovery. "His activity on all occasions was wonderful," Bostwick added.[6]

William Hull and Nathan Hale hadn't stayed in contact much, if at all, post-Yale. But Hull would play a pivotal role in Nathan's life in the next year. For Nathan, having a man such as William Hull, the first lieutenant of the Seventh's Second Company, to fall back on when he needed advice turned into a blessing. It wouldn't matter how much they'd corresponded in the past, or if they had kept in touch after graduation (Hull graduated a year before Nathan); what mattered more than anything was that the world they lived in now was a different place.

William Hull—called Billy—was two years older than Nathan, almost to the day. Hull's ancestors had emigrated from Derbyshire, England, settling in Derby, Connecticut, along the banks of the Housatonic River, a few miles west of New Haven and more than fifty miles from New London.

Like Nathan, Hull had pursued teaching after Yale, a vocation he later said provided him with "the happiest years of his life." But his parents talked him into leaving his schoolmaster's job to study theology. This failed to satisfy Hull's desire to travel and meet new people, however, and he instead opted to study law far from home in the hills of Litchfield, where he was admitted to the bar in early 1775.[7]

Upon returning home for a visit soon after receiving his law license, Hull's father approached him with a surprise. It was midsummer 1775. "Who do you suppose," Joseph Hull said to his son, "has been elected captain of the company raised in this town [Derby]?"[8]

Hull thought about it and rattled off several names.

"It is yourself," Joseph said with proud pleasure.[9]

Young Hull accepted the military post enthusiastically and without a second thought dropped everything to join Colonel Webb's company. Joseph, wrote Hull's daughter Maria Campbell, was "seized with a severe illness [during the summer of 1775], which soon terminated his useful life." When Joseph's will was read a short while later, he being a man of considerable wealth, it was learned that he'd left everything he owned to his wife and children. When William Hull heard that he had inherited quite a fortune, he paused, reflected, and "refused to receive any part of it," saying instead, "I want only my sword and uniform."[10]

As soon as Nathan and his men started their march toward Cambridge, he began a journal. Hiking toward Providence, Rhode Island, with his Seventh Regiment, Nathan documented the journey inside a large, leatherbound book he would rely on in the coming days for companionship, support, and, perhaps, a cathartic way of talking himself through what were sure to be the most trying times of his life. The first entry Nathan wrote was on September 23, 1775, a day after he and his unit departed New London: "Cannon[s] . . . heard from the last stage to the present; marched . . . arrived Waterman's (a private house & entertainment good) after a stop or two (6 miles)—tarried all-night."[11]

The Benjamin Waterman House, in Johnston, just a few miles west of Providence, was a popular overnight lodge for travelers along the Hartford Turnpike, located at a crossroad called Hughesdale. Nathan and his men had traveled about fifty-six miles to reach Waterman's. For a rebel army unit heading toward the theater of war, staying outside Providence, a major port city, was a tactical move. No army wanted to be sitting ducks for a regiment of General Gage's men, who were said to be roaming the region. Gage had sent several warships into Providence harbor and the surrounding ports to support a group of British troops heading into the area. An intelligent commander such as Nathan knew the danger of marching his troops into what could turn into a trap or ambush.[12]

Waterman's was a two-story inn, which allowed several of Nathan's men to stand guard on the second floor while the remaining troops set camp for the night outside, fed themselves, prepared a marching plan for the following day, and rested.[13]

By the early-morning hours of September 24, the Seventh had uprooted from Waterman's and marched through Providence amid a surprisingly warm reception of music, salutes, and cheers. "Having marched through the town . . . & made a short stop at the hither part, in the road, came 4 miles further to Slack's and reached Daggett's in Attleborough & put up, depositing our arms in the meeting House."[14]

Major Jonathon Lattimore joined Nathan at Daggett's residence. Daggett was a cousin of former Yale president Naphtali Daggett's. Storing a majority of their artillery at the local meetinghouse (church) was something Washington's troops learned almost immediately would keep them out of British hands, simply because the British would never suspect the hiding spot. With arms so scarce, the last thing a regiment wanted to do was be taken prisoner at night and have to hand over their arms.

After stationing several of his men for the night at Daggett's, Nathan and his officers dined at Eliphalet Slack's house in Rehoboth. Slack later noted that Nathan had paid him "five shillings and ten pence lawful money for the use of my house & other trouble by said Company."[15]

Money and, as Slack explained it in his receipt to Nathan, "trouble" (unruly, drunken soldiers) would become two of Nathan's chief concerns as they closed in on Roxbury, a town Nathan would soon come to know as camp. As they marched, Nathan earned his soldiers' respect. One night, Nathan took a walk through camp to check on his men and make sure they were acting as soldiers should. As he looked in on each group, he came upon a gathering of several men playing cards. They were loud and loquacious. Possibly even intoxicated.

"What are you doing?" Nathan asked sharply.

Gambling and drinking were strictly forbidden. Card playing led to both, Nathan knew. He himself had done his share at Yale.

"This won't do!" he exclaimed sternly, upset the men hadn't listened when he'd explained the dos and don'ts before leaving New London. As he spoke, the men sat staring at him like a pack of children caught playing spin the bottle.

"Give me your cards," Nathan said next.

Describing this scene later, detailing what Nathan had said, one of the soldiers explained, "They did so, & he chopped them to pieces, & it was done in such a manner that the men were rather pleased than otherwise."[16]

Roxbury was about forty miles from Rehoboth, and by nightfall the following day Nathan and his men staggered into town without having faced one skirmish or loss along the way. They were tired, sure. But they were healthy, well fed, and ready to fight.[17]

Just before sunset on Tuesday, September 26, the Seventh pitched their tents in Roxbury. "At our arrival in Camp," Nathan wrote ("5 minutes before breakfast" the following morning), "I found that 200 men had been draughted out that morning for a fishing party." A fishing party consisted of men spreading out and scouring the land for provisions: meat, linen, gunpowder, arms, or anything else they could plunder from the British or purchase from local merchants. By Wednesday, "12 or 15" of the men had returned with "11 Cattle & 2 horses." The team that scored this wonderful bounty was under the direction of Major John Tupper, who had returned and reported he had spied a British "pleasure-boat . . . belonging to some British officers" being prepared for launch along the shores of what they called Cambridge Harbor. Several of Tupper's men lit the vessel afire, he said, and looted whatever they could find in the immediate area after the officers ran away in disgrace.[18]

It took Nathan's regiment four and a half days to travel 106 miles northeast to Roxbury, a town that had become a staging area for a majority of the brigades and regiments filing into the region from all points north, south, and west. Here, plans were made and provisions collected as Washington's troops exchanged pleasantries and talked of what was going on four miles north in Cambridge. For the first time, Nathan felt that he was a soldier at war. There's no way to tell how many men were at Roxbury during this period, but perhaps as many as five thousand men from all walks of life— "farmers; shopkeepers; and rich merchants; ministers and convicts," wrote one historian—mingled, telling stories of how they were going to best the British at the first opportunity. Many of the men had no concept of what war involved, as they had never been involved in a tavern brawl, much less seen combat. But here, life as a soldier began to take on shape and meaning, for Nathan as he contemplated his role in, and dedication to, "the great cause." The perils of combat eclipsed any romantic image of war Nathan had ever read about or heard. Blood was going to be spilled on this land— they were hearing stories of death already. Men had come in off the line with missing limbs and shot-off faces, the survivors telling anecdotes of

other unimaginable horrors. At any moment a troop of redcoats might engage and prove how superior firepower worked in the field. But it wasn't
only the terror of battle that rattled these unsteady, scared men. "I am sorry
to have occasion to notice," wrote rebel surgeon James Thatcher of actions
he'd witnessed taken by the British, ". . . the following occurrence. The
body of a soldier has been taken from the grave, for the purpose, probably,
of dissection, and the empty coffin left exposed. This affair occasions considerable excitement among our people; both resentment and grief are man-
ifested." This display of contempt and disrespect for the dead, Thatcher
noted, impressed on the Americans who witnessed it "the idea that a soldier's body is held in no estimation after death" by the enemy army.[19]

On Friday, September 29, Nathan led his men into Cambridge and "encamped on the foot of Winter Hill," just a short jaunt from the more famous Bunker Hill, where the war had begun just three months prior—the
very foundation of the Revolution, a section of land that, even this early in
the war, had taken on sacred significance. By midmorning on the twenty-
ninth, Nathan met with General John Sullivan's three companies, including
Major Nathaniel Shipman's, and Nathan's new friend Captain Elisha Bostwick. As Nathan surveyed the camp, keeping tabs on his men, he gave orders to the men to keep busy and stay out of trouble. The next day Nathan
learned Roxbury, just moments after they had departed, sustained "considerable firing."[20]

The situation in the entire region near Roxbury was volatile, at best. Both
sides remained camped next door to each other, sending volleys of cannon-
balls over to the other at inconsistent intervals. The only sense of civilian life
the American soldiers got was on Sundays, when chaplains came in and
preached sermons. Throughout it all, most soldiers relied on what had been a
daily part of life back home: a devout belief that God was on their side. As
one private later put it, "By the best accounts they fired above one hundred
balls and our men fired 3 cannon from our breast . . . and one of the balls
went into Boston amongst the house but through the good hand of Devine
providence in all their firing they did not kill one man nor wound any except
one or too slightly." God was working on the American side—it was either
that, soldiers believed, or He had sent angels to watch over them.[21]

Meanwhile, Gilbert Saltonstall, a good friend of Nathan's from New London, was at home waiting for his call into action. As Nathan spent his nights in camp anticipating orders, he wrote to Saltonstall. He had asked in a letter a week prior if Saltonstall had heard anything from Stephen Hempstead, a fellow from Yale and neighbor who lived in New London, whom Nathan hadn't heard from in quite some time. Nathan vaguely described the situation in Roxbury and Cambridge, telling Saltonstall he would write more in the coming days as he began to understand the structure of the army, which was then constantly realigning and changing.[22]

As Nathan grew comfortable with his role in the army, he corresponded with those he viewed as valuable military resources: men who thought like him and were likewise dedicated to the effort. In Gilbert Saltonstall, Nathan felt he was conversing with someone who would become a close ally, a friend in whom he sensed a germ of greatness—an assessment history would prove to be somewhat accurate. Saltonstall, a future brigadier major who would join the rebels during the summer of 1776 with his father, a colonel and brigadier general in charge of nine militia units, was destined to see his share of brutal combat. In one instance, while serving as a captain of the marines aboard the navy warship *Trumbull* in the seas off Bermuda, Saltonstall and the crew took a savage cannonade one afternoon from a passing British warship and barely made it out alive. "It is beyond my power," Saltonstall wrote of the shelling, "to give adequate idea of the carnage, slaughter, havoc and destruction that ensued," adding, "Let the imagination do its best, it will fall short."[23]

When Saltonstall returned Nathan's letter, he focused on business for the most part, which Nathan surely appreciated. Saltonstall said he had heard that a regiment in St. John's, Canada, had taken a terrible bombardment and a mutual friend, Guy Johnston, had been killed in the engagement. "We every Hour expect to hear [the British] are in possession of St. Johns."[24]

Although Saltonstall was wrong (the soldier who lost his life was another man named Johnston), Nathan appreciated the news; he yearned for the cold facts, as dedicated military leaders understood them. He wasn't afraid to know what he and his men faced, or what was going on beyond Cambridge and Roxbury. Nathan had always thought ahead, which was likely one of the reasons why his superior officers viewed him as such an important addition to their command. They included him in much of the American strategy because they felt he could not only keep quiet about it, but offer essential advice; otherwise, he would never have been invited to dinners and meetings with generals and colonels.

Further on in his letter, Saltonstall asked Nathan to send him the "Rank of the Regiments in the Continental Army; I hear it is settled and handed about in Printed Handbills." Congress had spent some time on structuring the army the way it wanted and, when it finished, made sure to send out a sort of "memo" letting soldiers know their place among leaders. Saltonstall wanted to be in the loop. He mentioned to Nathan that he had traveled to Lyme the previous week and run into Nathan's brother David and several "girls," who "expressed a regard for you which I thought but few removes from Love." It was discouraging to Saltonstall to think he wasn't among those in Cambridge in the thick of the action and was clear from his letter that he wished to be with Nathan, describing the atmosphere around New London in light of the war as "quite barren—We are extremely dull—Sunday reigns thro' the Week."[25]

By mid-October the American army had settled on a base of command. Not much had changed in the branches of its leadership. Congress had originally thought thirty thousand troops were going to join Washington in Boston; yet a revised estimate promised no more than twenty-two thousand.[26]

The major change occurred not on the American side, but the British. General Thomas Gage was summoned back to England as his replacement, Major General William Howe, took his place. Part of Gage's job had been to keep order in Boston and make sure its ports were not being used by colonists to import or export goods. But as the strain between the armies escalated, Parliament realized it needed a leader who could match Washington's poise, competence, wit, and military knowledge, which it saw in Howe, "a man almost adored by the army," William Paine wrote, "and one that with the spirit of a Wolfe possesses . . . genius."[27]

Gage had been ordered to keep watch on Rhode Island and take possession of the city if he could. But as both sides knew, the City of New York was much more important. The British needed to take control of New York as soon as possible, which Parliament had expected of Gage. But Gage complained in a letter to Lord Dartmouth that he didn't have enough men, and the men he did have were "too weak to act in more than one point." He urged Dartmouth to send as many warships as he could to New York at once, as "that city could be easily defended, and supplied by a water communication." The problem was that the British couldn't imagine retreating from Boston and leaving it in the hands of the rebels. They had to make a stand and prove themselves all-powerful. England believed it could split its forces and occupy both cities at the same time. Before he sailed home, Gage agreed with Howe that it was an impracticable notion and instead commissioned upward of seventeen thousand additional troops to help try to make the split happen.[28]

Though not sure what the British had planned, Washington knew the standoff that had been going on since April would not continue. Sooner or later, the British were going to devise a plan to try to undermine the American effort. With that, Washington needed his own plan.

For the first time, Nathan began to understand what a battlefield during actual wartime was like. Although he had yet to be in any combat himself, he was stationed around intermittent episodes of fighting taking place near Winter Hill. On October 7, he reported hearing "firing from Boston Neck," a port about two miles from Cambridge. The Neck, as it was called, had been controlled by the British and commonly saw clashes. The next day, Nathan recorded that "Near 100 Cannon fired at Roxbury from the Enemy," and Nathan saw a man with his arm "shot off" and a cow blasted to tiny bits of flesh, bone, and blood.[29]

Still itching to be closer to the action, Gilbert Saltonstall wrote to Nathan again on October 9, beginning the rather long letter with "I see you're Stationed in the Mouth of Danger." Saltonstall viewed the location of Nathan's regiment as a "situation more Perilous than any other in the Camp." He mused over a decision by commanders to put lower-level officers such as Nathan in the line of fire and believed any officer was more beneficial to the

cause if held back and, in a sense, protected by front lines of common soldiers. Saltonstall explained how the troops in Norwich and Stonington had
taken several small ships, providing tons of provisions and powder for the effort. The same was true, he noted, for regiments to the west in Albany and
south in New York. In what had become a habit, Saltonstall included several
newspaper clippings with the letter, of which he noted, "There is nothing
material in [them], but that you'll see for yourself."[30]

October had produced many days of cold, wet weather, which of course
quelled much of the fighting. With not much going on around him,
Nathan's life became a structured routine of mundane chores: "Morning:
Clear & pleasant, but cold—exercised men." The next day, "rainy, no meetings." Clergy had showed up to read the Scriptures, Nathan wrote, which
he had taken great delight in. His nights consisted of dining with other officers, discussing strategy over pints of ale and jiggers of rum. At some
point, he asked for a leave, which was quickly granted, only to be told a day
later that it was completely out of the question.[31]

Heading into mid-to-late October, Nathan wrote and received letters
from several officers who were still stationed in Connecticut awaiting orders
to march. Each officer had a story to tell regarding some sort of "Divine
Providence" that had saved a soldier from death. Nathan found this an extraordinary comfort. He had, by this point, seen his share of fatalities and
destruction, but had not yet contributed one live musket ball to the cause.
Quite bored, when he wasn't dining with higher-ranking officers, he spent
his days training his men, keeping them fit while preparing them for combat. Saltonstall wrote again near the third week of October, a short note to
let Nathan know that Thomas Poole, whom Nathan had lived with at one
time in New London, had married Elizabeth Adams, a young lass whom
Nathan had himself once courted.[32]

On October 19, Nathan sat down in one of the officers' tents and wrote
a letter to Betsey Christophers. He had known Betsey from his days in New
London, and the two had become good friends. He wasn't writing for any
specific reason, he said, other than to express gratitude for her friendship
and catch her up with what was going on in Boston. It's possible that once
Nathan heard of the nuptials between Poole and Adams, he felt perhaps

further from civilian life than he had since marching east. It had been four weeks since the Connecticut Seventh left, but amid the war it seemed much longer. He realized the New London he had left behind would be a different place upon his return. Writing to Betsey was one way to keep those memories close by. "What is now a letter would be a visit were I in New London," Nathan wrote. "I once wanted to come here," he said, referring to Boston, "to see something extraordinary—my curiosity is satisfied. I have now no more desire for seeing things here, than for seeing what is in New London, no, nor half so much either. Not that I am discontented—so far from it, that in the present situation of things I would not expect a furlough were it offered me."[33]

Just a month at war had changed Nathan from a modestly practiced young man, eager to prove his devotion to his country, into a pragmatist who knew war was more mundane and tedious, wrapped around quick flashes of savage bloodshed, than anything else. "I would only observe," he continued, "that we too often flatter ourselves with great happiness could we see such & such things; but when we actually come to the sight of them, our solid satisfaction is really no more than when we only had them in expectation."[34]

He was surprised and disquieted by the perils of war and how violent and merciless men could be to one another. He'd had a different image of the battlefield in his mind upon leaving, an image perhaps instilled in him by the military history he had favored. Now he was part of it all—a player, a possible casualty, a devoted disciple, maybe even a pawn—and the idealized image of being a soldier had completely left him. The romance of war was just that: a fiction.[35]

In hearing from so many friends in New London, Nathan understood how hard it was for the females in town to watch the men they knew and loved head off to war. The army had taken just about every able-bodied male the town had. "I am a little at a loss how you carry on at New-London," Nathan wrote to Betsey, adding a bit of humor to soothe the melancholy. "The number of Gentlemen is now so few, that I fear how you will go through the winter, but I hope for the best."[36]

Chapter 10

SIEGE AND COUNTERPLOT

WITH THE END OF October came a kaleidoscope of fall colors that gave way to naked, leafless trees and a dull and morose mood over Boston. Thunderstorms, cold rain, and even snow made conditions difficult as the siege continued into the first weeks of November. Soon, bone-chilling winds and drifting snow would turn otherwise strong-willed, strapping men into shivering, ill-equipped soldiers, both discouraged and on the verge of mental breakdown and desertion. Washington pleaded with Philadelphia for blankets and warmer garments, as he sent teams of men out into wooded areas to locate hay and firewood, while warning his officers that few things were more brutal than a New England winter. Beyond that, the commander in chief knew the enemy was "strongly fortified," he wrote, which made it "almost impossible to force their lines." One historian later referred to these delicate moments as "siege and counterplot—one army in a city, shut in from every direction but the sea, another around that city building entrenchments."[1]

With all that was going on around him, Nathan began to worry seriously for the first time. His anxiety, however, wasn't rooted in the weather, or a sense that his unit, within musket shot of the British, was going to be surprised by a cannonade. Instead, he was concerned about a rumor floating through camp that the British—patient, resolved, and building in numbers—were at that moment deploying "25,000 [additional] troops from England" into the Boston region. If this was true, the daily bombardments he and his fellow soldiers had endured with few casualties would turn into an assault that could end the rebellion before it even had a chance to get fully organized.[2]

Other problems were made worse because many of Washington's troops had lost their sense of sure success. Some soldiers packed and left without word or warning. In other cases, as Nathan noted in his diary quite casually, "A Sergeant Major deserted to the Regulars . . . a sergeant left and deserted." Among several officers, the feeling was that by January 1, 1776, there would be no American army to speak of.

Gilbert Saltonstall wrote again, describing a schooner that had been captured in St. John's, Canada, with "all ye men kill'd & . . . 8000 bushels of wheat" shipped to Norwich. And so it seemed that for every piece of bad news circulating through Nathan's division, in his writings he somehow balanced it by noting the few minor victories the rebels could claim. Much of the news Nathan shared with his men was to motivate them. But now, as cold weather blanketed the region, a night shivering inside a drafty tent was no match for the warmth of a hot fire and a cup of tea back home. Nathan was one of only a few officers who could claim a zero desertion and fatality rate among his men.[3]

To add to the uncertainty, many soldiers who had signed up for a year tour weren't reenlisting at the rates Washington had expected they would. Congress had sent a committee to Boston in mid-October to consult on the new organization of the army, promising an additional thirty thousand troops after the first of the year. Washington sent a note to his officers, reminding them of his strict orders to convince as many men as possible to reenlist, if only from December 6, 1775, to January 1, 1776. Among the officers Washington scolded, Nathan observed in his journal, was Colonel Charles Webb, who had explained to Nathan that the army was planning to receive a large coalition of militia early in 1776, which did them no good now. In addition, Washington demanded the name and rank of each man declining to reenlist, along with a detailed explanation as to why each soldier was leaving. Then he sent word to the leaders of the colonies throughout New England that British sympathizers would not be tolerated. "Why should persons," Washington wrote to the governor of Rhode Island that fall, "who are preying on the vitals of the country, be suffered to stalk at large, whilst we know they will do us every mischief in their power?"[4]

William Hull arrived at Winter Hill a few weeks after Nathan. Upon entering the camp, Hull learned quickly that the American military could be quite a humiliating experience for an officer unfamiliar with the realities of the battlefield.

Not long after Hull and his company marched over a ravine in Roxbury and set foot on "the Hill," he and Nathan began dining together, drinking wine and taking long walks through town, no doubt reminiscing about their days at Yale and contemplating the rough road Washington's army faced in the coming days. On one such night, a rumor among troops was that a "body of the enemy had landed at Lechmere's Point," a small inlet in Boston harbor just east of Winter Hill. Hull and his men expected the regulars to advance toward Cambridge. As word made its way through camp, every unit in the area was ordered to fall back to its respective station. Most of Webb's men, mainly the subalterns, showed up dressed in "long cloth frocks, with kerchiefs tied about their heads." Apparently, Hull had not been told of this sudden change in the dress code and wore his captain's uniform, the same as Nathan, who was stationed farther west, closer to home base at Winter Hill. Several of Hull's soldiers asked him why he was in uniform: "The regiment is going into action . . . you'll be a mark for the enemy's fire."

Hull told his biographer that he quickly snapped back, "I thought the uniform of an officer was designed to aid his influence and increase his authority over his men . . . more particularly so in the hour of battle."[5]

"In the French war," one of Hull's men exclaimed, "it was not customary, and they had never worn it."[6]

Hull thought about it. After a moment, he sent his servant back to camp to fetch him a kerchief and frock.

Not long after Hull changed, Washington rode in. The commanding general had constantly been on the move, checking on his troops, evaluating their readiness and ability. As soon as he made it into Hull's fort near Lechmere's Point, the general asked who was in charge. Looking around, he couldn't distinguish the commanding officer from his men. Recalling the episode later, Hull explained, "With feelings of inexpressible mortification, I came forward in my savage costume and reported that [I] had the honour of commanding the redoubt."[7]

When Washington left, Hull changed back into his uniform. His regiment waited four to five hours, but the British never made a move. Later, when he talked about the episode, Hull "resolved never more to subscribe to the opinions of men, however loyal and brave in their country's service."[8]

Any hope Nathan had that his unit would escape Boston without sustaining a casualty or traitorous element was quickly quashed when, within twenty-four hours, he not only lost a man to a surprise gun attack, but the enemy, he wrote, "kill'd another . . . with 6 or 7 more wounded." During the attack, one of his men, a private, deserted on the spot after seeing the carnage around him. Then Colonel Webb issued orders for any man infected with smallpox to be removed from camp at once. Nathan noted two who were ill. Beyond what must have seemed like several days of dismal news, however, Nathan found comfort in the simple things, such as watching the sun set, or taking a stroll through town. During one of his morning walks into Cambridge, Nathan bumped into, as historian Thomas Jones called him, an "old illiterate farmer" friend from Connecticut, General Israel Putnam. Talking to Putnam, Nathan relayed the bad news that not one soldier in his unit was planning on reenlisting. Putnam wanted to know why.

"The state of the regiment," Nathan explained, "was through ill usage upon the score of provisions." His men were worried that they would starve or freeze to death. Putnam assured Nathan he would get back to him later that day and let him know what to do.

After the meeting, Nathan dined in town and "drank 1 bottle wine," then visited a friend of the family's before heading back to camp for the night.[9]

Stories of how tough army life was going to get in the coming days trickled through camp as Nathan made his way around, talking to his men and comforting them. One anecdote comes from a forty-year-old major, Return J. Meigs, a proud Connecticut Yankee like Nathan. On Thursday, November 2, 1775, on a "fine, clear, and warm" afternoon, Meigs was marching northwest through upper New England en route toward Quebec with a division put together by Benedict Arnold and Washington. If the British took control of the St. Lawrence River, they'd control the war. Arnold and Washington sent several regiments north to cut them off. At some point Meigs and his men stopped along the east bank of the St. Lawrence. Up until then, Meigs's journey had carried on without too much trouble or interruption; but provisions were running scarce in many units, as Meigs's men were completely exhausted and starving. In recent weeks, an embargo on shooting geese had been put into effect by Congress, with warnings of stiff penalties and fines for soldiers caught disobeying. Hunting wasted much needed ammunition.[10]

As Meigs settled his unit by "a low sandy shore or beach," several of his men "darted from the ranks" and ran toward a patch of greens off in the distance. The vegetation—especially at this time of the year—was a welcoming sight to Meigs's depleted troops. "With their fingers," Meigs recorded in his journal, "they dug up the roots of the plants and ate them raw."[11]

Watching starving men gnaw like rabbits was not at all unsettling to a military leader who understood the perils of life along the trail of battle. But it was nothing compared to the desperation Meigs witnessed next when he and his men met up with a second unit farther upriver. There, one of Meigs's soldiers had been passed a bowl of "a little broth, given to him by some friends." They called it bleary, or bear's broth, which was said to be made from boiling dirt and polish off leather shoes and other wares, likely in addition to any decomposing animal corpses collected along the trail. If that wasn't bad enough, on this day Meigs was shocked to notice that the broth had a "greenish tint" to it.[12]

The surly major wondered why it appeared so unappetizing and vile, only to find out the broth had been made from dog meat. "I passed a number of soldiers who had no provisions," Meigs later wrote, "and some that were sick, and not in my power to help or relieve them, except to encourage them. One or two dogs were killed, which the distressed soldiers [ate] with good appetite, even the feet and skins."[13]

It was quite a different scene from months earlier when it seemed a blissful time to be an American rebel soldier. Unity and democratic enthusiasm extended throughout New England, spreading to villages and townships alike. Washington and his army were poised to engage one of the largest, most disciplined military forces in the world, and in their hearts believed they could, at the least, stand up to them. Yet now, as winter settled on them, many thought the worst had come.[14]

Once again, the everyday habits of army life turned dull and unsatisfying for Nathan. When no alarms sounded, there was little to do. One could only read the Scriptures, tell tales from the trail of battle, or drink so much wine, rum, or ale. Nathan became so bored with life at camp that he staged wrestling matches between opposing regiments. Nathan invited another unit to his camp one night to compete. "View to find out best for a wrestling match to which this hill was stumped by Prospect, to be decided on Thursday," he wrote of the tie. In one instance, he allowed his men to omit "evening prayers" (a grave sin in those days) for wrestling. The next day, his unit wrestled Prospect Hill again, for fun this time, "no wager laid," but he failed to note who won the match.[15]

William Hull and Nathan walking together became a familiar sight around camp, be it to meetings, to dine in town, or just wandering the area. At times Nathan and Hull wrestled with their men, playing games, laughing and joking. Several soldiers had a problem with this and reported them. "Some dispute," Nathan wrote, "with the Subalterns, about Captain Hull & me acting as Captains."[16]

Scolded by Colonel Webb for not presenting themselves as distinguished, dignified officers, Nathan and Hull were said to have been told to act as their rank and uniform dictated. They shouldn't be parading around like common soldiers. When the brigade major heard what was going on, he agreed: The two men should be setting an example.

This admonishment rattled Nathan, who soon presented a petition to General Washington on behalf of "Hull & myself, requesting the pay" of captains be increased.[17]

His demand was promptly refused. The army had barely enough funding to purchase essential provisions. Frustration and stress were likely driving Nathan as much as monetary concerns. When several of his men announced they were going home because they couldn't get a raise, Nathan split his salary among them to increase their wages and keep them. "Promised the men if they tarry another month they should have my wages for that time."[18]

By the end of the first week of November, on a day when it rained "constantly, sometimes hard," what Nathan described as a "flying report" surfaced in camp. Congress had allegedly declared the colonies' independence. But other than that hopeful piece of news—which was, unfortunately, untrue—little else inspired the increasingly disillusioned captain. To his utter shock, Nathan saw a man from another unit accidentally stabbed in the neck by a bayonet one afternoon. With nothing but time on his hands, he marked the days and nights by playing checkers, exercising, and marching his men in proper formation, keeping them disciplined, in shape, and ready to engage.[19]

Meanwhile, the British were deciding whether to pull out of Boston. After taking control from Gage, General Howe suggested to Lord Dartmouth that Boston "should be evacuated, and the force designed for that place removed to Rhode Island." In surveying the region, Howe knew "the project of penetrating the Country" could more easily be executed from Providence. Because Samuel Adams and John Hancock had been planning the rebellion, arranging militiamen, express riders, and spies all throughout northeastern Massachusetts for months, all Howe's men could do at this point, he wrote to Lord Dartmouth, was defend the city. There was little chance of taking control of the area. "The possession of Rhode Island," Howe insisted, "would, moreover, put Connecticut in jeopardy." Part of Howe's strategy was to keep as many Connecticut divisions in that state as possible, to "induce that colony to keep its army at home for self-defence."[20]

Meanwhile, Washington was beginning to see his army disband, as insubordination, thievery, desertion, and treason spread like fever. He seemed unsure how to handle the low morale and dealt with things case by case. On one day he'd sentence a man to ten lashes on the bare back, while on others, he'd order his officers to make sure the groups of militiamen marching toward Cambridge were paid a stipend for bringing common essentials such as blankets and coats.[21]

Although the British considered withdrawal from Boston, Lord Dartmouth was still giving Howe strict orders to employ the harshest means necessary to establish control in and around the city. In a dispatch to Howe, Dartmouth directed him "in attacking and doing their utmost to destroy any towns in which the people should assemble in arms, hold meetings of committees or congresses, or prevent the king's courts of justice from assembling."[22]

Near this time, Tories from Portsmouth, New Hampshire, marched into Boston. This brigade probably included Nathan's cousin Samuel Hale, who was likely the only Hale in New Hampshire supporting the British. Many Tories were told that they could board a British schooner in Boston harbor and sail to other points along the East Coast where they were needed. Up until this point, Tories had been pretty much left alone by the Americans. When Washington heard Howe was preparing to herd them together and ship them south, he stepped in and gave orders for any soldier to "seize on those Tories who have been, are, and that we know will be, active against us" if he came upon them. Still, most of those northern Tories made it into Boston.[23]

Throughout October and into early November, save for a few minor exchanges, no conflict of real importance occurred near Boston. From what little intelligence Washington had received, the British appeared to be sailing part of their fleet of warships out of Boston harbor. Even so it appeared the British were staging a full-scale pullout from Boston, colonial citizens from Roxbury and other villages surrounding Boston harbor continued to pack up and leave the region. Helping the retreat along, the British torched houses, smashed windows, and scared away residents by riddling their homes with musket balls. One doctor in town later reported, "Nothing struck me with more horror than the present condition of Roxbury; that once busy, crowded street is now occupied only by a *picquet*-guard." The French term *piquet* was used during the war to describe standing rebel guards who were said to mimic "sharp-ended tree trunks and posts driven into the ground to form a defensive stockade."[24]

For Nathan, nothing was less fulfilling than "military duty out in the countryside," he wrote in his journal, "keeping watch over movements of the British army quartered in the city." He despised the tedium associated with such work, although he knew how essential it was to the greater good of the cause. What Nathan yearned for was action, tactical maneuvers that could bring the Americans closer to their goals. He was desperate to be part of it.[25]

As it continued to rain and snow that November, Nathan yearned to go home, if only for a brief visit. He had been at camp now for two months, and army life hadn't been at all what he had imagined. In a show of unity, he and several officers put their names down first on a list of soldiers reenlisting, proving to his men that the best thing they could do for their country was to repledge their loyalty. By now his days were filled, when not on guard duty, with more checkers and, as he put it, "jabber." He also started reading more, which passed the time, but did little for his spirits. When literature became uninteresting, he began to think about how the Americans lined up against the enemy. One afternoon, while sitting in his tent wasting time, Nathan mused about the state of his army, "It is of the utmost importance that an Officer should be anxious to know his duty, but of greater that he should carefully perform what he does know: The present irregular state of the army is owing to a capital neglect in both of these."[26]

His superiors suggested that Nathan study the manual of arms, a book of camp etiquette established by an order of "His Majesty in 1764." Some of the rules of fighting included, "To stand straight and firm upon . . . Legs; Head turned to the Right; Heels close; Toes a little turned out . . . Seize the Firelock with your right Hand, and turn the Lock outwards, keeping the Firelock perpendicular." It was a way to make sure every soldier knew his job along a column.

Beyond noting that he read the manual, Nathan wrote, "Rained pretty hard most of the day," on November 7, ". . . spent most of it in . . . my own and other tents in conversation—(some checkers). Studied the 1764 method of forming regiment for review, manner of arranging ye Companies, also of marching round ye reviewing Officer."[27]

The next day was wet and dreary, made especially glum by the dark clouds, cold mist, and ankle-deep mud around camp. That day, Nathan cleaned his gun, played some football and more checkers. "Some people came out of Boston via Roxbury." During the visit, Nathan drank wine, rum, and scored a load of hay, a few head of cattle, and several pounds of poultry for his men. What's more, a visiting soldier told him the rebels had taken control of St. John's, Newfoundland. Albeit small, it *was* a victory. Within the daily chitchat, as Nathan was in his tent polishing the handle of his weapon, came the most cheerful news he had heard in quite some time: General Washington had decided to give all of his officers furloughs.[28]

Chapter 11

OF THEE I SING

NATHAN WAS WALKING THROUGH camp on a Thursday afternoon in November, near one o'clock, when several soldiers approached him with a warning: A pack of regulars were on the move toward Lechmere's Point.[1]

Almost immediately, the Connecticut Seventh sprang into action, rushing hurriedly to their posts, struggling against an early-winter wind that made it difficult to pack their muskets with powder and ready them to fire.[2]

When they came upon Prospect Hill and a dairy farm just south of Lechmere's Point, the water table was so high in some areas that Nathan's men had to wade through waist-high shoals of ice-cold seawater to make it to their fortification. Yet as the enemy shored their vessels and ran for cover, the Seventh, side by side with several other brigades, "gave them a constant Cannonade."[3]

After the firing ceased, Nathan's unit marched in two columns, one on each side of the hill, toward Lechmere's Point. As they made their approach in perfect formation, with a dead-on view of the regulars, upon seeing such a well-disciplined stride, the redcoats retreated, hopping into their boats, Nathan wrote, "as fast as possible."[4]

All was not clear, however. A rebel soldier on lookout had failed to put a telescope on a British warship sitting patiently in Boston harbor, poised to fire; and as the rebels continued marching toward the departing regulars, "they were exposed to a hot fire from . . . a floating Battery." In response, a rebel division stationed on the crest of Bunker Hill fired "a few shot," but the mild clash was over within what seemed to be a few minutes.[5]

The Americans lost one man, Nathan reported, who had died only because of his own stupidity. A private, the soldier had been sent to a tent near Lechmere's Point to guard a herd of cattle and several horses grazing by a natural spring. If he spied a regular, the private was told to fire into the air, which would hopefully send the redcoats packing and warn the rebels back at camp that the British were approaching. But instead of doing as he was told, the soldier pillaged a keg of rum and ended up inebriated inside his tent. When the regulars found him sleeping off the liquor, they surrounded his tent and shot him in the head, killing him.[6]

Beyond that one soldier and "3 men wounded badly & it is thought 1, 2, or more cattle carried off," Nathan noted, the rebels could walk away from the skirmish waving a victory flag.[7]

Responding to the growing problem of guards getting intoxicated and sleeping on duty, Washington ordered his brigade commanders to explain to their men what was expected of them at all times within camp. He sent his commanders a list of twenty-one "Directions for the Guards." Likely out of boredom and perhaps to help him remember them, Nathan sat in his tent on Tuesday, November 14, and copied each direction into his journal.[8] Washington's commanders spent the next few days demanding that each of their brigade leaders instruct his men on the basics of camp life. Granted, some of the directions Nathan copied down were obvious, but Washington insisted on spelling things out plainly for an army of mostly illiterate farmers who had never before been soldiers. "The Officer of each Guard must order their Centinals," read one of the more blatant directions, "to Challenge every person that passes by them after dark in the following manner, in a manly & Soldier like voice: WHO COMES THERE?"[9] Perhaps Washington was preparing for an influx of new militiamen due in Cambridge any day. The general made it clear to his commanders that he wasn't going to accept just any colonist with a gun, ordering, "Neither Negroes, Boys unable to bear Arms, nor old men unfit to endure the fatigues of the campaign, are to be enlisted."[10]

Another important task before Washington was the need to convince his troops to stay until the end of December. Realizing that asking wasn't enough, Washington made a promise: Any soldier who reenlisted would be granted a furlough at some point during the winter. In his General Orders, Washington was adamant about his desire to maintain an army that could meet the high expectations he had, which was vital to the long-term war plan he was developing. He saw no need, for the sole purpose of numbers, to employ an army of, as he put it, "wretched assistance." He didn't want "vagabonds" and "miscreants," he wanted dedicated men who believed in the cause; not a mob of drunken bandits who could not have cared less whether America liberated herself from the oppression of England but were more interested in killing a few foreigners for a good time.[11]

By mid-November, Nathan was given the good news that his men would be allowed furloughs within the next few weeks. Although "not more than 50 [men] at a time" could go home, it was comforting news to soldiers on the verge of psychological collapse. Then Congress approved a raise for everyone, which sent hats flying in the air and cheers throughout. Nathan and William Hull had been on a mission for the past two weeks to get their men more money and time off—and within a day, both objectives had been secured.[12]

A week before Thanksgiving, on the third Sunday of the month, a preacher captured Nathan's attention with a sermon he had titled "For how can I endure to see evil that shall come unto my people? Or how can I endure to see the destruction of my kindred?" As Nathan and his fellow officers discussed the preacher's ideas afterward, someone brought up the man-of-war *Asia*, a British warship said to be stationed near Governors Island in New York. According to a source, the ship had been taken by the rebels. Several soldiers passing the *Asia* in a small schooner, Nathan wrote later that night, detailing the stealthy mission, "came up . . . alongside the men, which were before concealed immediately, sprung up with their lances . . . and went at it with such vigor that they soon made themselves masters of the ship."[13]

With a winter bearing down on camp that many of the soldiers from the south had never seen, Nathan gave his men leave as December began. While he was at base camp one night getting his new orders, Nathan asked if he was also going to be allowed to return home himself anytime soon. To his utter disgust, his request was once again denied. In truth, Colonel Jonathan Lattimore knew Nathan well enough to use his dedication to the cause and willingness to please Washington against him. There was little anyone could say or do to Nathan that would force him to quit. His commitment to the cause was unbreakable. His officers knew it. On top of that, Lattimore was certain the army would be better served with Nathan at camp near Boston. It was cold. Wet. Fighting had all but ceased. But a war was still raging. Washington needed good men—his best—to stick it out and wait. Although other officers were allowed furlough, Nathan was forced to stay in camp.[14]

The opening days of December saw terribly harsh winter weather, which added to a growing feeling of discontent around camp. One soldier judged the entire Boston campaign during this period as to "exceed the possibility of description." Many brigades, wrote surgeon James Thatcher, were "almost in a state of starvation, for the want of food and fuel." Things got so bad, with troops "totally destitute of vegetables, flour, and fresh provisions," many were forced to "feed on horse flesh . . . by means of which they have become very sickly." To keep warm, houses in the region were torn down and burned, as well as church pews and other flammable material in and around the city. But for a soldier walking the streets or the thousands of displaced civilians roaming through town like refugees, staring blankly at the charred carcasses of their homes and businesses, Cambridge, Boston, and the surrounding villages became a war zone such as few had ever seen or even read about before.[15]

Captain Nathan Hale's regiment was stationed so close to a British line that many of his men could hear the redcoats digging in and setting up fortifications as they shuffled from one area to another. With most of his men on furlough, Nathan found himself standing guard more often than not.

Some days, he reported in his journal, he could hear redcoats discussing tactical plans. On certain afternoons when the wind cooperated, he could even make out the enemy's countersign, a short phrase, a previously agreed-upon signal, used to get into camp or address a fellow soldier you didn't recognize out in the field. Marching back and forth near the front line was an important part of stopping the British from mounting small sorties into camp to steal cattle and what little provisions the rebels had left. Almost daily Nathan noted in his journal his frustration as the impasse continued: "Mounted picket guard—mounted main guard—slept little." If he was lucky, he'd encounter a problem he could fix, which always made a day easier to tolerate. "A number of men, about 20 in the whole confined for attempting to go home," he wrote of a group of deserters. He reported happily that he had talked his men into staying until January 1, 1776, which his commander had asked him to do.[16]

Those vital reinforcements Washington had been waiting on since early winter started arriving on December 11, as "a party of militia, said to be about two thousand," marched into camp, one soldier observed. On top of the two thousand getting settled, three thousand more were said to be on their way. New enlistments were filing into camp, too, but in far lower numbers. Even worse, these recruits had little to offer besides body and soul. "So destitute are they of fire arms," James Thatcher wrote, "that it has been found necessary to take the arms by force from the soldiers who retire, paying for them, in order to supply the recruits."[17]

Nathan traveled into Cambridge one night as Christmas approached to retrieve orders and meet with his superiors. It started out as a pleasant night, as he and a few fellow officers stood around talking as the sun set behind their shoulders. "Last night 2 sheep killed belonged to the Enemy," he wrote. The following morning, while still in Cambridge, there was "Considerable firing between the Centuries," he added. "A Rifleman got a Dog from the Regulars." For the most part, things seemed rather run-of-the-mill.[18]

Walking out of camp, Nathan ran into two generals he knew. They were discussing a higher-ranking officer, Colonel Jedediah Huntington, a man Nathan was quite familiar with. Jedediah, from Norwich, was the Reverend Joseph Huntington's first cousin. Thirty-two-year-old Jedediah, a Harvard man, had been in Cambridge since the opening of the Boston conflict, almost eight months now. He and his wife, Faith, had been inseparable until the start of the war, when Huntington left home. Since that day, however, he hadn't returned or even visited with Faith, who was staying in Connecticut. He promised to send for her when he felt Boston was secure enough to accept outside civilians and family members of the army's colonels and generals. Just a few weeks ago, Huntington had finally made plans for Faith's trip, and she had arrived at camp without complication. They had been staying in Dedham, outside Roxbury.[19]

Since her arrival, Faith was in a bad spot emotionally. She had been "delirious," Nathan heard, "for the greater part of the time [Colonel Huntington had] entered the Service." When the colonel first saw his wife, he determined that she was "as rational as ever." He thought she appeared quite normal, considering she hadn't seen him in so long. Yet "within an hour after he left her" and returned to the field, Faith became "melancholy" to the point of a breakdown. Her servants had a hard time containing her or even talking with her. She wanted to be by herself, she insisted. So they allowed Faith some time alone, only to summon Huntington from the field when she said she needed him back in Dedham. But proving clearly that the war was affecting more than just the soldiers who fought on the front lines, when he arrived, it was too late: She had "hanged herself," Nathan wrote.

Nathan became ill near the middle of December and spent several days in his tent recovering from what was likely a bout with the flu, or a slight manifestation of smallpox, which had taken a grave toll on soldiers in and around Boston. "A little unwell yesterday and today," he wrote on December 12, "some better this evening."[20]

A week later, he felt strong enough to travel and made one of his routine trips into Cambridge to see about the furlough he hoped for. If there was ever a time to take leave, Nathan pleaded with his commanders, it was now. Little fighting was going on. It was the middle of winter. Each side was more interested in staying warm and finding food than defending its fortifications.[21]

While at headquarters, Nathan ran into Stephen Hempstead for the first time in months. He had met Hempstead at Yale and known him later while teaching in New London, where Hempstead lived. A sergeant in Nathan's brigade, Hempstead had been in Cambridge for a few weeks, and now here they were together once again. Nathan was delighted to see his old friend. "The Hempstead family tradition is," George Dudley Seymour wrote, "that Stephen fairly idolized Nathan, and though only a year older, felt that he was a sort of big brother to him." To Seymour, Nathan was more "warmly attached" to Stephen Hempstead than to any other friend, especially after they reconnected that winter in Cambridge. Within the next ten months, Hempstead and Nathan would become inseparable.[22]

On Saturday, December 23, Nathan was told he could finally take leave, but was ordered to be back in camp within thirty days. He had been hoping to hear this news for weeks, but he was broke; he had spent every last cent he had among his men hoping to keep them. Thus, with no money, after packing in preparation for his trip home, he was forced to borrow "76 Dollars" from one of his fellow captains, "giving him an order on Col. Webb for the same [amount] as soon as my advance pay for January should be drawn." And so, with $76 in his pocket he "set out from Cambridge" at 3:45 P.M. that afternoon. With any luck, he'd make it to Coventry before the end of December.[23]

If the first leg was any indication how his trip would go, Nathan seemed destined to spend the 1775–76 winter season along the trail like a gypsy. "At Watertown," he wrote in his journal, "took the wrong road and went two miles directly out of the way, which I had to travel right back again." Four hours into his trip, Nathan had made it eleven miles to Newtown, where, he said, the "entertainment was pretty good," meaning the food, drink, and dance at the inn lived up to his expectations.[24]

On Christmas Eve day, at 6:30 A.M., Nathan left Newtown in a blinding snowstorm and made it eight miles in "ankle deep" snow. After a short break, he made nine more miles, then, at a place called Stone's, drank cider and ate biscuits as tough as beef jerky. Quite fatigued already, after trekking two more miles he realized he had to turn around and head back to Stone's after having discovered he'd forgot a few things.[25]

Several days before he had left camp, he had received a letter from his good friend Gilbert Saltonstall. Nathan had written to Saltonstall in mid-December, describing the dire situation he saw in and around camp. Nathan often used Saltonstall as a sounding board. In return, Saltonstall appreciated the interest Nathan showed in his life. Saltonstall sympathized in his letter with his friend for the lack of discipline and dedication to the cause some men were exhibiting. Things were worse, however, back home in New London, Saltonstall insisted.[26]

> Women wringing their Hands along Street, Children crying, Carts loaded 'till nothing more would stick on posting out of Town, empty ones driving in, one Person running this way, another that, some dull, some vexed, none pleased, some flinging up an Entrenchment, some at the Fort preparing ye Guns for Action, Drums beating, Fifes playing; in short as great a Hubbub as at the confusion of Tongues.

What had spawned such a dramatic reaction from the townspeople was "the appearance of a Ship and two Sloops" in New London harbor. But as Saltonstall told it, the panic that had spread throughout town was all for naught. The vessels turned out to be friendly.[27]

Saltonstall spoke of his high regard for Nathan's service, as he was patiently waiting himself for orders to sail. He praised men such as Nathan, "persons of Candor, Reason, Justice and Sincerity with their attendant to Virtues." Thinking of such men, not to mention *knowing* one personally, gave Saltonstall a "generous glow within," he explained. He ended the letter noting that more than a few of the "young girls" Nathan had taught in New London wished to send their "Master . . . compliments."[28]

Nathan arrived home, fatigued and feeling a bit sickly, on December 26, "after sunset," with "one heel string lame." No matter how difficult the trip had been, Nathan was among family now for the first time in what had been almost a year. After spending some time with Enoch and his father, Nathan visited his old tutor Joseph Huntington, several family members and friends in town, then returned home a bit sicker than he had felt when he left camp. "Unwell" was all he said about the sudden return of his illness, "tarried at home."[29]

After spending three days in bed, Nathan managed to get on his feet again to take a ride to his uncle Strong's in Salmon Brook and, from there, head north to Granville, Massachusetts, to make a call on an old college mate. When he returned to Coventry a day later, he settled in for about a month, yet failed to keep track of his time in his diary. Not until January 24, 1776, a Wednesday, did he again pick up his journal, writing quite simply, "I set out from my Father's for Camp on horse back."[30]

During the month he spent at home, Nathan received letters from two sergeants and several soldiers from his unit. They wanted to keep him abreast of events back at camp. George Hurlbut told him on December 28, "I Joined our Company Last Sunday and found them all In Good Spirits, I was very much Disappointed in not Seeing you Hear, I am now A Going to Set Out for Bunker Hill But I Shant Go with So much Pleasure as if You was to Be With me." A few days later, Hurlbut wrote again, saying how disappointed he was that he hadn't yet heard back from Nathan. He explained that Stephen Hempstead had left camp, adding, "It was nothing but the effects of Bunker Hill." Hempstead had been quite ill himself, suffering from a bad cold. "Sir, I hope the next Time I See you, it will be in Boston . . . Drinking A Glass of wine with me. . . . If we Can have A Bridge we Shall Make a Push to Try our Brave Courage." Hurlbut then spoke of a private, Charles Brown, one of Nathan's men Hurlbut had arrested and confined for "Attempting to Run one of our men through the Heart with A [bayonet]." Before ending the letter, Hurlbut warned his commanding officer to be mindful of men he enlisted, as it seemed many of the new recruits were unsavory, shady characters, looking to cause trouble around camp, pillage local homes, and harass civilians.[31]

Eager to get back to Boston and take control of his men, Nathan left Coventry along with his childhood friend Asher Wright, who would work as his "servant," the work being similar to that of a modern personal assistant. Asher said many years later, describing the end of Nathan's first six months of service, "His time was out, and he come up here (Coventry) in December, and had a captain's commission. First of January, he enlisted for a year. I engaged under him."[32]

Nathan left his horse in Ashford so it could be returned to Coventry. He and Asher were not far from the home of Nathan's friend Captain Thomas

Knowlton, after reaching town late in the day on January 24. From there, they marched three and a half miles to Pomfret, where Nathan and Asher met up with "9 Soldiers from Windham and spent the night." The following morning, after accepting, Asher explained, "several recruits from Windham, New London, New Haven and some from Long Island," they set out for Roxbury at 6:30 A.M.[33]

In his absence, Congress had appointed Nathan captain of the Nineteenth Regiment of Foot, a brigade under the command of Colonel Charles Webb, his superior. Before his departure from Boston, Nathan had expressed interest in a new commission by putting his name among those of ten other officers offering their services for an additional year.[34]

On Saturday, January 27, Nathan, Asher, and the soldiers they had traveled east with were about thirty miles south of Roxbury, after having traveled twenty-six miles in two days. At a place called Clarkes, Nathan ate breakfast and had a spot of brandy to warm his blood, then marched five and a half more miles into Jamaica Plains. Before reaching Roxbury later that day, he stopped again to eat. "Being refused entertainment, was obliged to betake ourselves to the Punch boll, where leaving the men," he traveled to Roxbury by himself and, an hour later, "retired to Winterhill." According to Asher Wright, he and Nathan spent the next month at Cambridge, before heading back to Roxbury.[35]

Nathan was once again among what was left of his regiment, ready for new orders. The battlefield hadn't changed since he'd left over a month ago; it was still confused, with more shoot-and-run altercations than any sort of structured military action. It seemed things might be escalating, however, after a conflict erupted near the middle of February as a "party of Regulars made an attempt upon Dorchester," Nathan observed, "landing with a considerable body of men, taking 6 of our guard, dispersing the rest & burning two or three houses."[36]

Washington was dealing with a fresh body of recruits and thousands of militiamen during the months of February, March, and April 1776, as colonists taking up arms against the British marched into Boston from all points. By now, the City of New York was considered the prize of the American battlefield; whichever side secured Long Island and the city would have control over the war. Foreseeing this, Washington and his cabinet discussed sending part of the American army south. With such a considerable change of soldiers taking place in Boston, the general pointed out, "It is not perhaps in the power of history to furnish a case like ours . . . and at the same time to disband one army and recruit another within that distance of twenty British regiments, is more than probably was ever attempted."[37]

Major General Charles Lee, one of Washington's top three officers and advisers, had set out for New York at the beginning of January and had, by the end of the month, made it to Stamford, Connecticut. Forty-five-year-old Lee was sent ahead to set up defenses in the city. "New York," he wrote to Washington back on January 5, "must be secured; but it will never, I am afraid, be secured by direct order of the Congress." Lee added, "The consequences of the enemy's possessing themselves of New York have appeared to me so terrible, that I have scarcely been able to sleep. . . . You have it in your power, at present, to prevent this dreadful event."[38]

Lee knew what he was talking about; he had spent a number of years as a British officer, some of which he had served the king under General Thomas Gage, before resigning his commission in January 1775 and accepting an appointment as second major general of the rebel army in Boston.[39]

Washington respected Lee's advice and believed he could foresee what the British were planning, mainly because he had spent so much time among them. In his instructions to Lee three days later, Washington said he had "undoubted intelligence" that a fleet of British with a large body of troops "must be destined for a southern expedition." It was quite clear, Washington further stated, that William Howe and a majority of his army were not, as many believed, heading to Halifax to regroup, resupply, and head back to Boston; but were instead sailing due south and making a beeline for New York. "I am persuaded I need not recommend dispatch in the prosecution of this business," Washington wrote near the end of his instructions. "The importance of it alone is a sufficient incitement." Consequently, as soon as Lee could report back an assessment of the city and the "state and condition of the fortifications up the North [Hudson] River,"

Washington promised a majority of the rebel army in Boston, growing every day, would sail south to join him.[40]

Asher Wright had a different, more biased, view of the British withdrawal from Boston. He later said it was the rebels who had scared the British into retreating—and that Nathan's regiment had played a crucial part in the final conflict that led to their departure. "Went to Dorchester in the spring of [1776]," Asher recalled, "and built a breastwork." These temporary fortifications, quickly put together at chest level, were a common means of hasty defense for both sides. "Snow had gone off," he continued, "and was no frost on the ground." The next night, after he, Nathan, and the brigade had burrowed into their makeshift fortification, "some fools went down to the Neck within a half-mile of British and made up fires." This alerted the redcoats, of course, who "began to send over balls." It was either a coincidence, or the rebels must have bested their foes on that day, because, Asher reported, "Soon the British took the hint and evacuated Boston, went to Halifax, received reinforcements; [and] in the latter part of summer, landed on the west end of Long Island." Although this minor skirmish could have contributed to or seemed to take place coincidentally around the same time as the British retreat from Boston, Asher Wright gave Nathan's regiment a little bit more credit than it deserved—because in no way did the British leave Boston because of this battle, as Asher seemed to suggest. In truth, cannons from Fort Ticonderoga were brought in clandestinely at some point during that dark night, thus putting the British fleet within reach of rebel guns.[41]

The British, knowing that whichever side made it to New York first would have the upper hand in the war, wanted to get there before Washington. Howe could foresee that if he made it to the city first with the massive fleet of British warships, he could perhaps cut off New England from the American forces in the south and west via the North and St. Lawrence rivers, essentially boxing them in, thus ending the buildup of rebel forces before they had time to engage.

Chapter 12

Independence Day

IF THE AMERICANS LEARNED one thing from the siege in Boston, it was that without trustworthy tactical intelligence an army was constantly on the defensive. As the theater of war moved to New York, several different resolutions underlining the need for intelligence were written into the congressional record. Back on November 29, 1775, the Second Continental Congress had created the Committee of Correspondence, later renamed the Committee of Secret Correspondence. The group was made up of five persons "appointed for the sole purpose of corresponding with our friends in Great Britain and other parts of the world." Among the chosen few were Benjamin Franklin, Benjamin Harrison, Thomas Johnston, and James Lovell, a man who knew firsthand how important intelligence gathering was after he had been taken prisoner by the British at Bunker Hill and charged with spying. During this critical period, the committee devised several measures that would affect Nathan's life in the next several months. The committee employed "secret agents abroad," who "conducted covert operations, devised codes and ciphers, funded propaganda activities, authorized the opening of private mail . . . established a courier system, and developed a maritime capability apart from that of the Navy." Congress had created a colonial version of what would become, centuries later, the Central Intelligence Agency.[1]

Twenty-four-year-old Harvard graduate Isaac Bangs, a lieutenant surgeon with a militia regiment sent to New York from Harwich, Massachusetts, was a dedicated soldier who took copious notes of what was going on around him during that pivotal moment of the American Revolution when the Americans and the English were preparing to do battle in the City of New York.

On July 6, 1776, Bangs sat "merrily playing" and drinking wine with several officers at a New York City "publik house."[2] Inside was a party: music, rum, fresh ale, people dancing and enjoying themselves. The officers Bangs sat with had good reason to be merry. That morning word had funneled into New York that the "United Colonies were being Declared free & Independent States by the Congress," he wrote. A declaration of American independence from Great Britain had officially been signed into order; the colonies had agreed to cut the chain binding them to King George III. It was a grand moment of eternal fame, unrelenting vigor, and public unity—a cause for celebration.[3]

Upon hearing the news twenty-four hours later, a mob of New Yorkers, led by the Sons of Liberty, hit the streets near Bowling Green (the lower end of Broad Way), waving their tricorns and cheering wildly. The declaration was being read before roll call to soldiers on the front lines. In reply, a cascade of "loud huzzas" was reportedly heard from one camp to another. In the spirit of collective patriotism, later that night the Sons of Liberty, with torches in hand and the courage of new independence, lassoed a gilded lead statue of King George near Bowling Green, tore it down, and dragged it through the dirt roads behind their horses.[4] As the figure made the rounds through the Bowery, Broad Way, and up Old Colonial Post Road, the crowds coming out to see it roared.

Although Washington believed the pressure of "the continents" was now weighing entirely on the backs of his soldiers, support throughout the colonies for the effort seemed unwavering. Americans were liberated—from the general's perspective, unwilling to live as British "slaves" any longer.[5]

"Last night the Statue on the Bowling Green . . . was pulled down by the Populace," Isaac Bangs wrote. "In it were 4,000 pounds of Lead, & a Man undertook to take of 10oz of Gold from the Superficies, as both Man and Horse were covered with Gold Leaf. The lead, we hear, will be run up into Musket Balls for the use of the Yankees."[6]

After a tour of the Bowery, scraping and bouncing along the muddied pathways of the city, the statue was transported by wagon to Connecticut and dropped at the house of Oliver Wolcott, who lived in the hills of Litchfield. Wolcott's daughters and a few friends melted it into some forty thousand musket balls and bullets and sent the ammunition south to patriot camps in New York. Morale for the rebel effort could not have been more concentrated and resolute. The colonies were united. Nearly everyone believed liberty, gaining momentum, would soon prevail.[7]

With the drafting and signing of the Declaration of Independence, Congress set up the Committee of Correspondence's chain of command. John Adams, Thomas Jefferson, Edward Rutledge, James Wilson, and Robert Livingston were chosen as the gatekeepers of intelligence law and what to do with those who deserted. If a rebel soldier turned double agent, Congress felt it needed laws to deal with such disloyalty. In late 1775, Congress had added a death penalty to the Articles of War to deal with patriot soldiers convicted of espionage. The first Espionage Act was enacted on August 21, 1776, and stated, "All persons not members of, nor owing allegiance to, any of the United States of America . . . who shall be lurking as spies . . . shall suffer death, according to the law and usage of the nations."[8]

Despite what appeared to be several politicians in charge of the army's intelligence operations, the actual weight of the organization fell entirely on the shoulders of one man, General George Washington, who "retained full and final authority over Continental Army intelligence activities." Washington could delegate various responsibilities to any officer of his choosing and had the last word in any matter of importance concerning intelligence.[9]

Both sides needed spies. Washington and Howe knew this. They also understood spying was not only unpleasant trickery, but had won wars in the past. Spying wasn't new to the battlefield. The earliest evidence of spies exists in Egyptian temple drawings, Terry Crowdy wrote in his book *The Enemy Within: A History of Espionage.* Ancient carvings depict the battle of Kadesh, where "two kneeling figures are Hittite spies being beaten by Rameses' officers."[10] Some contemporary historians claim that spying led to the start of the French and Indian War. When the French were caught deep in the Ohio River Valley, Washington, a young officer, warned them that they were trespassing on English territory. Papers later found on the Frenchmen proved they were indeed spying on Washington's association with the Indians.[11]

In one instance later on during the Revolutionary War, General Washington placed Nathan's friend Benjamin Tallmadge in charge of guarding John André, a British spy, as he was being prepared for court-martial. Tallmadge found André a most pleasant prisoner and had long conversations with him. "The ease and affability of his manners," Tallmadge, then a major, said, "polished by the refinement of a good society and a finished education, made him a most delightful companion. It almost drew tears from my eyes to find him so agreeable in conversation on different subjects, when I reflected on his future fate, and that too, as I feared, so near at hand."[12]

And yet as Tallmadge and André were riding on a trail side by side one day, André asked Tallmadge about what lay in store for him. Tallmadge did all he could to ignore the question. But after André pestered him, urging his captor to give him explicit details of what was going to happen, Tallmadge stopped his horse and, quite emotionally, said, "I had a much-loved classmate in Yale College, by the name of Nathan Hale. . . . General Washington wanted information respecting the strength, position, and probable movements of the enemy. Captain Hale tendered his services . . . and was taken."[13]

Recalling the conversation with André at a later date, Tallmadge explained that he had paused at that specific moment and then, rather abruptly, while staring André in the eyes, snapped, "Do you remember the sequel of the story?"

"Yes," André said.

"He was hanged as a spy!"

"But you surely do not consider *his* case and mine alike?" André said. Because he had been treated so humanely and many didn't consider André an actual undercover agent like Nathan, he obviously didn't see the comparison—that a spy is a spy, no matter what his mission, or how and where he is captured.

"Yes, precisely similar; and similar will be your fate."

As André sized Tallmadge up, despair washed over his face as he realized, perhaps for the first time since being taken prisoner, that he was going to die. And with that "he endeavored," Tallmadge later said, "to answer my remarks, but it was manifest he was more troubled in spirit than I had ever seen him before."[14]

Philadelphia was the nerve center of political discourse in the first week of August 1776 regarding troop buildups by both sides in and around New York. Joseph Reed, a lawyer, had been in the city for months working with Congress to establish a governing body to support the war effort. In Reed, George Washington saw a patriot who could potentially help him deal with the problems he was having with certain members of Congress—those not providing his troops with the essential stores and wares they needed. That April, Washington had written to Reed, asking for his immediate attendance in New York, fearing Congress was not keeping its eye on what Washington described as the "divisions and parties which prevail with you, and in the Southern Colonies on the score of Independence." This logistical divide worried Washington. Furthermore, that the war had become politicized admittedly made the general "tremble" with fear to think of the consequences such action would ultimately have. He was torn. "Nothing but disunion can hurt our cause," the general warned. He wanted Reed as far away from the political backbiting as he could get, knowing his skills were much more valuable to the effort in the field and that he would eventually be debased by what was going on in Philadelphia.[15]

Born in Trenton, New Jersey, on August 27, 1741, Reed had moved to Philadelphia after graduating from Princeton in 1757. He was admitted to the bar six years later after studying law with Robert Stockton. Reed had traveled to England twice and married an English-born doctor's daughter, Esther De Berdt. For eighteen months, Reed held the position of president of the Second Provincial Congress. With his boyish good looks, he appeared to be a man of little agitation or rigidity. But Reed was a tough administrator, one not afraid to speak his mind when he thought the good of his country was at stake. Since Washington had taken over command of the army, Reed had served him as personal secretary. But he had returned to Philadelphia in October 1775 as things in Boston seemed to slow to a standoff. Now the war was heading into what Washington was sure would be its most brutal and bloody period yet, and he realized that one of his best men was no longer by his side, but was now being influenced by conservative members of Congress.[16]

When Reed failed to show up, the impatient general rode to Philadelphia to talk Reed into traveling with him back to New York. Washington pled his case to Congress and Reed was appointed adjutant general. Reed was now one of Washington's top advisers, who would, in the following days, cross enemy lines and meet with Howe to discuss a possible peace treaty.[17]

Nathan's life was an archetype of patriotism, as men for centuries after him followed in his footsteps. This was never more obvious than in his letters home or in the entries in his army journal. He was more interested in giving the men of his company credit than promoting his own reputation. Winning a war was not going to be decided by a single man's effort, or even a single victory in battle. Nathan knew that each regiment had to collectively contribute to further Washington's larger agenda.[18]

"Last Friday night," Nathan wrote to Enoch that summer, "two of our fine vessels (a sloop & schooner) made an attempt upon the shipping up the [North, or Hudson] River."

The event Nathan described took place at a time when chaos reigned in the city as women, children, and the infirm still in New York panicked at the sight of a fleet of British warships slowly cruising up the North and

East rivers. "When the men-of-war passed up river," Washington wrote of this day, "the shrieks and cries of these poor creatures running every way with their children, were truly distressing." Washington was concerned that such a display of power would have "an unhappy effect on the ears and minds of our young and inexperienced soldiers."[19]

In what seemed like one crushing blow after another by the British, minor displays of gallantry were indeed taking place, such as the one Nathan had described. Among the brave were five men from Nathan's brigade who set out on the cavern-dark night of August 16, 1776, to wreak some havoc on several of the British men-of-war.

On that night, Nathan explained, fog hovered at eye level, limiting visibility. The wind, he added, "was too slack for the attempt." Ships and schooners were having trouble sailing. The soldier responsible for what Nathan called a moment of pure divine Providence was Sergeant Thomas Fosdick, who had, ever since joining the rebellion, yearned to prove his worthiness to Nathan, a commanding officer Fosdick had tremendous admiration for. Fosdick had written to Nathan in December 1775 when Nathan was at Winter Hill awaiting word on furloughs for his men. In that letter, Fosdick had made quite the impression on Nathan, saying, "Ever since the uneasiness, which I have heard, persisting amongst the Connecticut Troops, I've form'd a Resolution to go down to the assistance of my Countrymen." Fosdick wanted Nathan to know he was willing to die for the cause.[20]

Nathan had known Fosdick from his days in New London and had always liked him. He could tell Fosdick had a sense of what being a true patriot meant. Fosdick was so captivated by Nathan's charm and dedication he had resigned from a sergeant's post in another regiment to join Nathan's unit. "I make no doubt, Sir, that you can assist me to some such office," Fosdick had said, "as I should choose to be in that Station, under you in particular—if not, I am determined to come down—a hearty Boy, undaunted by Danger."[21]

At the time Fosdick had written Nathan, Connecticut soldiers were fleeing the cause as if jumping from a runaway stagecoach. The officer whose regiment Fosdick resigned from in order to join Nathan's unit sent the captain a letter assuring him that if he accepted Fosdick, he would not be sorry. "I Should be Glad if you would be kind enough To Give him the Chance," wrote George Hurlbut, "[Fosdick] is a Good hearty fellow, And Them are the Men we want."[22]

Fosdick had joined Nathan's company back on June 8, 1776, and, after landing from Boston on Long Island, journeyed with them to a post near Brooklyn. On that night in mid-August, Fosdick led a group of four other soldiers from the regiment up the North River in an attempt to destroy one of Britain's most venerated and well-equipped warships, the *Phoenix*. The big-bellied British fighter had been in the river with dozens of other ships and men-of-war, positioning itself to shell rebel fortifications along the coastline and assist what Washington knew would be an onslaught of British troops against Long Island and the city any day. "The schooner which was intended for one of the ships had got by before she discovered them," Nathan wrote to Enoch, "but . . . she run athwart a bomb-catch which she quickly burn'd. The sloop by the light of the former discovered the *Phoenix*—but rather too late,—however she made shift to grapple her." A *bomb ketch* was a vessel used in the seventeenth and eighteenth centuries to carry heavy trajectory-type rounds of ammunition; a floating platform, in other words, with a mortar that could toss shells of explosives like a catapult might launch stones.[23]

The wind wouldn't cooperate with Fosdick's crew or the British fleet, so the *Phoenix* was forced to sit around in an area upriver near Tarrytown, New York, waiting for the gales to kick up. But in doing so, she left herself vulnerable. "The *Phoenix*," continued Nathan, "after much difficulty got her clear."[24]

Fosdick's goal was to burn the *Phoenix* and the *Rose*, another British warship nearby. Because the night was so foggy and dark, Fosdick had a hard time navigating his small boat. Soon, the *Phoenix* saw them coming at her, but did not "perceive our vessels till they were near aboard of them." Fosdick intended, without the crew of the *Phoenix* noticing him, to connect his boat to the ship and light her on fire. Yet things did not go as planned; his torches would not cooperate. After about twenty minutes of trying, Fosdick untangled his boat from the *Phoenix*. The mission was not a total loss, however. Before leaving, Fosdick was able to reach onto the *Phoenix*'s deck and light a small pile of her provisions afire. As he watched the flames spread rapidly aboard the massive ship, somehow one of his men fell into the dark waters, quickly grabbed hold of a burning timber nearby, but floated away.[25]

After searching for the missing soldier, Fosdick and his crew lost sight of the man. Forced to sail or be pummeled by the *Phoenix*'s cannons as the deck of the ship burned, Fosdick retreated back to base camp without the man. "This gallant enterprise," the *Pennsylvania Evening Post* reported three days after the event, "struck so great a panic upon the enemy, that they thought it prudent to quit their stations."[26]

Fosdick and his surviving crew members had escaped. When the winds picked up the following day, amid a considerable rainstorm, many of the British warships had to cut and run, while under fire from "a great number of well-directed shots from our batteries," the *Evening Post* continued, "in and near New York, which no doubt must have damaged them much." As spectators from New York's coastline looked on from the tops of their homes, the British fired back on the city, "but very little damage was done to the buildings, nor any lives lost upon the occasion."[27]

Washington made public how pleased he was and rewarded the bravery of Fosdick and his remaining crew, Nathan wrote, "with forty dollars each except the last man [Fosdick] that quitted the fiery sloop who had fifty."[28]

In his Orderly Book on August 18, 1776, Washington mentioned the effort, noting, "Though the Fire Ships which went up the North River . . . were not successful as to destroy either of the Men of War . . . the General thanks the officers and men for the spirit and resolution which they showed in grappling the Vessels."[29]

In a second letter to Enoch in late August, Nathan explained to his favorite brother that he was in the thick of a major predicament as the Continental Army prepared to make a swift retreat from Long Island. "I have only time for a hasty letter," he wrote. "Our situation has been such this fortnight or more as scarce to admit of writing. We have daily expected an action—by which means if any one was going, and we had letters written, orders were so strict for our tarrying in camp that we could rarely get leave to go and deliver them."[30]

By now Britain's highly touted commander in chief, General William Howe, was on Staten Island, setting up camp and preparing to begin his invasion of Long Island and the City of New York. Rumors throughout camp, Nathan said, were that Howe was preparing to make an offer of peace, but the soldiers were confused. Some were saying Howe was going to launch a terrific cannonade, firing on the American troops now settled along the east and west shores of the city. The peace offering had to be a speculative rumor, Nathan considered. While word of it circulated, Howe ordered every warship and man-of-war the British had in the region to begin trolling the North and East rivers. If he was planning on offering peace, why was he preparing for what looked to be an attack?[31]

Washington warned his troops that Howe's words were likely "calculated . . . probably to lull us into a fatal security." The general made clear that "no such offer has been made . . . but on the contrary, from the best intelligence . . . the Army may expect an attack as soon as the wind and tide shall prove favourable."[32]

Additionally, he wanted "every man's mind and arms"—the wet weather of late had proved disastrous to the army's stock of gunpowder—"prepared for action, and when called to it, show our enemies, and the whole world, that Freemen contending on their own land, are superior to any mercenaries on earth."[33]

He also offered a bit of sobering advice to his men, hinting at what to expect in the days ahead: "The Brigadiers are to see the Spears in different works, under their command, are kept creased and clean."[34]

Nathan explained to Enoch that they had expected the enemy hourly for the past "6 to 8 days." Like Washington, he noted how the "wind and tide" had most likely hampered the British effort. In what would no doubt have made Richard Hale proud when he later read the letter, Nathan said he was certain that the British attack was an "event we leave to Heaven. Thanks to God! we have had time for completing our works and receiving our reinforcements." Nathan believed the Americans were ready for whatever the British were staging.[35]

By now, many of the Connecticut troops promised by the state's governor, John Trumbull, had arrived, and more men, Nathan told Enoch, marched in every day. "We hope under God, to give a good account of the Enemy whenever they choose to make the last appeal."[36]

The summer of 1776 had yielded one of the most reduced harvests the New England colonies had seen in years. Not because of a drought or poor fertilization, but the loss of laborers. Men across New England were off to war. This labor shortage put a tremendous strain on the women of each farming household, who were already working as many hours as they could sewing and spinning, keeping the army equipped with linen and wool. As Secretary of State Royal Hinman put it in his evaluation of the war in 1842, Connecticut "women became familiar with the use of the plough, hoe, axe, and sickle." Because farming responsibilities had fallen on the overextended women in the households, only a "small supply of seed had been put into the ground."[37]

While Washington dealt with the politics of the war, Nathan and his regiment dug in on Long Island near Brooklyn and prepared for what many assumed was going to be an invasion by the British any day. Since his commission to captain of the Nineteenth Foot, and perhaps even as far back as the day he first set eyes on Washington in Cambridge, Nathan had hoped to prove his merit to the general. With this in mind, he devised a plan to secure a load of much needed provisions for his regiment. If Congress was going to pussyfoot around and his men were going to be deprived of the essentials they needed to survive, Nathan was smart enough to know that he needed to take on the role of provider and show his men that a competent, dedicated soldier dealt with the circumstances presented, as much as shouldering a weapon and mounting a charge.[38]

When Nathan had sailed into Long Island from Boston via the East River, he had made note of a British sloop near the mouth of the Atlantic that was carefully guarded by a man-of-war. The warship keeping watch over the sloop was the impressive *Asia*, a ship Nathan and his men were quite familiar with from their days stationed outside Boston. The *Asia*, considered one of the most dominant ships of the British navy, was the same vessel that had fired on Nathan's regiment near Lechmere's Point shortly before he left camp on furlough.[39]

As Nathan settled in Long Island, fed up that not much had changed since Winter Hill regarding his men's lack of necessities, he conceived a plan to capture the sloop loaded with provisions floating near the *Asia*. He didn't share his plan with his supervising officers, for fear they would try to stop him. Nathan chose a few good men from his unit and set out on an unofficial scavenger mission.[40]

A few hours before daybreak, Nathan and his crew carefully crossed the brush on their way through to a shallow portion of the East River near hostile territory. Coming upon the shores of the enemy, Nathan heard the man-of-war watchman, who was standing guard aboard the sloop monitoring the area. He was saying something to his men while looking left, center, and right.

Then, in a moment, "All's well," the guard yelled.[41]

Standing in the water patiently, awaiting his chance, Nathan told his men to stay back as he made his move for the boat. Moments later, sure the guards had gone belowdecks and fallen asleep, Nathan stepped quietly through the water, climbed up and over the bow of the sloop, "seized the tiller," and headed toward the American side of the river.

He left a few of his men behind to keep watch as he steered the boat ashore to "the cheers of the patriot camp."[42]

Nathan had proven to his men—and his superiors—that he could fend for himself and his men if he needed to. From that day on, Nathan was the hero of his unit, a rebel soldier undaunted by the prospect of stepping within the enemy's reach. Additionally, he'd had his first real taste of action, which only increased his desire to be more involved.[43]

The capture of that British sloop made Nathan a champion around camp, the recipient of pats on the back and cheers from his comrades. With the constant praise Nathan began to feel, after nearly a year of service, that he was finally worthy of wearing the uniform. He had set a goal and accomplished it without difficulty. In the letters he received from home and from friends in New London during this period, not one friend or family member failed to applaud his gallant efforts—which meant that most of the letters Nathan had sent, of which sadly only one exists, included the story of his midnight raid across British lines to secure that sloop full of provisions.[44]

In one letter Nathan wrote to a woman he referred to by the initials P.H., he said, "I can't convey to you the grateful emotions excited by the tender concern you express for me when in danger. . . . The risqué I had run was not trifling. My escape demanded the most heartfelt gratitude." It's likely that P.H. was none other than Mary Hubbard, wife of Captain David Nevins. Mary's nickname was Polly. She and her family were respected in Norwich and New London. She was extremely attractive. Those in New London viewed Mary as a model citizen. Captain Russell Hubbard, Mary's father, was one of the proprietors of the Union School, where Nathan had taught while in New London. To a then twenty-one-year-old Nathan, Mary was an older woman, somewhere near thirty.[45]

In that same letter, Nathan responded to P.H.'s question as to how often he had run into his old friend Benjamin Tallmadge, asking how he felt about seeing him. "I am always glad to hear from Mr. Tallmadge," Nathan wrote. "But more to see him, which, Thank God, I have now the happiness frequently to do." It was important to Nathan that while in New York he surround himself with men he knew, and he did whatever he could to make that happen. Nathan had routinely run into his good friends Stephen Hempstead, William Hull, Tallmadge, and several other fellows from Yale and his days in New London. He felt a sense of security and kinship when around these men, which was something he had not experienced while in Boston.[46]

Sometime after William Howe landed his troops on Staten Island, his brother, Admiral Lord Richard Howe, took to the same shores with one of the most powerful fleets behind him the British had yet sent into action. The strategy of the British was to amass all the troops they could on Staten Island and, at the right moment, sail to Long Island. As the British made battle plans, figuring out the best time to make their move, pressure was mounting on Washington to react or face certain annihilation. Congress and the general knew that defending Long Island and the City of New York was impossible, considering the diminishing band of starving, unhealthy men they had. Yet the country's political leaders felt Washington needed to at least attempt it. What other choice did the Americans have?

Despite the stress he was under, Washington rarely ever displayed his concern openly. In his general orders during this critical period, he kept the focus on discipline and composure in the face of what were going to be the most trying days the army had yet faced.[47] In late August 1776, he wrote, "It is an incumbent duty therefore, upon every officer of every rank, to be alert and attentive in the discharge of the several duties annexed to his office; his honor, his own personal safety, and for ought he knows, the salvation of his Country. . . ."

Long Island and Brooklyn became the focal points for Washington and Howe. The severe heat the soldiers had endured throughout July and August lingered into September. August had been a rough month for Washington and his troops. By the end of the month, "the British and Hessian army," an officer recorded in his diary, "landed on the island under cover of their shipping. . . . The very judicious attack by the British generals was carried into execution with irresistible ardor and impetuosity." The British now had a fleet of "more than 130 vessels . . . combined with more than 24,000 men," reported that same officer.[48]

Washington was dealing with more than his share of issues. Not only were the British closing in on his troops, but mounting internal problems that Congress had not addressed were now interfering with the basic functioning of the army. The rebels had been beaten badly at Brooklyn Heights in what one historian later claimed was the "first great battle of the Revolution," as a combined forty thousand soldiers came head-to-head. Washington later wrote to Congress saying he had lost approximately a thousand men to either death or imprisonment during the battle.

Furthermore, stories and sightings of British soldiers bayoneting Americans through the chest and staking them to trees scared new recruits arriving from all points north and south. What saved Washington from total defeat was the weather. As the fighting at Brooklyn began, so did torrential rains, which momentarily put a squeeze on combat operations. As it poured, thunder and lightning moved through the region. Men were running in columns, soldier Philip Fithian wrote, to the front lines. "All the time the rain falling with an uncommon torrent." So bad was the rain that no one could fire because "the guns of the whole army are wetted."

Additionally, it was reported that soldiers were being struck dead by lightning while in camp waiting for orders to attack, some knee-deep in bunkers filled with water. An "uncommon lightning," one soldier reported, "one hard clap after the other; heavy rains mixed at times with a storm like a hurricane. . . . Upon the whole it was an awful scene." Three officers, he added, were struck dead in front of him as if dropped in their tracks by musket balls.[49]

In his army diary dated Wednesday, August 21, 1776, Nathan wrote of this extraordinary storm: "Heavy Storm at Night Much & heavy Thunder— Capt. Wyke & a Lieutenant & Ensign. of Col. Dougall's Regt. Killed by a Shock Likewise one man in town, belonging to a Militia Regt. of Connecticut."

The storm rolled through town for "two to three hours," Nathan observed. The flashes of lightning he witnessed were "perpetual . . . the sharpest I ever knew."[50]

As Washington sat in his tent at headquarters days after this intense storm, by candlelight he wrote about the dire situation he believed he faced if Congress didn't step in and send the troops and supplies he had been asking for: "The Enemy are forming a large and extensive Encampment . . . and are busily employed in transporting their cannon and Stores from Long Island. As they advance them this way, we may reasonably expect their operations will not long be deferred."

The general expected a worse bombardment than any the Americans had yet seen. Despite an erosion of morale among his troops, Washington had great will and composure. He would not give up or display any ill feelings, impatience, or discouragement in front of his men. If anything, he exhibited the polar opposite. He was seen day and night, trotting along the front lines on horseback, encouraging soldiers with words of praise, sometimes as the rains pounded his skin. He wanted Congress to believe in him the way his men did. Near this time, he stated, "Every disposition is making on our part for defence, and Congress may be assured that I shall do every thing in my power to maintain the post so long as it shall appear practicable and Conducive to the General good."[51]

Meanwhile, as the summer wound down, even though he was not writing to his family then, Nathan documented what he and his regiment were facing as word reached them that British troops had basically taken over Brooklyn Heights and burrowed into shallow ground near the East River. There the English were gathered together on the banks of the East River like a gang of protesters ready to break through a gate. "The Enemy landed some troops down at the Narrows on Long Island," Nathan wrote in his army journal. The Narrows was an area near Jamaica (present-day Queens) where a ridge of hills five to six miles long met a thick stretch of woods on a small rising. In the immediate vicinity were three roads, or passes, as General Samuel Parsons referred to them in a letter to John Adams: Flatbush and Bedford roads, and a cross section of the two cut on the southern side of a ridge.[52]

As Nathan noted the mass of enemy troops bottlenecked near Brooklyn, he praised a group of rebel soldiers suppressing the charge: "Enemy landed more troops—news that they had marched up and taken Station near Flatbush their advance guards being on this side near the woods—that some of our Riflemen attacked & drove them back."[53]

Any minor victory against Howe's men was short-lived, however, after a major crisis erupted for Washington. The army numbers were dropping, he wrote, "according to the tenor of their enlistments." As the British pushed from all sides and continued to sail warships in both rivers, seemingly closing in on the rebels and beginning a complete takeover of Long Island, American soldiers, scared and starving, who were serving short tours of duty began heading back home. Reenlistments were lower than commanding officers had expected. Money was running out. Food was scarce. Camp after camp was affected by disease. An uncertain army, with waning confidence, was in great need of continual restraint and reassurance.

"It is a melancholy and painful consideration," the general continued, "to those who are concerned in the work, and have the command, to be forming armies constantly, and to be left by troops just when they begin to deserve the name, or perhaps at a moment when an important blow is expected."[54]

When the rainstorms of August and the mild temperatures of early September passed, cold settled on New York with snow and sleet surely not far behind. This change in the seasons presented a more ominous set of circumstances for Washington; many soldiers needed winter supplies, and he had observed that in many camps "not a pan or a kettle" could be found. "Our situation is now bad."[55]

Governor Trumbull promised Washington that scores of Connecticut and Massachusetts militiamen, along with trained soldiers, were on the way. Although the assurance of coming manpower was comforting, Washington would have the problem of thousands of extra men to feed and shelter. "They, I am informed, have not a single Tent nor a necessary of any kind, nor can I conceive how it will be possible to support them."[56]

Meanwhile the British had built a solid, closely controlled military force, men who were well fed, well trained, and subordinate. However, when it came to strategy, especially early in the war, despite General Howe's assault at Brooklyn Heights, it appeared as if his commanders lacked the basic skills to plan an assault that could defeat the rebels. Howe would back the Americans into a corner and, for some reason, fail to drop the hammer. Whenever the rebels were on the verge of falling before Howe's more powerful army, they somehow escaped without being totally routed.

Despite their good fortune so far, Washington's chain of command was beginning to break down, and Congress hadn't been providing artillery, rations, and provisions such as tents and eating utensils. Washington would have to make the best out of what he had.

Nathan picked up on Washington's sense of honor, nobility, and duty, even though his observations were based on secondhand information. He lived by Washington's words, accepted those words with the utmost credulity. Unlike some soldiers, Nathan wasn't fighting for money or fame, or even to protect the rights he felt so deeply about; he was first standing on the front lines because he believed, beyond anything else, that it was what God wanted and expected from him and his countrymen.

He was not alone in his adoration of his commander. Just the sight of Washington could melt even the most solid of men. When surgeon James Thatcher witnessed Washington enter camp for the first time, distinguishing the general from his counterparts was as easy as spotting a redcoat in the brush. "His Excellency was on horseback," Thatcher described admiringly, "in company with several military gentlemen. . . . His personal appearance is truly noble and majestic, being tall and well proportioned. His dress is a blue coat, with buff colored facings, a rich epaulette on each shoulder, buff under dress, and an elegant small sword; a black cockade in his hat."[57]

Before the British had even landed on Long Island, Washington stood before his troops and addressed them, passionately describing what he expected from them and, even more, what they could anticipate out in the field:

> Be ready for action at a moment's call, and when called into it, remember that liberty, property, life and honour, are all at stake; that upon your courage and conduct rest the hopes of your bleeding and insulted country; that your wives, children and parents, expect safety from you only; and that we have every reason to believe that Heaven will crown with success so just a cause.[58]

With a strong sense of duty, Nathan understood that when his country called, he was supposed to answer without question, regardless of the task in front of him. Washington's words inspired Nathan, feeding his patriotic spirit. Though he did not yet have much hands-on battlefield experience, he still understood what was expected of him once he reached New York.

The rebel army Nathan had described to Enoch that summer was a functioning, albeit unstable, machine, its soldiers full of patriotic zeal and thirst for victory. They needed constant grooming and attention. In one letter, Nathan went into detail regarding what he believed was a growing effort, just now beginning to show promise and collective resolve. He was "not in Long Island" any longer, however, as Enoch had guessed in a letter he had written to Nathan earlier. Instead, Nathan said he was stationed "in New York, encamped about 1 mile back of the City." His regiment had, in fact, just been forced out of Long Island. "We have been in the Island and spent about three weeks there but since returned." By this point, a majority of Washington's army was stationed in the City, with more men on their way south from Connecticut and New York State. Upper New England was still controlled by the militia and the colonies. Howe and his military, however, had taken Long Island and were beginning to set their sights on New York City and, via Long Island Sound, coastal Connecticut and upper New England.[59]

Nathan explained where he had traveled over the past eight months, after he had left Coventry in January. "As to Brigades," he said, "at the beginning of the Campaign we were at Winter Hill . . . from thence we were removed to Roxbury . . . and then we marched from that place here . . . and on our arrival we were put in Gen Lord Sterling's; here we continued a few days and we returned to Gen Sullivan's, on his being ordered to the northward we reverted back to Lord Sterling, in whose Brigade we still remain."[60]

It might have seemed unclear to Enoch why Nathan mentioned Sullivan and Stirling; but both men, especially Stirling, had made a significant impression on the young captain.

Lord Stirling, as he was known by his men, was born William Alexander. According to a painting by Bass Otis, Stirling had an oval face, quite pudgy, with soft brown eyes above an elongated nose. A close ally of Washington's, he was born in New York City, but spent the better part of his life in New Jersey. His knowledge of New York's topography added considerably to Washington's tactical plans.

The story going around was that Stirling was the "rightful heir to the title and estate of" a well-to-do family in Scotland, where his father was born. Even though he could never prove the designation, his peers had referred to him as *lord*. Later, he would achieve distinction as a mathematician and astronomer.

Nathan, while serving under Stirling for a short time, realized the general was quite different from many of the other commanding officers he had met and served. Stirling displayed a "brave, discerning and intrepid" discipline, said Nathan, attributes the patriotic captain had hoped for in himself.[61]

The same could be said for Major General John Sullivan, a true minute-man, raised in Massachusetts after sailing to America with his family from Ireland. On June 4, 1776, Sullivan, a stocky man with dark hair and a profile similar to that of his commanding general, took over the army in Canada from Benedict Arnold, before being forced to retreat, ultimately heading south into Long Island, where Nathan's regiment joined him.

In retrospect, Nathan and his unit could be considered lucky, because not long after they crossed the East River into New York from Brooklyn, Lord Stirling and General Sullivan "were obliged to surrender as prisoners," while Nathan and his men escaped into the city unharmed. In a full-scale battle brought on by the British as they began their takeover of Long Island, Stirling and Sullivan surrendered to Howe's overpowering men—there was no way out.[62]

Nathan pointed out for Enoch that the regiment Nathan commanded, although intermittently at risk of collapse, was faring quite well. "It gives pleasure to every friend of his country to observe the health which prevails in our army, Doct Eli"—the surgeon enlisted in Nathan's unit—"told me a few days since, there was not a man in our Reg but might upon occasion go out with his Firelock."[63]

While Nathan and his men may have been spared, scurvy, yellow fever, and famine were spreading among rebel camps. The militia was a diversified group of ragged men and children (ranging in age from ten to fifteen years old), a majority of whom were untrained in hand-to-hand combat or bat-tlefield tactical maneuvers of any sort. Unlike Howe's orderly, subservient British troops, who had fought in several wars and dressed in sharp-colored red uniforms with sparkling gold buttons and carefully tailored and defined hemlines, firing only the latest weaponry, most of the Continental Army dressed in civilian clothes and shot long hunting rifles and squirrel guns. With troops coming into New York from the south, west, and north, the army had turned into a diverse group of American men and children, some dressed in the finest uniforms, while others donned slipshod rags, as if they were heading out for a day of hunting.[64]

Despite what Nathan saw as an army lacking raw physical strength, bat-tlefield experience, discipline, and even fine, matching garb, he believed he could help Washington turn them around. He imposed strict standards on his men. "Hale's promptness, activity, and assiduous attention to discipline, were early observed," wrote the historian Jared Sparks. "He prevailed upon his men to adopt a simple uniform, which improved their appearance, attracted notice, and procured applause."[65]

Enoch and Nathan's sister Elizabeth Rose had sent Nathan a letter that past June, excitedly explaining that she was going to make him a suit. She knew the summer months, heading into fall, were going to be brutal for Nathan, marching with all that equipment. The lighter his load, the longer the distance he could walk. Elizabeth Rose had asked Nathan if he wanted the garments shipped right away, so he could have them in time for the summer. But she had not heard from him.[66]

"Sister Rose talked of making me some Linen clothe similar to brown Holland for summer ware," Nathan explained to Enoch. "If she has made it, desire her to keep it for me." Nathan hoped to return home at some point.[67]

Chapter 13

A Necessary Purpose

A T THIRTY-SIX, THOMAS KNOWLTON was a colonel with the reputation of a general. He stood as tall as Washington, yet was in far better shape than the general, muscular and trim, sporting the square jawline of a superhero and the boyish good looks of a prince. Knowlton was rarely seen without his polished sword hanging from his hip. He had consistently proved his dedication to the cause and knew how to strategize and conduct successful clandestine surveillance operations. Born in Boxford, Massachusetts, to English parents whose ancestors were among the first settlers of Boston, Knowlton had enlisted as a soldier at age fifteen for service in the French and Indian War. He was known as a practical commander, a soldier who wasn't afraid to get his hands bloody and fight with his men on the front lines. This attitude drew Washington to him. In one skirmish near Bunker Hill during the 1775 campaign, Knowlton took a post with two fellow officers and wound up in a shoot-out with a redcoat brigade much larger than the unit he and his colleagues had put on the field. As the firefight raged, rebels were picked off and killed. When they had a chance to survey the battlefield after a break in the shooting, one of the men by

Knowlton's side later reported "the dead covering the ground" around them were "as thick as sheep in a foal." Despite losing twice the amount of men as his colleagues, however, with both officers by his side abandoning their posts, Knowlton stood his ground and continued to fight. As a British column stormed in for one final blow after reloading, Knowlton and his limited unit killed double the number of redcoats as the entire brigade before him and forced the remaining British to retreat. Known for such daring achievements—one of many Knowlton would be involved in—he rose up the chain of command quickly and, upon reaching New York a month later, was promoted to lieutenant colonel, then commissioned to form Knowlton's Rangers, the army's first organized elite unit, similar to the Green Berets.[1] Knowlton took orders directly from Washington and sent his men out on reconnaissance missions to scout where the British were stationing troops. Like Special Forces, or any other unique military unit of today, Knowlton's Rangers were generally the first unit into an assault and the last out.[2]

Nathan was a twenty-one-year-old captain in charge of over seventy men. What he couldn't tell Enoch as he wrote to him during the summer of 1776—and had shared with a select number of his own men only—was that Knowlton had chosen Nathan as one of his discreet intelligence-gathering rangers and that he was about to be asked to partake in an undercover spying mission the likes of which had not yet been attempted, as far as anyone knew, by either side. On paper Nathan's résumé dovetailed with the requirements of the spy job perfectly. A somewhat taciturn, albeit zealously dedicated soldier, Nathan was on a mission to prove to Washington what he could do for the war effort. Beyond a few skirmishes outside Roxbury, where he was first stationed, and the retreat from Brooklyn Heights, the committed captain had seen little action. Still, Knowlton was now in the market for a devoted soldier who could slip behind Howe's line, retrieve the information Washington needed, head back into camp, and help save the Americans from total defeat in New York. The mission would prove the soldier's devotion to the cause and to Washington. One of the problems—and several would be discussed inside the next few weeks—was that the man Knowlton was soon to choose had been "prostrated with illness" and was quite ill, probably too sick to undertake the assignment.[3]

George Dudley Seymour later suggested that the *Asia* episode Nathan spearheaded on Long Island had perhaps underscored his value enough to make him the perfect candidate for inclusion in Knowlton's Rangers and for Washington's spy mission. But Knowlton had likely chosen Nathan as a ranger because he knew him personally and had already selected two of Nathan's brothers for the special forces unit. In total, Knowlton picked 150 of the best men he could find in the American military. Nathan's knowledge of science and engineering, and his study of war strategy by means of the classics, would prove invaluable, and Knowlton knew it.[4]

After having relinquished their post at Brooklyn Heights with a measured amount of success, a majority of Washington's Long Island troops—some reports claim they were five thousand strong—settled at the tip of New York near present-day Wall Street. New York was then an open land of rolling hills, grass- and wetlands, trees and beaches, with numbered dirt roads running north to south from the Battery. Old Post Road, called the Grand Highway, snaked northward toward McGowan's Pass on the east side, and Bloomingdale Road on the west near Twentieth Street headed toward Bloomingdale Heights at about today's 115th Street. Spread about the island were acres upon acres of apple orchards. At the very tip of New York, just opposite Brooklyn, the city thrived: Broad Way and Broad Street were both part of the South Ward; and Dock Street and Hanover Square were inside the East Ward. Combined, the wards made up one square mile of actual downtown space. Buildings and homes, churches and public houses, filled blocks from about Twentieth Street south toward the tip. Near Duane Street to the north was the City Hospital. At the base of the city, where Broad Way started, stood Fort George, a "square bastioned affair" made of stone walls eighty feet long, thick enough to withstand multiple cannon shot. Inside this massive structure were barracks, magazines, and the mansion of the colonial governor.[5]

According to a census taken four years before the start of the war, the city and county of New York housed some 21,863 residents. The population had swelled to at least 25,000 by 1776, possibly even more. Now, though, with a majority of Washington's men having made the city their new post, about 30,000 people were there. With British swarming around them, the rebels were in a dangerously defenseless position. A good portion of Howe's army, which now included thousands of German Hessian troops, was positioned five miles across the harbor on Staten Island, as British warships armed with loaded cannons departed the island and headed up the East and North rivers, feeding Long Island on the east side with soldiers. If they wanted to, the British could land near Kip's Bay on the east side (Iclenberg on the west), form a column across the city at, say, present-day Fortieth Street, and the continentals, trapped at the city's tip, would be forced to swim the Atlantic or surrender.[6]

From his headquarters near what is today Varick Street, Washington kept Congress informed of the situation the Americans now faced. On September 8, he wrote a letter to the president of Congress, alerting him that he had called a council of officers "in order to take a full and comprehensive view of our situation." In one of the longest letters Washington had ever sent to Philadelphia, he admitted he was not certain what Howe was planning—any number of tactical scenarios could take place. "This [makes] it necessary to be prepared for each." Washington said his best defense at the moment was to try to outmaneuver the British and make them wonder what he was going to do next. It was "now extremely obvious from all intelligence from their movements, and every other circumstance, that, having landed their whole army on Long Island, except about four thousand on Staten Island," Howe was going to use Long Island as a staging area to take the City of New York and either pummel the Americans or send them packing. No matter what the British did at this point, one thing was apparent: Howe was planning a major assault.

As Washington wrote, redcoats were piling off ships, schooners, and men-of-war, splashing onto the shores of Long Island between the Narrows and Sandy Hook, near Brooklyn Heights, Newtown Creek, and Blackwell's Island. Washington wanted to "demonstrate that on our side the war should be defensive . . . that we should on all occasions avoid a general action, nor put anything to risk." He knew that at any time his troops could fall back to Harlem Heights [now Morningside Heights] after fighting their way through the city. Once in Harlem, however, a choice would have to be made: retreat entirely into the Bronx, surrender, or fight forward. The key to any decision was to find out what Howe was planning and, more important, where Howe's first large-scale attack was going to occur.[7]

To find out, Washington had summoned Knowlton. If the Americans had any chance of standing against the king's increasing number of troops, the commander in chief would need intelligence, a type of risky intelligence the Americans had yet to engage in. The city was brimming with civilians who supported the Revolution, while most of the Tories were still on Long Island.[8] Sending a spy—that is, a continental soldier dressed in civilian clothes—over to the enemy's side on a surreptitious spying expedition was dangerous. Up until this point, Washington had relied, for the most part, on what were called couriers, men who trafficked in information-swapping. A courier had traveled to Staten Island in late August to retrieve news of British movements from a citizen there, and the information had proven fairly accurate. At best, though, this type of intelligence was dependent on timing: If the courier couldn't make it back to rebel lines quickly enough, the information was useless. Washington wanted "regular Intelligence of the Enemy's movements." Maybe, he suggested, one of his officers could locate a few Tories who could be bought. "Perhaps," he wrote to two of his officers, "some might be got who are really Tories for a reasonable reward to undertake it. Those who are friends are preferable, if they could manage it as well."[9]

Quite frustrated that he couldn't obtain the intelligence he needed, Washington organized scouting parties and reconnaissance drives, which were highly unproductive. Sitting on hilltops with telescopes, scouts could warn of an oncoming invasion or how the British were setting up, but what good was a last-minute declaration that a line of redcoats had crested a hill and were about to surprise an American brigade?[10]

So Washington turned to Knowlton and asked him to find a spy, someone from his unit of rangers he could trust to slip behind enemy lines and find out what Howe was planning and, even better, when. Knowlton's first choice wasn't Nathan, but a dapper, well-disciplined soldier named James Sprague, an old French and Indian War vet Knowlton had known for years. Sprague, a cousin of Nathan's from his mother's side, was likely the first choice simply because Knowlton knew of Sprague's reliability from the earlier conflict they had fought in together. Knowlton trusted Sprague. Yet Sprague was quick to refuse his old friend, giving the popular opinion among rebel soldiers: Spying was the work of a scoundrel, a charlatan, or a fool. Asher Wright, who knew Sprague somewhat, since he was a distant relative, claimed Sprague was taken aback by the request, emphatically telling Knowlton, "I am willing to go and fight them, but as for going among them and being taken and hung up like a dog, I will not do it." Death wasn't just a possibility; it was a certainty if one was caught in civilian clothes behind enemy lines.[11]

Meanwhile, Nathan was part of a group of Knowlton's Rangers now stationed near the tip of New York. His struggle with influenza had knocked him down considerably once again; he was weaker now than he had been in quite some time. Since joining Knowlton's Rangers, following the rules of an intelligence agency, he'd stopped keeping his journal. In one of his last entries, Nathan wrote, "From their post" the British were burning hay, and several rangers intercepted them near Flatbush, Long Island, and "kill'd some of them." When news spread that the Americans had attacked a British regiment, more rebels showed up and "routed and drove them back [one and a half] miles."

Nathan had been seen around camp after that "rout" and the subsequent abandonment by the Americans of Brooklyn Heights, but for long stretches he had withdrawn into his tent to recover with only Asher Wright by his side. With so many men around him dying of yellow fever, starvation, and other ailments, this must have been a trying time for Nathan. He had been waiting for combat, yet here he was unable to contribute. Through his illness, coupled with the devastation he had seen since his days at Winter Hill, Nathan had developed a queer sense of wisdom one can acquire only through suffering. Nathan realized he was powerless as one man with a gun in his hand, but could be quite effective undercover. He had a lot of time to sit and think, read the Scriptures, analyze the battlefield, and recognize his new place in it—all of which undoubtedly contributed to the decision he was about to make.[12]

As the second week of September dawned, Nathan was still nursing his bout with influenza. While he recuperated in his tent, several new developments were brought before Washington, which Nathan was made fully aware of, even while holed up in his tent, because he was one of Knowlton's

Rangers. One of Washington's close confidants, Nathanael Greene, a general from Rhode Island who had led the Brooklyn Heights engagement, recommended burning New York City, after a peace conference between Howe and several American delegates proved futile. "I would burn the City and Subburbs," Greene advised. According to a letter Greene wrote to Washington, he believed "two thirds of the Property of the City of New York and the Subburbs belongs to the Tories." If this was true, and a majority of the city's residents were entrenched in a one-mile radius downtown, would torching it create chaos and throw off Howe's plans, whatever they might be? Still, what would destroying New York actually accomplish? Greene thought, "It will deprive the Enemy of an opportunity of Barracking their whole Army together."[13]

Some historians believe Washington was in total accord with Greene, but his superiors in Philadelphia wanted nothing to do with such destruction. And who could blame them? The Americans had already lost "eleven to twelve hundred" men, Nathan's friend William Hull reported later, during the retreat from Long Island, "more than a thousand of whom were captured." A decision was then made to spread the American forces, however sparse, throughout the city northward toward Harlem Heights. But it needed to be done promptly, before Howe's army made its next move.[14]

In the interim, Knowlton convened a secret meeting among those rangers he could gather on short notice. Word among the rangers—which James Sprague must have spread—was that Knowlton needed a spy, a man brave and smart enough to strip off his uniform, don civilian clothes, cross over to Long Island, and blend into society with the purpose of finding out what Howe was planning. Washington wanted maps, detailed plans, dates, troop numbers, and conditions. Washington's forces in New York were worse off than anyone could have imagined. Because so many rebel soldiers were stationed near taverns downtown, drunkenness had become a common way to deal with the poor odds facing the Americans. With shorelines exposed on both rivers, the fleet of warships seemed to go on forever. The sight was enough to send many soldiers—even entire units—running from the battlefield.

British "numbers" would become the subject of much speculation in the years to come. How many redcoats and Hessians were there, anyway? David Hale, Nathan's brother, wrote in his memoir that "the Commander-in-chief wished to ascertain 'the numerical strength . . . of the enemy,'" and this was one of Washington's main reasons for sending a spy to Long Island. But there was no question the colonists were outnumbered. What Washington needed to know was what Howe was going to do next and where was he going to do it.[15]

At no other time since the beginning of the war had the Americans been more exposed, vulnerable, and packed so tightly together in one region. For Washington, intelligence seemed the only hope for escaping New York without having to surrender, which he certainly wasn't prepared to do. Connecticut delegate from Congress Silas Deane had crossed the Atlantic on a secret ambassadorial mission and successfully secured arms and assistance from the French, but as Washington and his commanders knew, shipments were still a long time away.[16]

The British now had total control of Long Island, and Howe was moving a large number of his troops onto the island via Brooklyn Heights. Washington needed to know the details of Howe's plan, as well as how many men he had and where they were setting camp. James Sprague had already refused Knowlton. Thus, it was time for Knowlton to call a meeting of the rangers and find someone to take on the job.

At an undisclosed location, probably at a temporary fortification somewhere near present-day Fiftieth Street, Knowlton "assembled several of his officers" and spoke on Washington's behalf, relaying his urgent demands. This was the first time the rangers had heard about the spy mission directly from Knowlton.

Nathan had been told about the meeting, but was unable to attend, probably because he was once again battling fatigue from the flu. Asher Wright later reported that he and Nathan, at this point, "took tents at Grand Battery," about one mile back from the point of the city.

When the meeting began, Knowlton didn't choose any one particular ranger and ask him directly (he knew better). Instead, he opened in general terms, hoping, of course, someone would step forward and volunteer.

While Knowlton was still relaying Washington's appeal, Nathan stumbled into the blockhouse and asked what was going on. By every account, the ailing captain appeared pale, sweating, sickly, and barely able to stand on his own feet.[17]

After listening to Knowlton, "almost immediately" Nathan stepped forward with a confident gaze and, as the room went silent, looked toward him.

"I will undertake it, sir," he said.[18]

Whispers were followed by astonished looks. A well-respected officer was determined to take on what appeared to be a suicide mission. Besides that, what dignified soldier with any integrity and honor would assume the role of a spy? Only a rogue would volunteer for such a job.[19]

After a few moments, several other rangers voiced their objections and told Nathan the mission was a sure death sentence. "They at once closed around [him]," historian Henry Howe wrote of the meeting, "and remonstrated by every appeal with consideration and friendship could dictate, to abandon his purpose—the love of home, the ties of kindred, future fame, and a felon's death, were all in vain urged to dissuade him."[20]

When his fellow officers gave up trying to talk him out of it, Nathan stood back and collected himself. He took their concern seriously and surely appreciated it. But his sense of duty overrode the fear of the others. He was resolute—and no one was going to change his mind.

"I think I owe to my country," Nathan said to his colleagues, "the accomplishment of an object so important, and so much desired by the commander of her armies—and I know of no other mode of obtaining the information, than by assuming a disguise and passing into the enemy's camp."

Nathan explained part of his reasoning: "I am fully sensible of the consequences of discovery and capture in such a situation, but for a year I have been attached to the army and have not rendered any material services while receiving compensation for which I make no return."[21]

With that, he turned and walked out of the meeting.

William Hull was at his quarters not far from the meeting when Nathan pushed the door open and entered. Hull would later write extensively about his friend and detail their conference. He looked up to Nathan in many ways, viewing him as a true patriot unlike any other he had met while serving. "There was no young man who gave fairer promise of an enlightened and devoted service to his country, than this my friend and companion in arms." Both had marched from New London to Winter Hill and traveled to New York with the same brigade. Hull got to know Nathan intimately during this time, and understood him better than perhaps anyone else. "His heart was filled with generous emotions," Hull said, describing how well Nathan understood himself and how honest he was. Yet when Nathan appeared before him that afternoon and explained what he had agreed to do, Hull wasn't about to sit idle and allow his friend to sacrifice his life. "Like the soaring eagle, the patriotic ardour of his soul," Hull wrote, "winged the dart which caused his destruction."[22]

"I owe to my country the accomplishment of an object so important," Nathan told Hull as they sat and talked, "and so much desired . . . and no other mode . . . than by assuming a disguise." Nathan then asked for Hull's opinion of the mission.[23]

Hull was an idealistic young man, generally quiet and reserved. He could sense that his friend had already made up his mind. Still, he decided to at least try to talk him out of it. "I replied," Hull wrote, "that it was an action which involved serious consequences, and the propriety of it was doubtful." Hull believed that "although he viewed the business of a spy as a duty, he could not be required to perform it." No one could make Nathan take on the job, in other words. This was his decision and his alone. Furthermore, Hull explained, spying was "not in his character: his nature was too frank and open to deceit and disguise, and he was incapable of acting a part equally foreign to his feelings and habits."[24]

Hull knew the soldier's place in the war. He later wrote of something he had said to Nathan near this time: "But who respects the character of a spy, assuming the garb of friendship but to betray? As soldiers, let us do our duty in the field; contend for our legitimate rights, and not strain the honour by the sacrifice of integrity. And when present events, with all their deep and exciting interests, shall have passed away, may the blush of shame never arise, by the remembrance of an unworthy, though successful act, in the performance of which we were deceived by the belief that it was sanctified by its object."[25]

According to Hull, Nathan posed an important question at one point during their conversation: But what if he was successful?[26]

"Who would wish success at that price?" Hull replied. "Does your Country demand the moral degradation of her sons, to advance her interests?" To Hull, war strategy was something both the British and the Americans respected and understood. "There are feints and evasions," he said, "performed under no disguise." This was "lawful and advantageous, and the tact with which they are executed, exacts admiration from the enemy."[27]

After a continued argument by Hull, in which he warned Nathan that few "respect the character of a spy," the future general cautioned, "Should you undertake the enterprise, your short, bright career, would close with an ignominious death."[28]

Hull wasn't about to give in and, patting his colleague on the back, tell him the decision to spy was dignified and noble. He had to be honest.

When Hull finished, Nathan stood and explained why it was so important to carry out the assignment. He said he knew the consequences should he be caught. "I am not influenced by the expectation of promotion or pecuniary reward," he said. "I wish to be useful, and every kind of service, necessary to the public good, becomes honourable by being necessary. If the exigencies of my country demand a peculiar service, its claims to perform that service are imperious."[29]

"That such are your wishes," Hull replied, "cannot be doubted. But is this the most effectual mode of carrying them into execution? In the progress of the war, there will be ample opportunity to give your talents and your life, should it so be ordered, to the sacred cause to which we are pledged. You can bestow upon your country the richest benefits, and win for yourself the highest honours. Your exertions for her interests will be daily felt, while, by one fatal act, you crush for ever the power and the opportunity Heaven offers, for her glory and your happiness."[30]

Hull urged Nathan to "abandon the enterprise" immediately, "for the love of country, for the love of kindred." The "only end in the sacrifice will be of the dearest interests of both."[31]

Nathan paused at this thought. But then, grabbing Hull by the hand, he said, "I will reflect, and do nothing but what duty demands."[32]

Chapter 14

BRAVE RESISTANCE

Provisions and arms were still as scarce as confidence among soldiers, and Washington began to feel the patriotic enthusiasm surrounding the signing of the Declaration of Independence just a few months back deflating. The general knew the road ahead led to death and destruction, with much blood left to be spilled. His apprehension regarding an early celebration was never more evident than in his admonition days after the Declaration: "knowing that now the peace and safety of his Country depends (under God) solely on the success of our arms."

Early September saw a series of inconsequential, minor victories and hard defeats, while Washington amassed one-third of his army inside the city. But after a council of war, a determination to "abandon the city" was unanimously passed. The British now had approximately thirty-two thousand soldiers ready to take hold of New York and, in turn, control the Revolution. At best, according to most estimates, Washington had sixteen thousand. Near the end of the first week of September Washington drew back from the city and stationed his troops three miles north of Harlem, making his headquarters at the Roger Morris House, just south of Fort

Washington. As the general saw it, Harlem Heights was the most tactically vital location he could manage. If the British took the city, General Howe would undoubtedly cut off communication with New England, disabling the rebellion at its throat. If Washington lost contact with Philadelphia, the unofficial capital of the colonies, the Americans were finished. "The Heights we are now upon," the general wrote, "may be defended against double the force we have to contend with, and the whole Continent expects it of us."[1]

The British knew the importance of capturing New York. Some said Quebec was part of the king's New York plan. By taking both cities, the British could control all of New England by simply patrolling the St. Lawrence and North rivers with their impressive and intimidating fleet of warships, using the waterways as conduits to feed the rest of their army and prevent any merger between American southern and northern forces.[2]

While at Harlem Heights, Washington's troops were confused. One of the most pressing issues the general faced was what he referred to as the "great Waste of Ammunition," soldiers firing when they shouldn't and/or leaving powder out to be lost to the elements. His main concern was that "unless the officers will exert themselves to see justice done . . . a sufficiency [of ammunition] cannot be kept upon hand to supply them."

Beyond fatigue, starvation, scurvy, and smallpox, Washington was contending with large numbers of American soldiers—being pushed out of the city by British forces stationed on Staten Island and Long Island—throwing down arms and deserting. The general, of course, had little use for absconders. Washington saw only one type of punishment for deserters. When a Connecticut private, Ebenezer Liffingwell, reportedly ran from the battlefield in cowardice and, after being told to stop, pointed his musket at a commanding officer and misfired, the general promptly ordered Liffingwell's execution. After all, Liffingwell had made a mockery of the American effort, acting treasonously. As Liffingwell dropped his musket after trying to fire on Colonel Joseph Reed, the frustrated commander shouldered a gun and fired. But his firelock jammed. So Reed reportedly brandished his sword and slashed Liffingwell in the head, opening a large gash, before slicing off half of Liffingwell's thumb.[3]

"Ebenezer Liffingwell, being convicted of offering Violence to his superior officer—of Cowardice and Misbehavior before the Enemy, was ordered to suffer Death this day," Washington wrote.

After a court-martial, which included an argument on Liffingwell's behalf that he had not been running away after all, but going back to base camp for more ammunition, Washington, who had approved a sentence for Liffingwell to be put before a firing squad at the "head of the Army" and shot, no doubt feeling pressure from his soldiers, changed his mind.

"The General, from his formal good Character and upon the intersession of the Adjutant General, against whom he presented his firelock, is pleased to pardon him, but declares that the next offender shall suffer Death without mercy."[4]

Facing the British now on all sides, with British schooners and men-of-war cruising the East and North rivers and surrounding New York, the Americans were even more desperate for intelligence regarding the enemy's next major movement. It was imperative that Nathan get behind enemy lines as soon as possible. It was clear the British would stage an attack, but when and where would it arrive? Washington needed to know, so his army could escape New York without being totally destroyed. Although spying was viewed as a disgraceful digression from the common laws of war, Nathan wasn't going to be deterred.

Soldiers on both sides considered spies the scourge of the battlefield, viewing them as treasonous scum. Regardless of how his men felt about spying, Washington urgently needed the information a spy could bring back to camp and understood the benefits of this new type of intelligence. Up until then, spying consisted mostly of reconnaissance: men on hilltops with telescopes watching the movements of the enemy. Both sides participated—however, no soldier had actually (or, rather, officially) gone *behind* enemy lines under disguise with the objective of gaining an understanding of the enemy's plans and strength in order to use that information against them.

In sections of his last two letters Nathan wrote to his brother Enoch, he informed him of the dreadful conditions he believed the army was in at the time—a mood that hovered over the Continental Army as they had marched through Long Island and had been forced into the city and were now being pushed north.

Still, as the war carried on throughout the summer and into early fall, Nathan had always held out hope that things would get better for the colonial army. This was the nature of his character: Regardless of the discontent around him, the sight of men dropping out of the army every day and the meager supplies the Americans survived on, Nathan rarely focused on the negative, always looking at the good that could come out of any bad situation. "Maj. Brooks informed me last evening," Nathan wrote that summer, "that in conversation with some of the frequenters at Head Quarters he was told that General Washington had received a packet from one of the sheriffs of the city of London, in which was contained the debates at large of both houses of Parliament—and what is more, the whole proceedings of the Cabinet."[5]

One would have to ask, did Washington, by leading his troops north, know of Howe's master plan? Was this the reason he seemed so confident in the decision? Rumor circulating through camp, Nathan went on to note, was that Howe's "campaign" was "communicated in full" in the body of those letters.[6]

From his letter, Nathan clearly admired and was absolutely dedicated to the commander in chief and was prepared to do whatever was asked of him to serve Washington and the troops. Upon word that Washington had obtained such vital, primary intelligence, Nathan was thrilled; he saw how important a resource intelligence, on *any* level, could be to gaining the upper hand on the British. Regarding the information Washington had supposedly received, Nathan wrote, "Nothing has yet transpired; but the prudence of our General we trust will make advantage of the Intelligence." Further along, he told Enoch that General Horatio Gates had "gone to Philadelphia, probably to communicate the above," meaning that Gates was taking the intelligence to Congress. It appeared that one of Benedict Arnold's men in Quebec, George Merchant, had been captured by the British during the spring of 1776 and sent to a prison camp in England. With enemy "letters concealed in the waistband of his breeches," Merchant not only escaped from his British captors, but was able to sail back to America with the letters and deliver them to Washington.[7]

Washington did send Gates to Congress, along with the letters, which

Nathan accurately reported to Enoch. The letters contained "sundry matters of intelligence of the most interesting nature," Washington later wrote. "As the consideration of them may lead to important consequences, and the adoption of several measures in the military line."[8]

Two worlds were colliding for Nathan, one that put him behind the scenes and involved him in deeply secure matters, and another that placed him on the front lines with men who had no idea how much planning and strategy went into fighting a war. As he understood the importance of intelligence gathering, part of Nathan sensed the rebels were being bested on every level. "Some late accounts from the northward," he wrote in that same letter, "are very unfavorable, and would be more so could they be depended on. It is reported that a Fleet has arrived in the [East] River; upon first notice of which our army thought it prudent to break up the siege and retire—"[9]

As they retreated, the soldiers were "attacked," Nathan continued, "and routed." He wasn't sure how many had been killed, or how many casualties there had been, but he was certain the British had pillaged most of the rebels' cannons and "stores," taking from them perhaps the most important resource they had left: artillery. On the other hand, he had also heard that it could be just rumor, adding, "The account is not authentic: We hope it is not true."[10]

Leading up to the day he left camp, Nathan was certain that Washington's army faced a "critical Period." He saw how a disciplined army, ready to give their lives for the cause, was different from a group of untrained warriors running through the city, dropping their arms at the first sign of defeat, looting their neighbors' homes, and taking what they wanted. Nathan was dealing with tired, diseased men, fighting without pay. If Washington had ever wished for a man who could push his troops to the limit of their abilities, Nathan was certainly that leader. And if he had the guts and gift to convince his own men to continue a fight they believed couldn't be won, what would he do himself when called upon? "America beholds what she never did before," Nathan concluded to Enoch. "Allow the whole force of our enemy to be but 30,000, and these floating on the Ocean, ready to attack the most unguarded place. Are they not a formidable Foe? Surely they are."[11]

A while later Nathan once again wrote to Enoch. Nathan was still in New York—and still optimistic, even though the army was being boxed in and preparing its retreat from the city. Asher Wright, his childhood friend from Coventry—who, after becoming his aide, had spent some time with him in Boston and traveled to New York—was dedicated to his commanding officer and referred to himself as Nathan's "trusted servant." In 1836, facing death at age eighty-two, he sat down with R. N. Wright, a relative from Hanover, New Hampshire, who was visiting Asher in Coventry. In a text that would later become known as the "Testimony of Asher Wright," Nathan's good friend gave a brief account of their time together. Wright was terribly distraught over Nathan's last days in the military and the events surrounding his departure from camp—even sixty years after the events. R. N. Wright opened the testimony by stating, "[Even now] . . . besides the infirmities of advanced age, [Asher] has been affected in his mind, ever since the melancholy . . . [disappearance] of his young master, Captain Nathan Hale." Asher had been educated with Nathan at the Reverend Huntington's. Before Nathan left camp, Asher had shaved and clothed him. Although he wasn't the last person to see or talk to Nathan before Nathan departed Harlem, he was certainly one of the closest friends Nathan had to confide in before he left.[12]

In his last letter to Enoch, Nathan asked his brother to pay a visit to "Mr Wright," Asher's father. "Tell him Asher is well," Nathan explained. "I am in hopes of obtaining him a Furlough soon, that he may have [an] opportunity to go home, see his friends." Then he said that on the previous day Asher had summoned Nathan for a conversation upon his return from a meeting with several other officers. "Your brother Joseph Adams was here yesterday," he told Nathan [13]

Nathan explained to Enoch that he wasn't around that day. Upon a bit of checking, Nathan found out that Joseph was in Colonel (Samuel Holden) Parson's regiment, stationed not too far from his camp. "I intend to see him to day and if possible by exchanging get [Joseph] into my Company."[14]

Asher Wright had been by Nathan's side since they left Coventry at the end of January. Nathan's previous servant, a young man from New London, had fallen "sick of a fever" soon after he arrived at Winter Hill with Nathan.

The boy's father, Nathan told Asher, rode to Boston to fetch him. As the boy lay ill, Nathan knelt beside him many a day and night and prayed for his recovery. Asher had always considered Nathan one of the most devout men he knew, but he now began referring to him as the "praying man."[15]

I. W. Stuart described a spy as a "companion of darkness." There was no way of dressing the job up to appear less dishonest than it was. "If he moved in the light," Stuart wrote, "it is behind walls, in the shadow of trees, in the loneliness of clefts, under the cover of hills . . . skulking with the owl, the mole, or the Indian." One of the problems Nathan faced as a spy was that, on his best day, Nathan Hale was none of those. He embodied the spirit of that compassionate man Asher Wright described: the one who knelt by the bedside of a fellow, a devoted Christian who prayed for his servant as sincerely as he prayed for a soldier dying next to him in the marsh. He was not an impostor, an actor. However, Nathan's commitment to the cause overrode any of the hazards. He had made a decision and saw it as his duty as an American soldier to follow through with it. Nothing was going to change his mind.[16]

Years later, Asher Wright described the army's move from lower New York into uptown: "Latter part of Sept, we went to Harlem, perhaps five miles from New York." Washington had given the order to withdraw from lower Manhattan and set camp near Harlem Heights. According to historian Henry Howe, around this same period Nathan received instructions from and met with Washington. During this alleged meeting, of which no record exists and only oral tradition supports, they were said to have discussed "the points on which Nathan was to obtain information." And so, according to Howe, Nathan and Washington worked out a plan for the still unwell patriot captain to "cross over the Sound and land on Long Island."[17]

On either September 14 or 15 (some have claimed the date was closer to September 12, but there is no definitive record), Nathan met with Asher Wright to discuss his departure from camp. He wouldn't give Asher any details, other than he was *leaving*. "When he went away," Asher said later, "he did not tell me where he was going, but wanted I should take care of his clothes [and] if the army moved before he return'd to have his things taken along with it." After Nathan finished explaining what to do with his belongings, "Captain Hale went away."

It would be the last time Asher ever saw the praying man.[18]

Sergeant Stephen Hempstead had an odd look about him: a long, narrow face with a sharp jaw. He wore his dark hair slicked back. In the coming months of the war, Hempstead would be stripped naked and loaded into an ammunition wagon after being taken prisoner by the British. After the experience he was so traumatized he lay in bed for eleven months "as helpless as a child."

But while in New York, not yet changed by the horror of war, Hempstead was one of Nathan's close personal friends. Some nights during the fall of 1774, Hempstead's sister later remembered, he and Nathan would "lie flat on their backs in the New London meadow in the evening and watch the stars." Hempstead had lived right around the corner from the Union School.[19]

The Hempstead family were among the first settlers of New London, where the future sergeant was born on May 6, 1754. Young Hempstead was one of the few to be on the shores of Boston at the time the British evacuated and took great comfort in having had the "pleasure" of watching them go during the spring of 1776. When his first tour ended in December 1775, he immediately reenlisted under the condition that he be posted back into his friend Nathan's regiment.

When it came time to choose a traveling companion for his spy mission, Nathan asked Hempstead, and he agreed. The plan was to march north into Connecticut along the coastline and find the safest place for Nathan to cross the waters of Long Island Sound. Washington was said to have given Nathan a general order to allow him transport on any armed vessel of his choosing, a congressional mandate that permitted travel anywhere at any time.[20]

"You must go as far with me as you can," Nathan told Hempstead before they left the city, "with safety, and wait for my return."[21]

Hempstead and Nathan would travel on foot so as to not draw attention to themselves. Their ruse was rather plain: two friends—American New Englanders—who were pushed out of New York and heading home, one of whom was looking for work as a schoolmaster. Getting into Connecticut and finding a ship to board was not going to be a problem; the test would come when Nathan landed on hostile soil and began his sojourn behind enemy lines.[22]

Near this time when Nathan was preparing to leave camp, noted army surgeon James Thatcher recorded in his diary an anecdote that would later become an important allegory to Nathan's legacy. A German by the name of "Ledwitz," Thatcher wrote, who was "by his solicitation . . . appointed a Lieutenant Colonel in our army," had been unmasked as a British spy. Ledwitz had given another German, a man named "Steen," a letter to bring to Howe—a missive that contained what little Ledwitz knew of Washington's master plan. Unbeknownst to Ledwitz, however, Steen was a dedicated rebel soldier. After accepting the letter from Ledwitz, Steen rode straight to Washington's camp and hand-delivered it to the general. A bit taken aback by this infiltration of his organization, Washington read the letter at once. Ledwitz opened his treatise with his "compliments in a formal manner to Lord Howe." To explain his place with the Americans, Ledwitz said he had been "forced to accept his commission" in the army in fear that the Americans would kill him and his family. Then, in what should have guaranteed a noose around his neck, Ledwitz pledged his undenying devotion to "do all he could in his new capacity for his majesty's service." In an act that truly showed Ledwitz's intentions to commit treason, the spy demanded "two thousand [English] pounds sterling, to be paid in advance in gold . . . [which] might be immediately conveyed."[23]

"By this criminal act," Thatcher intoned, "the perfidious wretch had forfeited his life, according to the articles of war."

During a court-martial, however, proving a glimpse into perhaps how forgiving the Americans were when it came to treason, Ledwitz's "life was saved by the casting vote of a militia officer," and he was spared the penalty of death.[24]

As Nathan and Hempstead packed for their trip, Washington anticipated an imminent attack by the British. The general had supper on the night of

September 14 at the Apthorpe house, a three-story, English-style mansion built in 1767 at Ninth Avenue, between Nineteenth and Twentieth streets. Martha J. Lamb and Burton Harrison, in the *History of the City of New York,* claim that Nathan had dinner with Washington on this night and discussed his mission. Benson J. Lossing, in the *Pictorial Field-Book of the Revolution,* also says Nathan and Washington met on September 14, though Lossing claims the meeting took place at the Murry House, where Washington had made his quarters. Most scholars and historians dispute that Washington and Nathan ever had dinner together, simply because no documentation exists. However, a meeting between them would not have been documented because of intelligence concerns. It seems likely that Washington would want to speak with Nathan before he left camp, whether they dined together or not.

Nevertheless, as General Washington dined that night (with or without Nathan), New Yorkers packed their belongings and left the city in droves as fear of a British invasion mounted. Reports of residents stripping brass knockers from the doors of their homes, churches dismounting bells and packing them into wagons, and public buildings being stripped of any precious metals were common.[25] A few days before, the commander in chief had established an army hospital, he wrote in his general orders, because of "the difficulty of procuring Milk, and other proper Food for the sick." The hospital was a place "where those Necessaries can be procured in plenty." However, it was up to officers in the field to decide which soldiers should be sent to the hospital.[26]

On Sunday morning, September 15, as the wounded and sick soldiers— said to be near one thousand—were shuttled about the city to safer confines, a most incredible sight appeared over the horizon near the mouth of the East River. Heading north toward Kip's Bay, General Howe directed his attack, utilizing the ships *Phoenix, Roebuck,* and *Rose* to take control of the City of New York. It was a spectacular display of naval power. Private James S. Martin was there onshore, in awe at the sight:

> While lying here (Turtle Bay) we heard a heavy cannonade at the city; and before dark saw four of the enemy's ships that had passed the town

and were coming up the East River; they anchored just below us. . . . Half of our regiment was sent off . . . to man something that were called the 'lines,' although they were nothing more than a ditch dug along the bank of the river, with the dirt thrown towards the water.[27]

That evening, while the ships sat at anchor in the bay, Martin was entrenched so close to the *Phoenix* he could read her name painted on the bow. "They were within musket shot of us," he wrote. As he waited, he heard a British soldier relay a warning to no one in particular, yelling out loud into the darkness, "We will alter your tune before tomorrow night."[28]

After Howe and his troops landed at Kip's Bay, the Americans "opposed them, mostly militia," the following morning, "but then broke in a disgraceful panic and fled." Upon learning that his men showed such open cowardice, Washington was said to have "spurred to the scene in a frenzy of rage," brandishing his sword and "striking at the fugitives," while screaming words of "bitter scorn." To prevent Washington from being taken prisoner or killed, one of his assistants grabbed the reins of his horse and quickly pulled the stallion in the opposite direction.[29]

To the delight of the Americans, the British were slow on foot and missed a grand opportunity, as an American brigade, made up of several different regiments, rushed from the south and made it past the British without having to defend themselves. Soon, Israel Putnam and Alexander Hamilton pushed a large battalion forward and "in one or two slight skirmishes beat off the advance guard of pursuers." All was not clear, though. At the same time, Howe's men were piling off ships onto the shores of the city near Kip's Bay. The war had finally come to the Americans. With pandemonium breaking out near midtown, Washington sent a good portion of his troops farther north of Harlem Heights as he began weighing his options: take a stand and fight, or retreat northward into the Bronx and wait?[30]

In an impressive display of athleticism, on a clear afternoon one day before he left camp, Nathan had taken a ball and kicked it over the tops of the water beech and locust trees dotted along the dirt road that connected the

Bowery to present-day Roosevelt Park. Those soldiers who had witnessed it were said to have been astonished by Nathan's show of strength. In the past ten months, he had revealed to his colleagues how well he could wrestle, but this recent display proved to them how strong he was, even though he was still suffering from the flu. As Nathan and Hempstead left the city and marched into the Bronx before or on the night of September 15, 1776, unaware of the British attack in the works, if there was ever a time in Nathan's life when he needed that ability, it was surely right now.[31]

Upon his departure, Nathan dressed in "a frock . . . made of white linen, and fringed." Most officers from the Northeast had skipped the traditional colonial manila and blue with epaulets and instead opted for the same plain garments Nathan wore. The higher-ranking officers—colonels and generals—generally wore those multicolored uniforms of blue, yellow, and white that have become synonymous with revolutionary garb. Nathan believed that dressing like his men kept him on the same level. But as much as he wanted to show by example that he was one of them, he couldn't hide or suppress an air of valor about him. When Asher learned months later why Nathan had left camp, he said, "He was too good-looking to go . . . he could not deceive. Some scrubby fellows ought to have gone. He had marks on his forehead, so that anybody would know him who had ever seen him—having had powder flashed in his face." Those marks, or scars, were a permanent sign of who Nathan was: giving away his identity to the first redcoat who saw him. Any perceptive British soldier or Tory, upon meeting Nathan, would ask, Why does a Dutch schoolmaster (the identity Nathan was said to have taken) have a powder flash on his face that only soldiers in the military who had recently fired a musket would have?[32]

"It was at a most gloomy period of the war of independence when Hale departed from the American camp," historian Henry Howe wrote in 1859. Indeed, as word among officers spread that Nathan was preparing for a clandestine mission, it sent a "thrill of temper through those who were aware of its nature."[33]

Despite all that was against him, Nathan looked at the situation far differently, saying shortly before he and Hempstead left, "A sense of duty urges me to sacrifice everything for my country."[34]

As Hempstead and Nathan crossed into the Bronx and made their way to the shores of Greenwich, Connecticut, Nathan's plan was to cross over into Long Island at his first opportunity. At the time, sailing in the waters near Westchester County and southern Connecticut were hostile warships, American fighters, and merchant ships still trying to conduct business under incredibly unfriendly circumstances. Norwalk, Connecticut, about fifty miles from where they had started out, was the first point where Nathan felt he could cross the Sound without being intercepted.[35]

Norwalk is located between present-day Bridgeport and Stamford, about twenty-five miles east of White Plains, New York. During the eighteenth century the town was made up of largely Dutch colonists who supported the Revolution. Nathan would fit right in.

Wandering through the port of Norwalk, Nathan came upon the armed sloop *Schuyler*, captained by Charles Pond. It was the perfect vehicle for Nathan. The shores of Long Island were one gusty west wind and a few hours away. Pond, who had grown up a few miles east in Milford, Connecticut, was a captain in Nathan's former regiment, the Nineteenth Foot, so there was a good chance they already knew each other.

The *Schuyler* had been an important vessel in Washington's water war. Just a few months before Nathan and Hempstead set foot on her deck, Captain Pond had sailed the *Schuyler* near the shores of Long Island and seized "a Ship and a Sloop bound to Sandy Hook . . . with a Company of the 42" British. Apparently, Captain Pond and his *Schuyler* mates intercepted the ships with the help of another American schooner, whose captain quickly transported the captives to Rhode Island. Captain Pond reported five commissioned officers, two ladies, and four privates taken, on top of all of the ship's provisions. By all means, a great catch.[36]

Before boarding, Nathan changed his clothes in a wooded area near the docks. Hempstead had brought along a package of civilian garments Nathan's sister Elizabeth Rose had made for him. In front of Hempstead, Nathan put on "brown clothes" and a "broad-brimmed hat," likely a felt Dutch cap. Nathan bent down after getting dressed and snapped off the silver buckles on his shoes, looking up, telling Hempstead, "These will not comport with my character of a schoolmaster." Handing his loyal friend his uniform and the buckles, the commission Washington had given him to board any ship he desired, his public and private papers, "retaining nothing but his College diploma," Hempstead later wrote, Nathan believed he was ready to play the part of a Dutch pedagogue seeking employment.[37]

The *Schuyler* then set sail with America's first official spy aboard. It was the middle of the night, September 15 or 16, 1776. As the sloop sailed out of the tiny Norfolk inlet, Nathan Hale, with Hempstead by his side and the blurry moon over their backs, turned to watch the coastline disappear into the mist of the harbor.[38]

Captain Thomas Knowlton and Nathan Hale had more in common than they, as friends and colleagues, perhaps realized. Besides being taller than their contemporaries at six feet and growing up in northeastern Connecticut in neighboring towns, both were committed soldiers: to their country, to the men of their regiments, to General Washington. With the battle for Harlem Heights under way as Nathan sailed toward Long Island, Knowlton was ordered to take a group of over 125 of his rangers into a section of Harlem Plains near Hollow Way, an area now heavily packed with redcoats. Knowlton's mission was to guard the American regiments already stationed there. On the night of September 15, Knowlton and his team slipped into the region without being seen. Once there, Knowlton set up camp, knowing blood would likely be shed the following morning.[39]

When he relayed a message to Washington that the number of British troops was far greater than they had anticipated, Washington sent in backup. Major Andrew Leitch soon led a division of his Virginians down a slope into the valley of Hollow Way. Leitch's job was to surprise the British in the rear while Knowlton and his men flanked the front. This difficult maneuver was designed to entrap the British in a small ravine. But when it came time to carry out the plan, Knowlton ended up in the rear, as an aggressive battle ensued between the two sides.[40]

All things considered, the Americans fared quite well in the fight, driving the British back. But not without suffering substantial losses. Both Leitch and Knowlton were wounded. Leitch, upon being shot, was carried from the battlefield in haste, mortally injured. Knowlton, witnesses later claimed, had single-handedly attacked a line of redcoats behind a fence, running at them, screaming and firing blind. As he reloaded, Knowlton was shot in the head, immediately falling to the ground, as one of his men approached. Offering assistance, the soldier explained to Knowlton that he wanted to drag him from the field and get him help. Knowlton, however, knew his injury was fatal. He said, "Continue to do your duty in the action for you can do me no good." Undeterred by his brave words, the soldier ordered a wagon to fetch his fearless commander. Before he died an hour later, Washington spoke to Knowlton, "commending him for his gallantry and good conduct on all occasions." Thomas Knowlton, Washington said, was "brave and gallant . . . an honor to any Country."[41]

It's likely Nathan landed on the shores of Huntington, Long Island, on the morning of September 16, which meant he and Hempstead had spent about a day in Norwalk. A logbook from the British twelve-gun vessel *Halifax* noted that "two rebel privateers" had been spotted cruising the Sound near Huntington Bay during the early-morning hours of September 15 (the *Schuyler* had never left port or sailed the open ocean during this period of the war without the *Montgomery* by its side). After getting word of the two sloops in the area, the *Halifax* went in search, but failed to locate them.

At daybreak, Nathan and Hempstead caught a glimpse of the heavily wooded contour of the Long Island coastline near Great Neck and Oyster Bay. Within a few hours, Nathan would be walking the shores of Long Island in search of the information he had been commissioned to obtain.

Still, what Nathan didn't know—and there was little or no chance of getting word to him at this point—was that the mission he had undertaken was, by now, of no value to Washington and the rebel army, who were retreating from Harlem Heights and bailing completely out of the City of New York.[42]

Chapter 15

THROWN INTO THE FLAMES

S TANDING ON THE BOW of the *Schuyler* during the early-morning hours of September 16, 1776, Nathan turned and faced his traveling companion, Sergeant Stephen Hempstead. Each man knew this could be the last time they saw each other. Hempstead was one of only a few people who knew for certain what Nathan was setting out to do; Nathan had trusted him with his life. As the wind whipped in from the west and the waves of Huntington Bay crashed up against the stern of the *Schuyler*, Nathan said his good-byes to Hempstead and, before stepping off the ship, dropped a watch into his hand. After doing so, Nathan saluted his fellow soldier. Giving Hempstead the watch was a gesture of friendship no doubt, as much as a way for Nathan to say thank you for accompanying him.[1]

"He went on his mission," Hempstead later reported, "and I returned back again to Norwalk, with orders to stop there until he should return, or hear from him, as he expected to return back again to cross the sound if he succeeded in his object."[2]

Huntington sat on an elevated plot at the mouth of an enclosed harbor between Eaton and Lloyd necks. The beach dissolved into a thickly settled countryside—some called this area the Cedars—overgrown with pine trees and scattered hedge plants, camouflaging access to the main road into town. Although a majority of Long Island was now controlled by British and Hessian forces, with more Tories than anywhere in the northern Colonies, for the most part the natives of Huntington supported the rebel cause. Just a few months earlier, at the announcement of the signing of the Declaration of Independence and a reading of the Resolutions of the Provincial Congress, loud applause had been heard in Huntington amid "animated shouts of the people who were present." When the gathering broke up, several on hand ripped down a flag hanging from the town's liberty pole, on which one side read LIBERTY and the other GEORGE III. When the flag was raised a few minutes later, King George's name had been stricken from it.[3]

Even so, the moment Nathan stepped off that boat, he was a Dutch schoolmaster looking for work, his Yale diploma tucked safely in his pocket to prove his credentials.

That Nathan took along his Yale College diploma has been the subject of discussion among scholars and historians. One might ask, Why did Nathan take this with him? Are we to assume he stepped off the *Schuyler's* small dinghy and entered Huntington under a disguise, but used his real name? It seems that for every intelligent decision Nathan made, he also made some poor choice that helped lead to his capture. Still, it being September, a month that even during the eighteenth century signified the start of a new school year, Nathan could be confident his subterfuge would work.

As Nathan walked from the shore toward town to begin the planned four-day journey, his mission was officially on track.[4] It is thought that Nathan's strategy was to head straight for Brooklyn and work his way into Howe's camps along the shores of the East River on the Long Island side. Once there, he could speak with soldiers and civilians and, with any luck, gain an understanding of Howe's troop strength and short-term plans. He could draw maps, take notes, and get a feel for how the British viewed the war. From Brooklyn, Nathan was prepared to cross the East River into the city via a merchant dinghy or small sloop, find out what Howe's men were up to there, draw sketches of British fortifications and camps, head back into Long Island, and meet up with Captain Pond near Huntington on September 21, per an agreement they were said to have made when Nathan stepped off the *Schuyler.*

The first dangerous task in front of the captain was to make it through a neighborhood in Huntington where Rachel Chichester, known as Mother Chick, had "made her house a rendezvous, somewhat famous, for all those Tories in her region."[5] Once past Mother Chick's without complication, Nathan made his way to a dirt path heading into the brush just over the dunes beyond present-day Huntington Beach. He was now on the east side of Huntington Bay. Traveling for approximately one mile, he came to an open field, where he saw an old farmhouse sitting by itself in the meadow. Approaching the door "with a quick and assured step," the owner, William Johnson, answered Nathan's knock and, after realizing he was nothing more than a harmless schoolteacher, furnished him with a "hearty breakfast" and a bed to rest on "for a few hours." Then, as a Johnson relative later told I. W. Stuart, "When the morning had somewhat advanced, the stranger departed."[6]

Washington and his troops were stationed at Harlem Heights, more or less waiting for what the general believed was an imminent attack by Howe's men. Responding to gut feeling, along with a bit of dependable intelligence, the general sent several commanding officers, with "no less than twenty men from each regiment," out into the field to set up a line of defense on the right side of the Heights up to the Morris House. "Should the Enemy attempt to force the pass at night," he wrote, the rebels would have troops in a position to push them back and give the others time to react.[7]

On the morning of September 17, Washington thanked those men who had fought alongside Major Andrew Leitch the previous day, "who first advanced upon the Return of Killed and Missing in the Nineteenth Continental Infantry." The general praised their bravery, saying that their "Behavior . . . was such a Contrast to that of some Troops the day before." He asked everyone—officers, privates, militia—"to act up to the noble cause in which they are engaged, and to support the Honor and Liberties of their Country."[8]

Although in Washington's view the rebel army's defense had not been a total loss during the battle for Harlem Heights, he was quick to lash out at some troops he believed had not followed orders. "The Loss of the Enemy . . . would undoubtedly have been much greater," he wrote in his general orders, "if the Orders of the Commander in Chief had not in some instances been contradicted by inferior officers, who, however well they mean, ought not to presume to direct." The thought of his soldiers not only questioning his orders, but totally ignoring him, was infuriating. Staging attacks was *his* call—no matter what an officer thought about the decision. For an officer to change orders and instruct his regiment differently from what Washington had specifically directed was to defy his authority. After analyzing the results from the battle at Harlem Heights, Washington warned his troops that insubordination would not be tolerated. From this point on, he warned, his general orders were to be "delivered by the Adjutant General, or one of his Aide's-De-Camp, Tench Tilghman, or Col. Stephen Moylan the Quarter Master General."

There would be no more excuses. Disobedience would be dealt with severely. Especially during such a volatile time.[9]

For more than a century leading up to the American Revolution, Long Island was about two-thirds colonized by Dutch, who had settled the sandy, dunelike terrain in 1636. From the Huntington region, heading southwest, Brooklyn was a forty-mile hike. Whereas most of Long Island had become a mixture of Dutch and English throughout the eighteenth century, Brooklyn held to its Dutch roots. This helped Nathan as he made his way from the woods outside Huntington under the guise of a Dutch schoolmaster heading for Brooklyn, where he was hoping to "find work." Throughout his trip southwest, though, Nathan would pass through a considerable amount of British-occupied territory, with Tories eager to bring in any rebel they could snatch up and serve to Lord Howe. One detail he either completely overlooked or disregarded in total ignorance was the gunpowder flash on his cheek that Asher Wright reported. As Nathan crossed enemy lines under the mask of a schoolmaster, a redcoat might be suspicious. After all, soldiers and hunters were more inclined to have such pockmarks. Nathan was pretending that he was neither.[10]

Major Carl Leopold Baurmeister, a Hessian commander encamped on Long Island, had written to a friend in Germany describing the layout of the land and its people, many of whom he had socialized with as part of his daily rounds. In his view, the Long Island Dutch were a calm, pleasant people known for kindness toward just about anyone. They were passionate about caring for their property and their personal belongings, nurturing the land, and building only the finest houses. He was especially impressed by the women he met, whom he called "universally beautiful" and dressed routinely in the most popular European fashions: "Indian lace, white cotton and silky gauze." Most of the ladies, he observed, traveled with a Negro farmhand accompanying them. He had never seen this before. Each farm had separate quarters to house slaves, Baurmeister wrote, "who cultivate the most fertile land, pasture the cattle, and do all the menial work." The community of Long Island, as a whole, he thought, was a friendly lot, even as the war raged around them. The Dutch had a long-standing dispute with the English over rights to Long Island. Because of that, they didn't want the British there, but stayed neutral throughout the war.[11]

Stationed somewhere near this same region of Long Island where Nathan began his journey was Major Robert Rogers, an American. With his elongated nose, bulgy eyes, and pockmarked face, Rogers was a physically imposing brute of a man, who had the shoulders and barrel chest of a veteran British deckhand. His reputation stemmed from the no-nonsense, hands-on approach he had assumed for combat. His British commanders looked to Rogers for his brutal, bloodthirsty reputation and plain, soft-spoken method of talking people into doing what he wanted. It was neither nobility, integrity, duty, or even devotion to the king motivating Rogers; more than anything else, he was in it for the thrill and the money. Rogers had recently escaped from American custody and had been on Long Island just a few weeks with orders from Howe to recruit Tories for his newly formed unit, Rogers Rangers.

George Dudley Seymour called Rogers's life "a chapter of truculent ambition," branding him a derelict who lived by his own set of morals. Based on a 1937 novel by Kenneth Roberts, the film *Northwest Passage* (1940), starring Spencer Tracy and Robert Young, fictionalized Rogers's life during the French and Indian War, in which he was portrayed as a quasi-American-folk-hero.

Known as a loner, Rogers grew up in Londonderry, New Hampshire, but quickly left town to pursue a life in the British military. During one conflict in the Great Lakes region in the early 1760s, Rogers was said to have "scalped the dead within the sight of a French garrison and murdered a prisoner too badly wounded to march." Rogers fell right in line with what Howe needed in his field leaders. Up until 1775, Rogers had spent five years in England, in a sense proving his loyalty to the British, serving in their army. His courage was famous. While riding in a coach one afternoon near the town of Hunslow Heath, Great Britain, a highwayman "thrusted a pistol through the coach window [and] demanded the purses and watches of the occupants. The "bold American" grabbed the bandit by his shirt collar, yanked him into the coach, and held him down with his feet on his chest until the coach made it into town, where the thief was promptly arrested.[12]

As Nathan made his way out of Huntington toward Brooklyn, Rogers was lurking about the island in the same region, working under orders from Howe to sniff out any Americans willing to jump sides. Beyond that, if Rogers could be considered an expert at one thing within his large repertoire of military skills, it was deception. He was an expert liar and con man—the ideal agent, the perfect hunter, and ten times the secret agent Nathan would ever be. Rogers, for example, had no qualms about buying information. And yet, similarly, Nathan was not immune to paying informants or buying intelligence. In his army account book, he noted that he paid a man in New York for "the secret." What intelligence he actually bought was never noted; a spy would, of course, never document intelligence.[13]

Rogers had established his headquarters on Long Island near Flushing, about twenty-five miles from where Nathan had set out on foot from William Johnson's farm. During most of his time on Long Island, Rogers spent his days trolling the waters of the Sound—probably in through Eastchester Bay to King's Point and Glen's Cove—in a sloop provided to him by Howe. Rogers was a recruiting officer, combing the region for loyalists looking to join the winning side. However, he liked to gamble and drink. He spent much of his free time in taverns throughout the Flushing region, talking to patrons, looking for men to support what he talked up as Howe's eventual pummeling of the Americans. As Nathan made it through the area, he did not cross paths with Robert Rogers, who would surely have questioned what he was doing on Long Island—but would have to soon pass through the region again on his way back.[14]

Nathan made it to Brooklyn on or about September 18. South Brooklyn was largely made up of swampland, which came down to the East River like a set of large, earthen steps. English descriptions of the landscape called it a peculiar place, "presenting strong contrasts of high and low land." A section of the town, near Nevins Street and Wallabout Bay, jutted out into the river like a peninsula. The City of New York was about a mile directly across the river. According to Asher Wright, he later heard that Nathan "passed all their guards on Long Island [and] went over to New York in a ferryboat." In fact, Nathan could just as well have talked his way onto a British sloop or merchant ship. From there, he no doubt began his journey through the streets of New York near the South Street Seaport area, where he was now officially looking for work.[15]

Heading into New York was risky business. Nathan had spent five months stationed in the city, and although he was sick for a better part of that time, he had mingled with the populace regularly. What if he was recognized now? The British had pushed the American troops back to Harlem Heights by this point (though Nathan didn't know this upon entering the city). Howe and his troops had taken control of the city and had since set up several fortifications. Shopkeepers, merchants, slaves, common people, kids, clergy, innkeepers, and farmers would run into Nathan around every turn. For most soldiers in Nathan's position this may not have been a problem. But as his friend Elisha Bostwick described him, Nathan was in many ways *different:* He stood out. He walked with the presence and posture of a well-trained soldier. If he was going to enter a British-occupied environment and make drawings and notes, it was imperative he keep as low a profile as possible. One misspoken word or a chance run-in with someone he knew could mean certain death. City people were suspicious as it was:

Washington and his troops had fled, the British had moved in. Nerves were raw. It was going to be hard to trust anyone.[16]

A few days before Nathan left for Long Island, Nathanael Greene suggested to Washington that torching the city would solve several problems for the Americans. After Greene made the recommendation—with the general's blessing—to Congress, its body of governing officials quickly shot it down. The political fallout would be disastrous, the destruction to the city unforgivable.

During the first two weeks of September there had been a few intermittent smatterings of precipitation, and one "severe shower of rain . . . that produced a sudden change in the temperature," Colonel David Humphrey wrote as his regiment left Brooklyn. Generally, conditions around the city had stayed dry. The city's cedar buildings were dangerously flammable. Sometime after midnight on September 21, under a clear sky, an arsonist showed up in the city, though his or her identity is unknown.

John Joseph Henry, an American imprisoned on the British sloop *Pearl*, was supposedly one of the first to see the flame that would soon set the city ablaze. It originated inside the Fighting Cocks Tavern, a brothel and watering hole on the east side. Sitting in his cell, Henry looked out the small porthole and spotted a shimmering light off in the distance no bigger than a candle's soft flare. That flame was enough to set fire to a better part of the city and grant Washington and Greene their wish.

By two in the morning, civilians and British were running through the streets in confusion as shingled homes burned, rippling and cracking as if made of dry hay. No sooner had the fire started than a southeast wind rushed across the river and turned what could have been an easily containable fire into the worst blaze the city had seen in over 150 years. To make matters worse, all of the city's bells, some of which were used to warn of fire, had been taken down before the British took control of the city so they wouldn't be melted into munitions, and any bells left over had been melted down by the rebels or British, whoever got to them first.[17]

The fire created havoc. Residents soon awoke to pandemonium in the streets as the British directed civilians to help put out the fire. Yet the dry conditions and wind were overwhelming, and as each minute passed, the fire grew larger, its flames licking one rooftop after the other.

Redcoat lieutenant Fredrick Mackenzie was sleeping when he awoke to look out his window and see the city burning before him. He dressed quickly and ran to his major's quarters before dashing two miles into town. "When I got there the fire had got to such a head," Mackenzie wrote in his journal, "there seemed to be no hopes of stopping it—and those who were present did no more than look on and lament the misfortune."[18]

Mackenzie was frantic, yelling and screaming at New Yorkers to grab buckets of water and at least *try* to extinguish the blaze. Most refused. The people of New York were loath to accept the British occupation to begin with. Although they stood and watched their lives and livelihoods turn into ash, they knew the British would leave as soon as the fire subsided. "From a variety of circumstances that occurred," Mackenzie wrote, he could tell that the city had been "beyond a doubt . . . designedly set on fire." According to Mackenzie, as the fire raged near him, several of his soldiers caught civilians torching buildings that had somehow, luckily, escaped the original flames. "Many were detected with matches and Combustibles under their clothes. . . . One Villain abused and cut a woman who was employed in bringing water to the engines." Another woman, MacKenzie reported, who had been caught cutting off the handles of water buckets the British were using to fight the fire, "was hung up by her heels . . . [and] thrown into the flames."[19]

Some would later ask, Had Nathan Hale been sent to New York to set the fire? Was Nathan the chief arsonist among them? Although it's highly unlikely Washington would send a captain into the city via Long Island to set a fire, mainly because a common soldier was easier to replace if he was caught, it is certainly possible. More likely, though, it was a coincidence that Nathan was in the city on the same night the fire erupted. In addition, to send a captain via Long Island into the city to light it on fire was, logistically speaking, not something Washington would have contemplated. If he wanted to torch the city, he would have had his men do it before they retreated to Harlem. On top of that, he had asked Congress and been refused. To ask and then go against his superiors would have put his reputation at stake.

The question cannot definitely be answered, but what's clear is, as the fire burned itself out during that day, Nathan was already on his way back through Long Island. Captain Pond and the *Schuyler* were scheduled to meet him near Huntington on September 21 or 22. With maps and notes already tucked underneath the soles inside his shoes, all Nathan needed to do was hike the forty miles back across Long Island, and his mission was complete.[20]

Surgeon James Thatcher reported over one thousand homes, "some of the most superb buildings, being about one quarter of the whole city," burned to the ground. The fire was so hot that not one person could get near it to help put it out. Another man called it the "amazing blaze."[21]

Washington was, of course, thrilled—and probably more so because he could explain to Congress that, as far as he knew, the fire had accidentally been set. Yet, in private, writing to his distant cousin Lund Washington, the general put a different spin on it, waxing sarcastically about the inferno, saying, "Providence, or some good honest fellow, has done more for us than we were disposed to do for ourselves."

Chapter 16

Pretended Friend

B Y VIRTUE OF A natural-born instinct toward bravery on the battle-field, in addition to a dedication to his duty as a soldier, Robert Rogers was promoted to lieutenant colonel during the summer of 1776. The tough-ness Rogers exhibited, despite what could be a crass attitude at times, was no doubt one of the reasons why most civilians—and fellow soldiers—he came in contact with on Long Island viewed him as an intimidating, selfish man. Part of his reputation for disobedience came from his having sued Thomas Gage for wages Rogers claimed he had never received. How could a man honor the king and, at the same time, sue one of his generals?

Rogers hadn't developed this pragmatic though paradoxical attitude dur-ing the Revolution or even the French and Indian War, as many of his fel-low soldiers believed. He was born into a world, historian Caleb Stark wrote, "inured with the hardships of frontier life."

Being such an infamous ruffian, however, came with its with advantages, as Rogers took to the dirty work of the military—guarding prisoners of war, transporting loyalists to jails, and sniper killings and lying and decep-tion. Yet at times the cool and reserved Rogers could intimidate without even having to deceive or tell a falsehood. One night, for example, Rogers was with several British officers in England at a social event. As they were standing around after dinner, they agreed that whichever man could tell the greatest tale or the most unlikely story would have a free night on the others. When it came time for Rogers's tale, he warned his fellows that the story he was about to relate would—hands down—win the friendly wager. When he was a boy, Rogers explained, his father had set out one afternoon for a hunter's camp deep in the forest near Haverhill, Massachusetts, to fetch the hunter and invite him to dinner. The hunter had been making surveys of the land, and no one had seen him for quite some time. Upon approaching the hunter's camp, the elder Rogers, rustling the bushes and cracking twigs underneath his feet, startled the hunter. Not expecting a visitor, the hunter believed a bear had picked up his scent. With the fear of death clouding his thinking, the hunter poked his musket through a firing hole in the side of the cabin and shot the elder Rogers, killing him instantly. Not too long after, Rogers continued, his mother was walking through the forest when a hunter locked onto her tracks, which had been set in a fresh blanket of knee-high snow, and thought they were those of a wolf. In a blinding snowstorm, with drifts kicking up all around him, the hunter soon picked up his pace, and when he came upon a silhouette of a figure he felt certain to be a wolf, he fired and killed the woman.[1]

Amid belly laughs and pats on the back, the group cheered Rogers on as they paid his tab. However, both stories, he later claimed, were the absolute truth. He had made nothing up.[2]

One of Colonel Rogers's men once referred to him as "subtle"; but within this outwardly simple man lived an angry human being, the soldier pointed out, filled with an evil as "deep as hell itself." Rogers could snap in an instant and order an execution, as he routinely did during the French and Indian War when his prisoners lagged behind. Or if an Indian scalped one of his men, Rogers would scalp two or three Indians. Still, regardless of what people thought of him, those same ruthless characteristics would make him famous.

On Friday, September 20, Nathan and Rogers brushed shoulders as the rebel spy made his way back toward Huntington, probably marching through Great Neck, Glen Head, and East Norwich. Rogers and a detachment of men had been aboard the *Halifax* on September 16, 17, and 18, then they were dropped off at Sandy Point, near Flushing, at 10:00 P.M. on the night of the nineteenth. Rogers had several informants along the northern coastline of Long Island and even as far as across the Sound in Norwalk, Greenwich, and other points along the Connecticut shoreline. He had been paying these men to feed him information since the beginning of September. Rogers knew someone had landed at Huntington on September 16, but didn't know who he was or what type of business he had on the island. Once he heard that the mysterious stranger was back in the region asking questions of the locals, Rogers wanted to get closer to him and find out what his purpose was.[3]

It wasn't only Nathan that piqued Rogers's interest. A Tory storekeeper from Connecticut named Consider Tiffany, who was in Huntington at the time, recorded in his diary that Rogers "detected several American officers" in and around Flushing on that same day. *Detected* seems to be a disingenuous term; Rogers either roughed people up and forced them to talk or paid a sizable reward for the information. His nature was to bully people into giving him what he wanted; "an enemy in disguise," one of his early biographers called Rogers, a man "with no principles that would deter him from selling out his opportunities, if it could be done with probable success."[4]

Upon his arrival in Huntington, Nathan spoke to local merchants, tavern owners, and natives. He was trying to find out, Tiffany recorded in his diary, "whether the Long Island inhabitants were friends to America or not." This seems like a rather foolish query on Nathan's part. If he had already obtained the information Washington had sent him to fetch, one wonders why he started sniffing around again, asking more questions, risking the entire mission, not to mention his life, when he was merely a breath away from stepping back aboard the deck of the *Schuyler*.[5]

When Rogers heard that Nathan was asking questions of people in town, he guessed the so-called Dutch schoolmaster was up to something. "Colonel Rogers, having for some days, observed Captain Hale . . . suspected that he was an enemy in disguise," Tiffany wrote. Rogers then came up with a plan to "convince himself," using Nathan's inexperience at espionage against him.[6]

Nathan likely rented a room for the night at a local tavern. He wasn't expecting to meet Captain Pond and the *Schuyler* until the following morning. Most taverns in colonial New York–Long Island were homes converted into rooming houses that offered food and drink, similar to what we might today call inns. We know Nathan did not camp in the woods. Several of his early biographers, relying on interviews with local Tories, claimed Nathan dined and slept at a Tory-owned tavern and, it was believed, was betrayed by its owner.[7]

Rogers was quite well-known at this time. He had been written about in all of the newspapers and had parlayed his reputation into a high-paying job with the British. When he walked into the tavern after a report from one of his sources indicated Nathan was sitting by himself having a drink, there's no doubt heads turned, as most locals already knew Rogers by sight.

After entering, Rogers sat down next to Nathan and introduced himself as a fellow American soldier. Important to this pivotal moment, Rogers spoke with the same dialect as his mark. He knew America well, having been raised in New England. Moreover, he could play the role of a rebel quite warmly. He had fought in the French and Indian War alongside Washington and had even once written to the general, "I love America; it is my native country and that of my family, and I intend to spend the evening of my days in it."[8]

After he introduced himself, Rogers "fell into some discourse concerning the war," Tiffany reported. Then Rogers explained how he had been troubled ever since the start of the war, adding, "I was being detained on the island."[9]

Around Nathan and Rogers the tavern was noisy with men getting drunk. Yelling across the table, Rogers shouted, "The inhabitants sided with the Britains against the American Colonies."[10]

Rogers knew exactly what to say. His words must have been comforting to Nathan, who hadn't—that we know of—spoken to anyone throughout his mission that seemed to understand the nature of his assignment in the same manner his new friend perhaps could. Rogers knew what Nathan had experienced. Maybe, Nathan began to consider, he could explain his purpose to Rogers and convince him to help his cause.

Still, it seems almost impossible that Nathan, a veteran captain in the American military, would not have heard of the infamous Robert Rogers. There's no way Nathan could have known what Rogers looked like, beyond a vague description from one of his superiors. But a more experienced spy would have been on the lookout for Rogers, or at least men like him. Furthermore, Washington knew that Rogers was on Long Island recruiting Tories for the British. So it's likely that because Nathan was a captain and now a spy, not to mention a ranger, he was also made aware of this. In a letter Washington would send to Connecticut governor Jonathan Trumbull just a week after Nathan and Rogers met, Washington lamented, "Having received authentic advices from Long Island, that the enemy are recruiting a great number of men, I have directed an expedition to the island, to check and suppress, if possible, a practice so injurious to our cause. Several persons have been detected of late, who have enlisted to serve under [the British] banner, and the particular command of Major Rogers."[11]

And yet without asking anyone in town about this mysterious man who had just appeared at his table, Nathan fell right into Rogers's trap and began to talk openly with him.

When Nathan asked Rogers what he was doing on the island, Rogers said quite brazenly, "I myself am upon the business of spying out the inclination of the people and motion of the British troops." Rogers spoke with confidence and ardor. He sensed Nathan hadn't recognized him or guessed his true purpose for being in the tavern. "This intrigue," Tiffany reported, "not being suspected by the Capt, made him believe that he had found a good friend, and one that could be trusted with the secrecy of the business he was engaged in."[12]

As they sat, drank, and discussed the rebel effort in detail, much like two old French and Indian War buddies, at some point Rogers raised his mug and asked Nathan to join him in a toast to the "health" of Congress.[13]

Without hesitating, Nathan obliged his new friend.

After that, they clanked goblets as Nathan began to candidly talk about his mission, "informing Rogers of his business and intent." Knowing that Nathan had a penchant for alcohol while at Yale and later in New London, one wonders if Rogers made sure Nathan was drunk, which might have loosened him up. It seems strange that after having made it this far, Nathan would have put the fate of the entire mission in the hands of a stranger—without, that is, being a bit seduced by alcohol.[14]

Rogers listened attentively, thrilled that he had netted himself a bona fide American spy. General Howe, he knew, was going to be much delighted.

After Nathan finished explaining where he had been and where he was headed, Rogers said, "I'd like to invite you to dine with me tomorrow morning at my quarters."[15]

Without another word, Nathan said he'd be there, bright and early.[16]

Before Consider Tiffany's diary was discovered, the most widely accepted story surrounding the capture of Nathan Hale, which all of his previous biographers told in some form, was that while Nathan sat in this tavern having supper and a drink, his cousin Samuel Hale walked in and, hiding from Nathan, recognized him and quickly left the tavern and returned to camp, where he then told his commander who Nathan was and what he was likely doing in town. Samuel was definitely stationed in or near Huntington. Samuel and other Tories felt comfortable in the tavern, as it was a known hangout for the British.

Young Samuel had been a popular lawyer with a prosperous career ahead of him. Had he chosen to conceal his devotion to the British and continue his law practice, he would have been considered one of the most prominent attorneys in Portsmouth, and maybe all of New Hampshire. Instead, during the 1775 siege, he traveled south into Boston with a group of loyalists and from there made the trek to Long Island.[17]

It's possible Samuel could have turned Nathan in at the same time Robert Rogers figured out Nathan's purpose, though Samuel later denied any involvement. One has to give Consider Tiffany's account a bit more credibility, however, simply because it is so well documented and falls perfectly in line with Rogers's character and the documentation we have supporting where Rogers was and what he was doing at the time. No documentation supports the claim that Samuel turned Nathan in—only oral tradition and rumors that were passed down from one generation to the next. We can be certain that if Samuel had been the Tory responsible for Nathan's capture, Tiffany would probably have corroborated on this point. It would have been further proof—perhaps the most solid the British had—that Nathan was lying about his intentions of opening a school. Additionally, E. E. Hale, who became the Hale spokesman for Nathan's legacy during the 1800s, said, "In the rage and distress of the excitement of the time, the rumor spread that Hale was betrayed by a Tory kinsman. But the narrative in [the witness's text] . . . gives no room for any such treachery; and I know no evidence for it, beyond 'it is said.' I know that my father did not believe the story of treachery: I did not think his father did."

The City of New York lay in ruin, smoldering after an inferno that had incapacitated the city. General Howe made his quarters in the neighborhood of present-day Fifty-first Street and First Avenue, inside the James Beekman mansion, which hadn't been touched by the fires. Beekman had been a member of the Provincial Congress of New York, his magnificent home fitted with arched windows, whitewashed clapboard, and a front porch that ran the entire length of the home. On the roof was a balcony covered with tiles made of white fir, where Beekman entertained his guests as they looked out on Turtle Bay, the shores nudging up to the back face of the home. On the opposite side of the estate was the Kissing Bridge. On the west side of the mansion was Beekman's greatly admired glass and iron greenhouse, surrounded by a flower garden, with the De Voor Mill stream gurgling placidly by in the back. Built only a few years before the war, the greenhouse was "the first upon Manhattan Island," historian William Aitken wrote. The Beekmans harvested lemons in the greenhouse that Washington and his staff had watched servants pick and then squeeze into fresh lemonade during the brutally hot summer months of 1776. Before the Beekmans left the property, as the British took control of the city, they buried all of their silver and china underneath the greenhouse. Now, though, the city's famed conservatory was no garden at all; it had been turned into a holding cell, which was about to house one important prisoner of war.[18]

Scattered about the Beekman estate, as well as all over the area, were enormous elm trees standing alongside columns of apple and beechnut trees. Slaves maintained the Beekman property and much of the vegetation around the estate. In what used to be a region of prosperous farming, where horses, oxen, and cattle grazed freely, "so many draught animals had been stolen by . . . officers and men," twentieth-century historian Stephen Jenkins noted, "that enough animals could not be found to drag the stores and artillery." Any cannons and wagons that had to be moved were pulled by relay teams of men. Despite the battle-zone environment around it, the Beekman mansion was considered the ideal location for Howe to manage his takeover of the city. The Americans were pushing north, heading into the Bronx. If Howe was going to close off New York via the North and East rivers, being stationed at Turtle Bay, just about in the middle of the city, would prove to be the ideal location to leave at a moment's notice and watch over the migration of his troops from New York into Westchester County.[19]

Things seemed to be going Howe's way, and one of Washington's biggest problems was now his military officers, who were more interested in the politics of the Revolution than in the safety of those men who were fighting for liberty. Chief among them, Stephen Jenkins pointed out, was Major General Charles Lee, whom Jenkins called a "conceited and egotistical braggart, so prolific of plans, schemes, and criticisms, and [yet] so barren of results." Reading Jenkins's assessment of this decisive period of the war, one would think the Americans were doomed to implode under a balloon of their own hedonistic ignorance.[20]

There was a divide between some of the leaders of Congress and field commanders. By now, arguably eighteen months into the war, it was clear to Washington and Congress that the Americans could not defeat the British and German forces by themselves. It would take a mightier force: men determined to win at any cost; more money; reliable artillery; food; supplies; simple everyday provisions. And if help didn't come soon, Washington knew, the rebels would be in more trouble than they had been when choked up down at the point of the city.[21]

Washington's adjutant general, Joseph Reed, bemoaned how ill-prepared and unskilled, however courageous, the Americans were. Writing to his wife on September 17, Reed spoke of a close call he had himself had that day. He had mounted his horse and ridden "down to our most advanced Guard." While he was there assessing the troops, talking to an officer, "the

Enemy . . . fired upon us at a small Distance," he explained, adding that his men had "behaved well" and returned fire, but were soon overpowered by the sheer numbers of redcoats. The horse Reed had ridden in on was captured by the British—and Reed found himself running for cover. What had disgraced the Americans most, Reed observed, was that as the rebels ran in all directions, like spooked hens running from a wolf, the oncoming British "sounded their Bugle Horns as is usual after a Fox Chase," laughing at the fleeing rebels.[22]

Fatigued and bitter, Reed was deeply insulted by this. "I never felt such a sensation before; it seem'd to crown our Disgrace."[23]

As the morning of September 21 broke, smoke from the mammoth fire in the city still billowed a blanketing, smoggy haze over the entire region. "A vast cloud . . . ," the *Boston Gazette* reported, "the consequence was that Broad Way from the New city hall to white hall laid in ashes," an area that would run today from about Forty-second Street, east to west, all the way south to the Battery. In the coming days, Washington would tell Governor Trumbull he wasn't sure who had started the fire: "By what means it happened we do not know." Rebels caught behind enemy lines were accused of igniting the blaze, Washington reported. "Some of our countrymen had been punished with various deaths on account of it, some by hanging, others by burning . . . alleging they were apprehended when committing the act."[24]

When Robert Rogers left Nathan at the tavern the previous afternoon, he went about setting up a posse to ensnare the rebel spy. The plan was simple: invite Nathan to a chosen location for breakfast, make him feel comfortable, then take him as a prisoner of war. It wasn't going to be difficult. All Rogers needed was for Nathan to show up.

Although there's no official record of it, standard British practice would indicate that either Rogers himself or a few chosen men he gave orders to had stealthily watched Nathan throughout the night. Rogers certainly wasn't about to lose sight of his catch and risk the chance of Nathan deciding to head back to Connecticut early.[25]

At some point that morning, as promised, Nathan arrived at Rogers's quarters. "The time being come," Consider Tiffany wrote, "Capt Hale repaired to the place agreed on, where he met his pretended friend, with three or four men of the same stamp."[26]

Nathan believed he was walking into a friendly discussion about other rebels stationed on Long Island, one of whom he believed he was now sitting with once again, only this time enjoying a breakfast of biscuits, tea, and eggs. As they sat and ate, "after being refreshed," Tiffany reported, Nathan and Rogers "began the same conversation" they had parted on the previous night.[27]

As this seemingly innocent conversation carried forth, Rogers knew his plan was nearly complete. For as they talked, Tiffany said, a "company of [Rogers's] soldiers surrounded the house."[28]

Thus, Nathan Hale had just eaten his final meal as a free man.

Chapter 17

THE WILL OF GOD

R OBERT ROGERS WAS ABOUT to put a feather in his cap by capturing America's first official spy on the morning of September 21, 1776, somewhere in (or near) Huntington, Long Island. At some point over breakfast, Rogers convinced Nathan he was among friends and got him to admit he had been sent over the British lines by none other than George Washington himself.[1]

When the moment came, Rogers stood and accused Nathan of the most heinous crime a soldier could commit: spying. But Nathan quickly denied the indictment, Consider Tiffany wrote, "and the business he came upon," trying to lie his way out of his capture by returning to his Dutch schoolmaster story.[2]

"By orders from the commander," Rogers said sternly, standing, the back of his knees pushing the wooden chair out from underneath him. He then seized Nathan and ordered him to be taken to the City of New York immediately.[3]

Nathan continued to deny the charges as he was led outside in front of a swelling throng of onlookers. A local shipbuilder, Solomon Wooden, who had worked on several of the British warships, later said Nathan claimed to be "disgusted with the rebel cause." Being led away, Wooden added, Nathan tried one final time to protect his subterfuge, telling his captors, "I am a deserter. I didn't want to enlist. I want a school."[4]

When Rogers brought Nathan outside, several of the rangers surrounded him, poking their muskets into his face and chest, prodding and mocking him. While this happened, several people in town pointed at Nathan in jest and, Tiffany reported, "knowing him, called him by name." They had recognized him as the schoolmaster who had passed through the region several days before.[5]

Rogers ordered his men to shackle Nathan's legs together and tie his hands behind his back. He was an official prisoner of war now. At this moment, Nathan would have realized that the old wives' tale of the mole on his neck had come true: He was on his way to the gallows. Any man knew that if an active soldier was caught behind enemy lines wearing civilian clothing, he was going to be executed without trial—and nothing and no one was going to stop it.[6]

Beyond a desire to prove he was an asset to Washington, unlike many of his peers, Nathan Hale had a strong sense of what his true purpose was during the war. "Neither expectation of promotion, nor pecuniary reward," George Dudley Seymour wrote, "induced him to this attempt . . . a hope that he might in this way be useful to his country." Nathan had routinely discussed his patriotism with his fellow Yalies and friends from New London as the skirmishes between the rebels and the redcoats in Boston became an all-out conflict during the latter part of 1775. In one letter Gilbert Saltonstall wrote to Nathan, he noted the unity the two men shared regarding the political and social collapse of the colonies if men chose to desert the cause:

> You saw in the Paper the Address to the King from the Merchants. . . .
> Notwithstanding their pretending their resources are many, and so large
> that the American non-importation & exportation will be like the light
> dust of the Balance, Yet to every one who will turn it in his Thoughts,

it's utterly impossible but that ye prodigious Consumption of British Ware & Merchandise . . . I consider as already completed must affect them sensibly, and they must recognize the consequence of America.[7]

Here were young men discussing the implications of a British occupation, increased taxation, and the effect it would have on the future of American commerce. People would suffer greatly, Saltonstall believed. Through this discourse, Nathan and his comrade understood the reasons for war and how, in the end, bloodshed would benefit future generations: freedom, survival, prospering, and raising a family were all at stake. But more than any of that, Nathan and Saltonstall agreed, any man who chose to take up arms against the king should do so without condition, and yet they both recognized that a majority of their fellow colonists would ultimately cave in to the king's demands and choose immediate commerce over hard-earned independence.[8]

"I wish New York," Saltonstall continued in that letter, "was either razed to the Foundation, or strongly Garrisoned by the American Forces; I greatly fear the Virtue of the Yorkers whose Religion is Trade, & whose God is Gain."[9]

The politics surrounding the war had exposed an important point: Beyond a patriotic cause, it was also a merchant's fight, not just an ordinary citizen's. Still, Nathan wasn't heading to the gallows for any one group of Americans. In his heart, which was made clear by his writings over the years and those anecdotes his peers later shared about him, he wore the uniform for God first and all Americans second.[10] Nathan was under the impression when he left camp on his mission that, in the eyes of his commanders, he played a much larger role in the effort than he did, which was never more clear than when, as a prisoner of war, he saw the more than one thousand American prisoners of war the British were holding.[11]

As Nathan continued to claim he was not a continental soldier, he was placed in the brig on the *Halifax*, which would transport him to the city. He had his college diploma, and also, in the soles of his shoes, likely written in

Latin, the notes and drawings and maps he had generated during the first few days of his mission. One of the reasons why Washington and Knowlton likely chose Nathan was his wealth of scientific knowledge. His intelligence and Yale education were imperative to the assignment: to recognize the enemy's fortifications and draw scaled versions of British forts and columns, and to calculate the numbers of soldiers.[12]

The choppy sail across the Sound likely took a good part of the morning. After making the turn around King's Point, the *Halifax* was drawn into the East River current, through Hell Gate, and finally onto the shores of the city, reportedly near Fifty-first Street. Nathan was on his way to the Beekman mansion to face General Howe and answer the accusations against him. What went through his mind, nobody will ever know. Yet between the time he was captured by Rogers and the time he arrived at the Beekman mansion, Nathan chose to come clean, to admit his purpose, and to accept what he unquestionably believed to be the will of God.[13]

His death.

Chapter 18

Without Ceremony

According to General Howe's provost marshal, William Cunningham, the British executed 275 American prisoners, as well as what Cunningham later called "obnoxious persons," in New York alone during the years the British occupied the city. Predominantly, executions in New York were not public affairs, but Cunningham, standing at the gallows himself in London during the latter part of the eighteenth century, having been convicted of forgery, admitted there were twelve public executions during his tenure in New York, "which chiefly consisted of British and Hessian deserters."[1]

Although death by hanging was one way to deal with enemy captives, the British had other ways of punishing Americans, as Cunningham later noted: "I shudder to think of the murders I have been accessory to, both with and without orders from government." In one instance, Cunningham was part of a cluster of provost marshals who starved to death "more than two thousand [American] prisoners" in various churches throughout the city "by stopping the rations," which he then turned around and sold for personal profit. Churches had become the perfect structures for Howe's men to corral large groups of rebels into and keep watch over them from the wood and stone balconies and landings. Houses of the Lord had become dungeons. A common sight for those passing by the outside of a city church prison was the small openings and barred windows lined with human heads, packed tightly together. These were men so thirsty for fresh air they had climbed on one another's backs just to take in a short breath or two. Conditions were so vile inside that at night prisoners could not even lie on the floor together at one time. Food and fresh water were not available. Cunningham or other British soldiers would intercept the food—mainly uncooked, rotten pork, hardtack, and spoiled meats of various types—meant for his prisoners and sell it on the black market. The water he provided was muddy and served in bacteria-laced pails.[2]

In contrast, the British carried out private executions in a quite orderly manner. "A guard was dispatched from the provost, about half after 12 at night, to the Barrack street," Cunningham later explained. From there, the neighborhood would be sealed off as orders were sent out for anyone in the vicinity of the execution to "shut their window shutters" and extinguish any lamps or candles. Citizens were forbidden to watch, Cunningham claimed, or, as he put it, "to presume to look out of their windows and doors, on [the] pain of death." When the area was secure, the prisoners were "gagged" and hung "without ceremony" and generally buried on the spot of their execution by "the black pioneer of the provost."[3]

Nathan had never really experienced the cruelty Robert Rogers was capable of dishing out. Part of Rogers's ruse was to charm Nathan into admitting he was in fact a spy. Yet, Nathan was about to be put into the hands of a man notorious for his immorality and severity against American prisoners of war: Provost Marshal William Cunningham, who Howe had sent for once he heard that a reported spy was being brought to his quarters for arraignment. Cunningham was known as a drunk and a "monster," an enforcer, and all-around wretched man who wasn't afraid to carry out any grisly duty bestowed upon him. If Howe could count on any man to impose the utmost punishment on a rebel soldier who had been charged with one of the more detested war crimes, Cunningham was it. Cunningham had been a prisoner of the Americans for a time and was inhumanely treated, as one story went, by being dragged behind a rebel horse around Cambridge before he managed an escape. So revenge, in the form of hanging rebels, might have become gratifying for the provost marshal.

Before joining the British military, Cunningham was known as a scow banker, in the business of crating human beings and loading them onto ships headed to America from England under the promise of "great advantage" and a fuller life, only to sell them into slavery and work camps under a debt of passage once they arrived in Boston and New York. When he reached the colonies himself, Cunningham took up the business of breaking horses. After his escape from Boston, he boarded the *Asia* and was given the job of provost marshal because he had such a desire to "gratify his bloodthirsty instincts," nineteenth-century historian and prolific writer Danske Dandridge observed. "His hatred for Americans found vent," said an American pamphlet distributed after the war, "in torture by searing irons and secret scourges to those who fell under the ban of his displeasure." For Cunningham, the worst American was a spy.[4]

Howe's quarters were far enough away from the Sugar-House, one of the more ruthless prisons near the Beekman estate, and a row of church prisons, that the British commander could not hear the wailing of the Americans housed together in such tight quarters, starving to death. His job was to direct and manage. Strategize and give orders. Nathan was brought before the general (probably during the late-afternoon hours) on September 21. Around them the city continued to smolder, as the putrid aroma of burned wood and flesh permeated the thick air. Captain Quarme, who was responsible for transporting Nathan to the westside port of the City of New York en route to a court-martial in front of Howe, later said he was awestruck that "so fine a fellow had fallen into his power."[5] Once Nathan stood in front of Howe, his ruse was fully revealed. It's unclear who found Nathan's stash of writings and drawings, or if he turned them over to Howe, but when confronted with this proof of his mission, Nathan "at once declared his name, his rank in the American army, and his object in coming within the British lines," his friend and colleague Captain William Hull later reported. A British soldier at the meeting corroborated the story that Nathan "frankly acknowledged his rank and his purpose as a spy."[6]

"I regret," Nathan said, standing in front of the British commander, hands tied behind his back, his words firm and without alarm, "that I had not been able to serve my country better."[7]

According to that same British soldier, "the frankness, the manly bearing, and the evident disinterested patriotism of the handsome young prisoner, sensibly touched a tender chord of General Howe's nature."

Howe was a fair man. He was pursuing the king's will, not his own. Still, the "stern rules of war" dictated his decision—it wasn't up to him. He was not in a position "to exercise even pity."[8]

Howe immediately ordered Nathan's execution to take place the following morning. For now, he announced to the men around him as Nathan stared at the commander unflinchingly, the rebel was being placed in the custody of Provost Marshal Cunningham.[9]

Nathan spoke up. He had two requests. "The presence of a chaplain, sir?"

No, said Howe.

"A Bible?"

No, Howe said once again.[10]

Cunningham took Nathan to the greenhouse on the Beekman estate and placed him under protective custody, two armed guards standing outside the door. Later on that evening, Howe's chief engineer, Captain John Montrésor, heard that his comrades had captured a rebel who had made drawings and maps of key British fortifications. Montrésor was stationed in a tent near Nathan's "fatal spot," said to be at an artillery park just north of the Beekman property. Because of his interest in the drawings Nathan had made and Howe's eagerness to understand them, Montrésor was called in to consult. But when he looked at the drawings and notes Nathan had constructed, Montrésor asked Cunningham "if he might offer Hale the protection of his tent while" the provost marshal "made preparations" for his execution.[11]

After considering it, Cunningham agreed.

"And so it happened that Hale on his way to the gallows became the guest for a brief space that Sunday morning of Montrésor," George Dudley Seymour wrote.[12]

Nathan's capture and pending execution, one historian wrote in 1891, "attracted much attention on account of his high personal character."

Montrésor, whose father was the chief engineer for the Forty-eighth Foot, had joined the military during Braddock's famed expedition to Quebec, where the young boy from Gibraltar learned the engineering trade from his father. One of Montrésor's major accomplishments was a chain of redoubts he had built on Lake Erie near Niagara. Strong and well-built, with prematurely gray hair, he could take a hit and keep going. "A restless Ball," Montrésor wrote in his journal many years before he met Nathan, "in my Body after Incisions cut to extract it." No medicine. No anesthesia. No liquor. Montrésor took the injury in 1760 during a quest from Maine to Quebec. "A loss of appetite from derangement of my System," he added, "for having been distressed by Famine for 13 days." Tough, sure. But he understood the brutality and risks of war; and what it took to survive.[13]

On Sunday, September 22, a bright, hot morning, Cunningham and his men chose a tree in the artillery park near the Beekman estate, then located a lengthy section of firm twine and a sturdy wooden ladder. As they did, Nathan sat with Montrésor and talked. The engineer had several questions for the rebel. "A fine gentleman," Seymour said of Montrésor, "whose humanity provides the only bright spot . . . from the moment of [Nathan's] capture to his end." Moreover, Montrésor knew Cunningham was "hardened to human suffering and every softening sentiment of the heart."[14]

Nathan faced his final hours with honorable poise and self-respect. "He was calm, and bore himself with gentle dignity, the consciousness of rectitude and high intentions," Montrésor would later say of the prisoner. Apparently, Nathan had given in to death, accepting it as a cost of the war effort. There can be no doubt Nathan placed this day in God's hands. Based on his daily habit of prayer and Bible readings, it is likely that Nathan prayed and thought deeply about the people he was leaving behind. At some point he turned to Montrésor and asked, "Can you oblige me with writing materials?" He wanted desperately to write two letters: one to a family member, and a second to his commanding officer, Thomas Knowlton.[15]

Montrésor furnished Nathan with several pieces of paper, a quill, and an ink bottle. This was done in haste, as Cunningham would have forbidden a prisoner to send letters before his death. Despite that, Nathan sat in Montrésor's quarters, chained at his feet and hands, writing as best he could under the conditions.[16]

One of the letters was addressed to Enoch. Then, not knowing that Captain Knowlton had perished just days before during the battle for Harlem Heights, Nathan wrote a final report to his commander. By now it was past 9:00 A.M. Cunningham would be summoning Nathan to the gallows at any moment. Montrésor, impressed with the composure Nathan had displayed thus far, his facing death with such dignity, sat with him and continued talking.

"His humane, gallant, and courageous befriending of Hale that Sunday morning is," Seymour said of Montrésor, "the one redeeming feature in the tragedy."[17]

John Montrésor would soon cross enemy lines under a flag of truce and explain to a young Alexander Hamilton what had happened to Nathan Hale.[18]

Chapter 19

SWING THE REBEL OFF

B Y 10:30 A.M. ON what was a beautifully warm early-fall Sunday morning, the time had come for Nathan Hale to make his death march from Montrésor's tent at the artillery park near present-day Third Avenue and Sixty-sixth Street, to an apple orchard not too far away. For whatever reason, Cunningham was running behind schedule; Nathan should have been executed first thing in the morning. Yet, at 11:00 A.M., the schoolmaster was walking toward a shallow ridge Cunningham had chosen, as several New Yorkers assembled to witness the execution of an American spy. Most on hand agreed later that Nathan walked with the grace and stateliness of a man carrying out the will of his people, the will of his God.[1]

Historians disagree on where, exactly, Nathan Hale was executed. A British soldier and a ship workman reported that Nathan was executed at Rutgers orchard, about four miles south of the Beekman mansion, near Duane and Vesey streets (present-day City Hall). The location has perhaps been misinterpreted, considering the city had dozens of apple orchards in 1776.

Henry Rutgers had died in 1750, but his vast estate, encompassing the area from Vesey Street to Duane, over to First Avenue and Broad Way, was maintained until the British occupied the region. It was a well-kept piece of property, historian Hugh Macatamney wrote, "with elegant shrubbery in the geometrical style of rural gardening . . . long walks, bordered with box-wood and shaded and perfumed with flowering shrubs, extending in various directions." Rutgers's mansion had been turned into a barracks for British soldiers. Around the estate, mainly on the southern side, was an immense apple orchard, "while the pasture lands and cultivated fields extended toward the north." The orchard had been turned into a staging point for Howe and his troops, where soldiers could arrive from Staten Island and get settled before heading out into the field for battle. Solomon Wooden, referring to where Nathan was hanged, later wrote that "an apple tree in Rutgers orchard" was chosen by William Cunningham. Later still, New Jersey native Daniel Wandell, then ninety-eight years old, told a local newspaper that when he was thirteen he visited Rutgers orchard on a day when crowds of "patriotic and loyal citizens desirous of paying respect to the memory of Capt. Hale" were wandering about the scene. One slave gave him an apple that he said had been "grown on the tree on which Capt. Hale was hanged." Wandell added, "The old [native] was a witness to the execution" and said Nathan was buried a "few feet from the tree."[2] All that being said, why would Cunningham, who was running behind schedule, march Nathan four miles south to hang him?

Cunningham would not grant Nathan his final request that the letters he had written earlier be sent. Legend has always claimed that in an open display of condescension, Cunningham took the letters from Nathan and ripped them up in front of him, laughing at the patriot. In 1859, historian Henry Howe described Cunningham during this exchange as venomous and seething. Taking the letters from Hale, Cunningham reportedly said, "The rebels should never know that they had a man who could die with such firmness." This story then appeared in every interpretation of Nathan's life thereafter. But in fact, Cunningham took the letters from Nathan, but did not destroy them that day.[3]

Cunningham, a heavily built, red-haired Irishman, with a red nose brought on by years of hard drinking, was thought to be about sixty years old. On that morning, he walked with his prisoner to an apple tree as several armed soldiers, John Montrésor, and one slave closely followed him. Many men and women working in the region flanked them on the right and left. There would be no formal ceremony or dramatic display of gallantry, only the option for Nathan to make one final proclamation of his guilt before he was forced to leap from a ladder to his death.[4]

"Any last dying speech and confession?" Cunningham asked as Nathan took his place on the ladder.[5]

E. E. Hale later wrote that at this moment Nathan asked to be shot rather than hanged, but was quickly denied this more humane way of execution.[6]

Nathan accepted his sentence. He stood proudly, head titled skyward, posture firm, hands tied behind his back. Then, in a phrase that has been misquoted throughout the centuries and turned into a slogan for patriotism, he said, "I am so satisfied with the cause in which I have engaged that my only regret is that I have not more lives than one to offer in its service."[7]

This is perhaps the most often misremembered moment in the Nathan Hale story: What did he say moments before he was executed? The line attributed to him—"I only regret that I have but one life to lose for my country"—is only a paraphrase of what Nathan actually said, which was reported in the *Independent Chronicle* on May 17, 1781, as part of an article many believe William Hull narrated to the reporter. But contemporary scholars and historians have said the apocryphal quote was derived from the popular Revolutionary War play *Cato*. This poetic line fit with the heroism being created around Nathan's legacy at the time it became popular decades after his death. His peers wanted him to be remembered not as a failed spy, but as a hero who spoke with patriotic self-worth at the moment of his death. In contrast, the *Essex Journal*, on February 2, 1777, reported Nathan's final words as "You are shedding the blood of the innocent. If I had ten thousand lives, I would lay them all down, if called to do it, in defence of my injured, bleeding country."

After Nathan had finished speaking, Cunningham said, "Swing the rebel off!"[8]

British lieutenant Fredrick Mackenzie, who was stationed in New York at the time of Nathan's execution, paid tribute to Nathan in his diary on that day:

> A person named Nathaniel Hales, a Lieutenant in the Rebel Army, and a native of Connecticut, was apprehended as a Spy . . . upon Long Island; and having this day made a full and free confession to the Commander in Chief of his being employed by Mr. Washington in that capacity, he was hanged at 11 o'clock in front of the Park of Artillery. He was about 24 [sic] years of age, and had been educated at the College of New-haven in Connecticut. He behaved with great composure and resolution, saying, he thought it the duty of every good Officer, to obey any orders given him by his Commander-in-Chief; and desired the Spectators to be at all times prepared to meet death in whatever shape it might appear.[9]

Mackenzie was reporting the death of Nathan as he had heard it from sources who were present, one of whom was Tunis Bogart, an ordinary farmer from Long Island. During September and October 1776, Bogart worked for the British as a wagon driver and was in New York at the artillery park on the day Nathan was hanged. Ever since then, Bogart said in 1784, he had "never been able to efface the scene of horror from" his mind. "It rises up to my imagination always. That old 'Devil Catcher' Cunningham was so brutal, and hung him up as a butcher would a calf." Bogart said Cunningham's slave tossed the rope that would hang Nathan over the limb of the tree as the women in the crowd "sobbed aloud." As they cried out, Cunningham cursed at them, warning that if they didn't stop, one of them "would likely enough themselves come to the same fate."[10]

Nathan hung for three days, his flesh rotting in the unseasonably hot September sun as his corpse was mocked and spat on before a slave finally cut his body down and buried it, reportedly unclothed. Thus was America's first spy of the Revolution interred, somewhere near present-day Third Avenue, between Forty-sixth and Sixty-sixth streets, without ceremony or formal prayer inside a shallow, unmarked grave.[11]

Chapter 20

A Brother's Search

A T THE HALE HOMEstead 138 miles northeast of where Nathan had been hung, Enoch Hale sat down on what he called the "pleasant morn" of September 23, 1776, to write two letters.[1] Enoch was one of only two of Deacon Richard Hale's sons to be home (David Hale, also home with Enoch, was a toddler). Five of Richard's sons had dropped everything to take up arms against the British. As far as Enoch knew, Nathan was in New York. Enoch had written to him on August 15, sending the letter via a cousin who had joined the militia and, like thousands of young and eager colonists, headed south to help crush the redcoats in what was to be the first major battle of the war: New York. In his return letter, Nathan had sounded moderately cheerful, encouraged by General Washington's progress, if a bit anxious and indecisive regarding what the future held for the troops. "Our situation has been such this fortnight or more as scarce to admit of writing."[2]

Instead of focusing on the negative, which Nathan had never favored, he described for Enoch a story of great bravery exhibited by five men from his company (the Fosdick episode), then abruptly ended the missive because he had "other brothers to write letters to" and little time to do it.[3]

A week after Enoch penned that entry in his diary regarding writing to Nathan, on the morning of September 30, 1776, it finally hit Enoch—and the rest of the Hale family—that Nathan might be in trouble. No one had heard from Nathan in well over a month. It was unlike him not to write or at least send word home via a messenger heading through Coventry. On top of that, several Coventry residents returning from New Haven and farther south near the New York border had reported hearing stories of Nathan's demise. No one was certain what had happened, but it was said that Nathan had met death somehow.

Autumn was thick in the New England air. The leaves on the oak and maple trees scattered about the Hale farm had turned a shiny bronze. Cold air was on its way. Yet, despite the changing weather and concern for Nathan, there was work to do. Enoch was helping to build a new "mansion," as it would be known, in place of the smaller house the Hales had all grown up in. As soon as the last nail of the new house was driven in, the old place was coming down. Nathan, who was born in the old dwelling, had been gone so long by this point he hadn't seen any of the work on the mansion.[4]

Just twenty-two, Enoch had passed up a role in the Revolution for a life in the church. He had graduated from Yale with Nathan in 1773 and had taken a short teaching tenure in Windsor, Connecticut, while continuing his studies in theology. By October 10, 1775, the Windham County Association of Ministers had licensed Enoch to preach. Several months later, he returned from Windsor to Coventry and, same as many new ministers of the day, waited on a calling from a congregation that needed him. To keep in practice, he "preached and lectured" to neighbors, friends, and family.[5]

Enoch was devoted to Nathan, probably more than Nathan was to him. Indeed, in a letter to Nathan back on May 30, in sincerity, Enoch had complained to his brother that he wasn't paying much attention to him since running off to war. Nathan wrote back on June 3, reassuring Enoch it wasn't out of spite or malice. "You complain of my neglecting you," the captain wrote. "It is not, I acknowledge, wholly without Reason—at the same time I am conscious to have written to you more than once or twice within this half year. Perhaps my letters have miscarried."[6]

Enoch rode to his uncle's farm in Salmon Brook on September 30, 1776. Enoch was closer to the Reverend Joseph Strong, his mother Elizabeth's brother, than to anyone else in the extended Hale family. Since graduation, heading into a life of the ministry himself, Enoch had sought advice from the noted preacher on several occasions and practiced his lecturing skills on him. One of many chaplains serving soldiers in the Revolution, Strong was popular among members of his congregation. "Naturally possessed of great self-command, correct judgment and a penetrating mind, [Strong] was eminently qualified for ruling a church," a parishioner once said of him. "His ministry was crowned with remarkable success."[7]

Enoch had made several trips per week out to the Strong farm. One can be certain that with rumors of Nathan's death spreading throughout Coventry, on this day Enoch was anxious to find out if Strong had any information about Nathan. The reverend had split his time between his congregation and ministering to troops on the front lines. Perhaps someone had said something to him during one of his evangelical sabbaticals into New York. The last the Hale family knew, Nathan was leaving Long Island with his regiment and heading into the city via Brooklyn Heights. At some point he had once again fallen ill; not from smallpox or scurvy, which were spreading among rebel camps; but with a bout of influenza he had spent weeks trying to recover from, a virus Nathan had struggled with all year. But as far as the family knew, Nathan had been feeling better, even though he was unable to contribute to Washington's effort the way he had wanted to. He had probably given up quill and ink altogether that August and September while getting his strength back and joining Knowlton's Rangers.[8]

Like his brother, Nathan held a special place in his heart for the Strong family. In a June 3, 1776, letter to Enoch, he specifically ordered Enoch to "Forget not frequently to visit and strongly to represent my duty to our good Grand-mother Strong. Has she not repeatedly favoured us with her tender most important advice? The natural Tie is sufficient but increased by so much goodness, our gratitude cannot be too sensible."

Quite confused about Nathan's whereabouts and condition, not to mention those unsubstantiated rumors circulating through Coventry that he was dead, Enoch mounted his horse on September 30, said his good-byes to his father, Richard, and stepmother, Abigail Adams, joining them in a lengthy prayer, and began his journey to Salmon Brook. With any luck, he'd be able to return home with good news about Nathan. Perhaps everyone had misinterpreted Nathan's illness for something more dismal? Enoch knew there was only one way to find out.[9]

This solitary ride to his uncle Strong's farm in Salmon Brook, twenty miles northwest of Coventry, took Enoch Hale through Hartford, over the Connecticut River via the ferry. By that evening Enoch was sitting inside his uncle's farmhouse, reminiscing about family, thanking the Lord for getting him there safely, while later asking the question on everyone's mind back home: Had anyone heard from Nathan?

The news Enoch received upon his arrival could not have been hopeful. When he sat down that night to record the events in his diary, he wrote of how confusing the situation had become over the past week: "Hear a rumor that Capt. Hale, belonging to the east side of Connecticut River, near Colchester, who was educated at College, was seen to hang in the enemies lines at N York being taken as a spy—or reconnoitering their camp." It was the first time Enoch mentioned the possibility that Nathan had been hung as a spy. The rumors back home were centered on Nathan's having been killed in the line of duty. This was a different matter entirely—something Enoch had never considered, which made the story perhaps much more possible.

As might be expected, Enoch did not sleep well that night. His anxiety as he tossed and turned was born from an afternoon of uncertainty. Awake most of the night, he wrote of the current rumor, "Hope it is without foundation."[10]

When Enoch awoke the following morning, he was still fixated on the previous day's news. Enoch was known to obsess over things. The Reverend Dr. Dorus Clarke, a friend from Westhampton, Massachusetts, where Enoch would later begin his ministry, recollected how compulsive he could be at times. Speaking of Enoch's preaching skills, for example, Dr. Clarke said, "Mr. Hale . . . was calm and judicious, but not eloquent or moving. His habits were systematic and exact to a proverb."[11]

So mechanical was "Father Hale," Clarke went on to note, that he preached "with his accurate watch lying on the pulpit before him" to a prescribed length that rarely changed. But what set him apart most, perhaps, and spoke to how neurotic he could be, was his "simple rule" of having "twenty sermons on hand," each one carefully written and edited, "which he had not preached, so as to be prepared for any emergency which might befall him."[12]

Enoch would be celebrating his twenty-third birthday in a little more than three weeks. He was set to begin ministering to parishioners at the first church to have him. But with Nathan's fate unknown, he had no time to consider his own needs; he needed to get back home to Coventry and explain to the family what he had heard. Thus, after a "turkey dinner" with the Strongs, along with a promise to "exchange . . . Church next Sabbath," Enoch took the opportunity to hone his ministering skills by preaching the Reverend Strong a "lecture." Then, after being wished well by his uncle, he prayed, saddled, and rode.[13]

When he returned to Coventry on October 2, Enoch retired to the "meetinghouse"—the main church near downtown, in search of Joseph's brother, Elnathan. Uncle Elnathan was in town to visit family. He had moved from Coventry some time ago to the City of New York and would likely have more accurate information. The Hales couldn't abandon the hope that Nathan was still alive. Nothing less than a clear confirmation—and preferably some sort of proof—would change that. Status of a soldier or his regiment commonly became uncertain as the war waged on, with news often unclear by the time it reached home. After running into Elnathan at the meetinghouse, Enoch wrote, "Heard some further rumors of the Capt," which were in total disagreement with what he had previously heard.

Enoch was determined to find out for himself what was going on. Deacon Richard was fifty-nine, old for the time, and couldn't leave the farm. It was Enoch's obligation, as the only male in the household old and strong enough to ride. To abandon his brother now would not be in God's good graces. "The excellence of Enoch's example was proverbial," Dr. Clarke wrote. "His whole life was modeled upon the principles of the Bible."[14]

After a second trip to the Reverend Strong's a day later, the question of whether Nathan was still alive consumed the future minister's mind. Partly Enoch was uncertain because Connecticut and New England had no fewer than a half dozen Hale families, many of whom had children named Nathan and/or Nathanael. It posed great difficulty for Enoch, Richard, and the rest of the family during their search for answers: Was it *their* Nathan that people in town and relatives were speculating about?

Enoch returned again to Coventry and heard further rumors about Nathan during each trip he took for supplies or preaching. Though Enoch did not add any entries in his diary in those two weeks, it's likely that the Hales spent many a night praying for good news while waiting for word from Nathan. On October 14, Enoch traveled up the road from the Hale farm to see the Reverend Dr. Joseph Huntington, his and Nathan's former tutor and mentor, the one man who could offer him solace, comfort, and sagacious advice.[15] When Enoch reached his dear friend's house, he and Huntington searched for an answer in the Scriptures.

After Enoch left Huntington's later that day, he stopped at home for a brief period, then returned to Salmon Brook. The purpose of this third trip was to talk to Uncle Strong about obtaining a pass into New York so he could further look into what had happened to Nathan. By this time, New York was in the hands of the British, so it was suggested that traveling civilians acquire a pass to ride beyond or near enemy lines. The Reverend Strong may have had Tory connections, through which he could secure a pass for Enoch to safely travel wherever he needed to go. While waiting on the pass, Enoch preached "a lecture for Reverend Strong," then returned home. The following day, October 15, he rode back to Salmon Brook to pick up supplies (nails and other hardware for the new house), to find out if anyone had heard anything new about Nathan, and, with any luck, to get his hands on that pass to New York.

The reverend sent Enoch from Salmon Brook to East Windsor to call upon a local squire, William Wolcott, who had connections in New York. Wolcott, Enoch was told, could get him that pass. An hour after leaving Strong's, Wolcott came through and Enoch wrote in his journal of his plan to "ride to N York."[16]

On the same day, the Reverend Strong traveled south to New London to see if anyone in town had heard from their old schoolmaster. In New London, Nathan was esteemed, well liked, and had routinely received letters from his former students and friends. New London, although chock-full of

British sympathizers by that point, was closer to New York than Salmon Brook or Coventry. Chances were that if a rumor had traveled as far north as Coventry, someone in New London had also heard about Nathan.

With Uncle Strong on his way to New London, Enoch saddled for the sixth time in four days. But he wasn't heading home or into New York. Instead, he was taking a trip approximately twenty miles north of East Windsor, into Granville, Massachusetts, to see an old friend, a man whom he called Lyman, probably a Linonian peer of his and Nathan's from Yale. Lyman had just returned from New York, and Enoch knew he might either have run into Nathan or have news from soldiers in Nathan's regiment. Enoch hoped an answer was waiting for him at Lyman's so he wouldn't need to travel to New York.[17]

When Enoch reached Lyman's house in Granville on October 16, his good friend gave him dreadful news. "N York Accounts from my brother the Capt are indeed melancholy!" Enoch wrote that night in his journal.[18] Lyman reported that he had visited New York and had heard that Nathan had traveled near the second week of September to Stamford and crossed over Long Island Sound aboard a merchant ship. Word from soldiers on the front lines was that Nathan "had finished his plan but before he could get off [the island] was betrayed, taken & hanged without ceremony."[19]

Enoch had studied theology his entire life. He could recite many of the Scriptures from memory. Waiting on a church to call him for the pulpit, he had written sermons, preparing for the day when he would preach God's word. In one he had written that May, he indicated how he might have reacted to such alarming news. Enoch believed that having God in one's life was a "favor" the Lord had bestowed upon man, and that God had to be "delighted" with those who followed Him. As Enoch listened to Lyman, learning that his closest brother might have given his life for the cause of liberty, he knew that Nathan fell into this favorable light. Whatever had happened to Nathan, Enoch undoubtedly understood and accepted, was in the hands of the Lord.[20]

But Lyman had more information, the most distressing news that any of the Hales could have imagined. According to what Lyman had heard, Nathan had been betrayed not by a friend he had met while behind enemy lines, a loyalist, a Tory, or a British soldier who discovered his mission and turned him in, but by a member of the Hale family. "'Tis said [he was betrayed] by his cousin," Enoch wrote, "Sam Hale."[21]

Was it possible? Neither Enoch nor Lyman knew for certain. Lyman was reporting what he had heard from his sources in New York. None of it, he explained, had been confirmed.

Those who supported the Revolution, such as Enoch and Lyman, had little use for Tories. But thousands of farmers, merchants, and colonial citizens had remained committed to King George and England. Many kept it hidden from their colonial neighbors and kin. In some cases, as the war spread from Boston to Connecticut and into New York, rebels and Tories fought each other. Some clusters of rebel soldiers traveling through towns were said to have stumbled upon a Tory home and burned it to the ground. In response, Tories were known to sneak into rebel camps at night and cut off "the manes and tails of patriots' horses," which sidelined the animals for days, if not weeks. Some would also tear down rebel fences put up to mark territory and, if necessary, engage in violent firefights.[22] At one time, Washington had given orders for one of his aides to ride into Portsmouth, where a large Tory uprising was said to have occurred, and "seize every officer of the royal government, who had given proofs of an unfriendly disposition to the American cause." As the rebels were forced out of Long Island near the end of summer, the territory had turned into a haven for British sympathizers, among them young Samuel Hale. General Washington had heard from a number of sources that a large "body of Tories" was waiting on Long Island to "join the enemy's forces on their arrival"—many of whom were from Samuel's hometown.[23]

The mere thought that Samuel had betrayed Nathan would still have been a shock to the Hale family. Richard was especially hurt when Enoch returned to Coventry the following morning and relayed the news from Lyman. Richard loved his brother and respected and adored his nephew. But if this news turned out to be true, what would become of the family? How could one of their own betray Nathan, not to mention the colonial movement?

Back home, Enoch was now more determined than ever to confirm what Lyman had told him. After a good night's sleep, a solid meal, and plenty of time for prayer, he would rise before daybreak and ride once again, this time to New York, in search of Nathan.[24]

Chapter 21

Gloomy Dejected Hope

W ITH A PASS TO ride into New York, Enoch was prepared to journey into the center of the battle to find out what had happened to
his beloved brother. The suggestion that Cousin Samuel might have betrayed Nathan added insult to the already dismal news. It was too much to
believe: Nathan captured by the British and hung like some sort of criminal. Could it be true? It had been three weeks since the first rumor of
Nathan's death, after which Enoch had traveled across northern Connecticut nearly ten times seeking confirmation or repudiation of Nathan's condition or whereabouts. It seemed that everyone Enoch spoke to had something
to say. Yet few spoke with a certainty he could accept. No one in the family
had heard from Nathan since August, almost two months now.[1]

Since leaving Lyman's in Granville, having heard the most legitimate—
and the most grim—news since his search began, Enoch could view the situation objectively. "Some entertain all is not true," he wrote in his diary on
October 19, "but it is a gloomy dejected hope."[2]

Work on the Hale mansion, which would offer much needed extra space
for the growing Hale family, was nearly complete. A few minor projects

were still going on inside the house, but for the most part the shell of the structure and much of the detailed woodworking was finished. In the coming weeks, the old house, as it stood next to its successor, would have to be demolished and whatever could be salvaged stored away in barns for the winter. The mansion had been built in record time, surprising most in town.[3]

While dealing with the possibility that the first Hale casualty of the war might be Nathan, Enoch and Richard completed the immense Georgian colonial. The new home was a showpiece, a symbol of the wealth and re-pute Richard had in the community. A deacon at the First Meetinghouse since 1764, Richard had lost his seat in the General Assembly in Hartford to Ephraim Root, a local man, several years prior, but not his reputation among community members, and the mansion was a reminder that Richard Hale was still one of the most affluent men in Coventry.

As Enoch rode, big changes were taking place in the region where he was headed. From the Bronx, the Americans were being pushed north toward White Plains. The British, who had taken total control of the city, were positioning themselves to move on Philadelphia and New England next. While still stationed at Harlem Heights on October 15, Washington had to make several major decisions that could make or break the rebellion. If the British were allowed to cross into New Jersey via the North River and march on into Philadelphia, the war was over. Because of this, Congress and the general debated whether to evacuate New York entirely, or stay in Harlem and fight.[4]

As the middle of October came and went, the Continental Army fled to White Plains with a growing British army coming up their backs, an army that now included a large German Hessian force that had arrived in early summer.[5]

Although Enoch didn't know it yet, if the Americans were heading north into White Plains and farther into Connecticut and New York State, it was going to be much easier for him to locate Nathan's regiment, or a soldier from the unit, and get to the bottom of what had happened to the captain. Enoch assumed that if his brother had been hung, he would be allowed to take his body home for burial and collect his belongings.[6]

There was no telling how long Enoch was going to be away from home. After packing his saddlebags full of provisions, placing his Bible up front for easy access, he left Coventry a confused but devoted brother. By October 21, after the first full day's ride, he reached Southington, having traveled thirty-seven miles. Southington was a familiar place to the Hale family, and the perfect halfway point to rest for the night. William Robinson, a classmate of Nathan and Enoch's, had grown up in Lebanon, an hour's ride from the Hale farm, but had relocated to Southington after college. A cousin of Connecticut governor Johnathan Trumbull's, Robinson had accepted a teaching tenure in Windsor after graduation; he and Enoch had stayed in touch ever since.

When Enoch arrived in town, Robinson was, unfortunately, ministering in Hatfield, Massachusetts; instead Enoch sought refuge while in Southington at the local meetinghouse, where Robinson had family connections. Enoch preached to what was a fresh Southington audience. First thing in the morning, he was resolved to rise and hit the trail once again, hoping to log another thirty or forty miles. New Haven was a short distance south. If he had time, a stop at Yale would be in order. Maybe one of their old tutors had heard from Nathan.[7]

General Washington's aide-de-camp Lieutenant Colonel Robert Harrison Harrison wrote to the president of Congress, John Hancock, alerting him of the army's situation in Harlem, which appeared to be rather desperate: "I am directed by his Excellency to acquaint you, that we are again obliged to change our disposition to counteract the Operations of the Enemy, declining an Attack upon our Front, they have drawn the main body of their Army to Frogs point with a design of Hemming us in, and drawing a line in our Rear." To prevent such an attack, Harrison concluded, Washington and his officers determined "that our forces must be taken from hence, and extended towards East and West Chester so as to out flank them." General Charles Lee, Washington's second-in-command, had arrived a few days before and "strongly urged the absolute necessity of the measure." Washington wanted to leave a defensive force behind at Fort Washington, "and to Maintain it if possible, in order to preserve the communication with the Jerseys."[8]

The British were on the move, too, landing "their Artillery and Wagons" at the point, the Battery between Staten Island and the City of New York. Moreover, British warships and schooners were spotted all over Long Island Sound.[9]

With Harrison's letter sent off to Congress, Washington ordered his troops to "punctually execute" his orders by hastily packing their tents and stores and ammunitions and heading north.[10]

In mobilizing thousands of tired, malnourished, sickly soldiers at once and sending them toward the Bronx and White Plains, Washington was dealing with an army determined, it appeared, to collapse under its own misconduct. Plundering was rampant. Soldiers were, on occasion, breaking into civilians' homes and taking what they wanted, trashing the dwellings. More often than not it was out of necessity, but Washington and his commanders saw any violation of the law as a black mark on the army as a whole. One soldier, Corporal George Wilson, a ranger, had been warned, but still thought it acceptable to ransack and loot a house in Harlem. After he was caught, Washington sentenced Wilson to "39 lashes," to be executed upon sunrise before the troops marched through the Bronx into White Plains.[11]

Before the army packed and left, however, Washington made it known that loyalty and dedication to the cause would not go unnoticed. He offered praise to troops who had taken part in an ambush near Harlem Heights a week earlier, adding, "The hurried situation of the General for the two last days, having prevented him from paying that attention to . . . the officers and soldiers who were with him in the Skirmish on Friday last, that their . . . good behaviour deserved . . . as they are offered with great sincerity and cordiality." At the same time, Washington said he hoped "that every other part of the Army will do their duty, with equal . . . zeal whenever called upon; and that neither dangers, difficulties, or hardships will discourage Soldiers, engaged in the Cause of Liberty, and contending for all that Freemen hold dear and valuable."[12]

After crossing the Harlem River on the morning of October 23 Washington's Continental Army set its tents at White Plains, with officers counting their numbers, assigning new posts, and digging in. Through reports from his officers in the field, Washington realized that Howe was at Throg's Neck, either preparing to attack the rebels from behind, or carry on along the shores of Connecticut and mount an attack from the north. Throughout the entire trip, Washington led the way, mounted on his horse, scouting favorable areas for repositioning, while "reconnoitering the grounds, forming posts and choosing sites for breastworks and redoubts." The general finally chose an elevated section of land overlooking downtown White Plains on the east and west sides. The position offered mobility, a clear view of the south, but stretched for three miles, nearly into the Bronx, which made a good part of the location near the Bronx River vulnerable to ambush, yet put them in the best position they could be to defend themselves.[13]

Once again, the British had lost an opportunity to put a stranglehold on the rebellion, mainly because Howe was relocating his own forces at the same time. As the Americans began to establish their new position, Washington had a problem with discipline once again, as officers and soldiers were, the general noted, meddling with civilian horses. This after being warned that any "officer, or soldier" caught with horses "belonging to the public, or any other not his own property will be severely punished."[14]

Although only twenty-three miles north of Harlem Heights, White Plains was a world away for an army being forcibly displaced. Because they were unfamiliar with the landscape and terrain, not to mention that Washington's advisers couldn't be sure Howe wasn't planning to attack at any moment, the general made his commanding officers "call roll" three times a day.

> And the General begs the officers to exert themselves, to keep their men from straggling away from the Camp—Officers and men would do well to reflect that their safety, their lives, and the liberty of their Country may depend on their being at hand, in case of an Alarm—Any Man who is found half a mile from the Camp, not ON COMMAND, will be punished very severely.[15]

All officers were ordered to meet inside Colonel Israel Putnam's quarters at three o'clock on the afternoon of October 23 to assess the situation and plan a strategy. In total, Washington had seventy-one regiments under his control. Since the beginning of summer, troop numbers had increased three-fold to about 28,500 men, with the largest addition, 9,700, from Connecticut. Nathan's regiment, among the thousands of soldiers now in White Plains, was under the command of Brigadier General Oliver Wolcott. Colonel Charles Webb was out in the field guiding Nathan's men in his absence. Webb was from Stamford, a few miles up the coast into Connecticut across the border from New York.

Webb kept a detailed orderly book representing his duties during Washington's relocation effort. Throughout the summer, Webb had noted on several occasions that Nathan had not attended meetings because he was ill. During a meeting on August 16, though, Nathan was one of four captains present; the week after, however, Webb wrote, "One Col: & one Lt: Col: Sick; Two Capt Sick, five Lieut: Sick." On August 23 and again on August 31, Nathan dragged himself from camp and made it to the meetings. On September 6, he was too ill to attend. "Two Captains Sick, Three Captains on Command." By then Nathan was one of Knowlton's Rangers and was preparing to exit camp for Connecticut: "1 soldier on Command with Col Knowlton," Webb recorded. This would be the official record of Nathan's assignment with Captain Knowlton. By September 20, it appeared that not even Webb knew of Nathan's status behind enemy lines. "One Col: one Lt: Col:, & 1 Maj Sick—One Capt: on Furlough . . . & 1 soldier with the Rangers." On September 27, Webb again noted Nathan's absence without comment: "1 Col: one Lt: Col & 1 Major, Sick: absent: one Capt: on Furlough, one soldier on Command with Col: Tupper, 1 soldier Sick absent, 1 soldier with the Rangers."[16]

Without hearing word of his capture, thirteen days after Nathan had supposedly been taken prisoner by the British on Long Island, the first official word of his demise surfaced in Webb's journal:

Camp at Heights of Harlem 4 of Oct: N: B, One Colonel present unfit for Duty. Lt: Col: on Furlough—Major Sick absent:—2 Capts present unfit for Duty, one Capt on Command, 1 [soldier] on Furlough, 1 [soldier] with Col: Tupper, 1 [soldier] Sick absent, and 1 [soldier] Supposed to be Executed in New York—[17]

Enoch decided against stopping in New Haven and instead rode toward Fairfield ("45 miles thro' N. Haven") on October 22. After spending the night praying and resting, he proceeded to Titus Mead's lodge in Greenwich (another twenty-eight miles) the following morning. Mead, a messenger for the American soldiers stationed near his lodge in Greenwich, was "a man to be depended on." While at Mead's lodge, Enoch was only ten miles from White Plains. Within an hour's ride he'd be at camp.[18]

At White Plains during the latter days of October, General Washington's troops were welcomed by a community of "hardy yeomen inured to toil," most of whom fully supported the rebellion. The people of Westchester County as a whole were said to have "imbibed an ardent love of liberty." Spirits were so high, some in town claimed a "star of Independence arose in the east" on the day Washington and his troops marched into the region. There was hope, indeed.[19]

Before leaving Titus Mead's lodge in Greenwich on the morning of October 25, Enoch had a spot of tea and a few pieces of pilot bread (hardtack), an unleavened, crackerlike biscuit made from wheat flour and water. Once fed, he slung his saddlebags over the rump of his horse, stuffed his Bible into the front pouch of his saddle, and continued on.[20]

Within a few hours Enoch rode to a nearby camp just outside White Plains, where he was pleasantly surprised to meet his stepbrother, Joseph Adams, and his brother Richard Hale Jr. Both had been stationed in Westchester County, near White Plains, just as Nathan should have been, along with a majority of Washington's army, setting up posts and awaiting word that the battle for White Plains was officially under way.[21]

By that time, Howe had sent "the greater part of his army in boats" through Hell Gate, "landing on Throg's Neck, an arm of the Westchester coast," just near the shores of the outer Bronx. For days they had sat, hovering around the area like a swarm of mosquitoes, breaking off into separate units, strategizing and waiting for the perfect opportunity to attack.[22]

After visiting with his brothers, Enoch rode on to Rye Ponds, a little village on the perimeter of White Plains. In four days, Enoch would turn twenty-three. He had spent the past month riding, waiting, and wondering about Nathan. He was closer to an answer now than he had ever been.[23]

The area Enoch had entered on the outskirts of White Plains was isolated and thickly overgrown with shrubbery and pine trees interspersed with clearings of sand and waist-high marram (beach) grass. The only road into town was lined on both sides with a stone wall, likely built by the Indians during the late 1600s. White Plains and the Bronx were boxed in on three sides by water. At first it seemed that Washington couldn't have chosen a more vulnerable location to pitch his tents. He had positioned his troops at the point of an arrowhead, closed in by rivers that were beginning to fill with Howe's navy.[24]

Of course, rebel commanders didn't see things this way, especially those generals viewing the war from farther upstate and points west and south. General Lord Stirling, who had been released by the British and sent to Peekskill, New York, as part of the traveling Convention Committee, saw Howe's movements as a blessing. "There appears to me an actual fatality attending all their measures," he wrote to one of Washington's aides. "One would have naturally imagined from the Traitors they have among them . . . they would have landed much farther to the Eastward." In other words, farther up the coastline of Connecticut. "Had they pushed their imaginations to discover the worst place, they could not have succeeded better than they have done." The idea was that they were vulnerable all holed up in one small region of the state; they would have been better off heading up the coast and attacking the rebels from behind, instead of going straight in at them.[25]

Stirling was one of many generals to put his stamp of approval on troop deployments to White Plains. In the days leading up to Washington's retreat from Harlem and word that Howe was moving his ships into the area of Throg's Neck, Stirling had said, "In this they will undoubted be joined by the villains in Westchester . . . it is therefore of the utmost consequence

that a Force should be immediately detached . . . to occupy these ports."
Stirling believed he was doing the right thing. "Experience will make us
both have and win; and in the end teach Great Britain that in attempting to
enslave us she is aiming a dagger at her own vitals." The rebel strategy was
to face off against the British as close as possible to the Hudson—a path-
way into upper New England, Washington knew, that had to be defended
at all costs.[26]

Washington was ordering his troops to dig in and expect action any day.
It was thought that Howe hadn't yet made a move because he was waiting
for additional artillery. One of the first teams of military police was put into
action during this week to roam through camp, keep order, or flank outward
into the surrounding regions to scout for redcoats.

Robert Hanson Harrison, the general's secretary, took the opportunity,
under Washington's order, to write to Congress regarding the "withdrawal
of the army to its new position." Congress had suggested that Washington
do whatever he could to stop the British from controlling the North River.
Harrison explained that although the army had tried, given the weaponry
and untrained numbers of men they had at their disposal, it had been virtu-
ally impossible. "To prevent the Enemy from possessing the navigation of
the North River and rendering the Communication and Intercourse between the States divided by it, extremely hazardous and precarious by means
of their Ships of War[, i]t has become a matter of important consideration
how to remedy the evil and to guard against the consequences which may result from it."[27]

The risk of losing communication with Congress consumed the general,
Harrison reported, and "as a matter . . . has employed much of his thought."
Washington told Harrison to relay to Congress what he expected from the
leaders around him. During a meeting between the two men, as Harrison
sat and wrote under the fading light of an oil lamp, Washington explained
that it was out of "absolute necessity, that Two distinct Armies should be
formed. . . . One to act particularly in the States which lay on the East, the
other in those that are on the South of the River." The men needed to be
split up. Having them all together in one area was as good as handing them
over to Howe.[28]

Beyond that, Washington asked Congress for its input regarding what to do. "The whole," Washington said, "[is] to be raised on a General plan, and not to be confined to any particular place by the Terms of Enlistment."[29]

If his men weren't split up into separate armies, Washington worried, "the apparent difficulty and perhaps impracticability of succors being thrown across the River, while the Enemy can command it, have induced his Excellency to submit the measure to their consideration, not knowing how their Operations may be directed, and foreseeing that innumerable evils may arise if a respectable force is not appointed to oppose their Arms wheresoever they are carried."[30]

As Enoch rode into White Plains after leaving Joseph and Richard's camp near Rye Ponds, he broke a section of his crupper (a strap holding his saddle down) and lost the other half of it along the trail. Forced to stop, he found a stable master, purchased a new strap, and continued on. When he arrived near the boundary of town, just miles from Colonel Charles Webb's camp, something startled Enoch. Alarmed, he quickly pulled back the reins of his horse, turned, and rode five miles back to "the edge of Greenwich," he wrote. But he never mentioned in his diary what had scared him.[31]

There was a lot of movement in the region at the time. Likely, what had frightened Enoch was the faint rustling of Howe's move on White Plains. October 25, 1776, was a Friday. By noon the following Monday, the battle for White Plains would be under way. Also roaming the region where Enoch had set up camp for the night was a regiment of British soldiers led by none other than Robert Rogers, the man who had captured Nathan. It was likely a reconnaissance force, sent in by Howe to assess the situation at White Plains before his troops marched. Without knowing it, Enoch had made the right choice in darting back toward Greenwich.[32]

When Enoch awoke on the morning of October 26, he was able to ride into Colonel Charles Webb's camp in White Plains without complication, where at long last he reached Nathan's unit. "Go to camp," Enoch wrote that morning, "see officers of Col Webb's Regiment . . . [and speak to] some of my Brother's men."[33]

The first account Enoch heard seemed to confirm at least part of the rumors. "He went to Stanford [Stamford] and crossed over the sound to Long Island," one of Nathan's men told Enoch.[34] Enoch would have known that Long Island, at the time Nathan had sailed for it, was entirely controlled by the British. And yet Nathan had written to him in late August saying that he had left Long Island. Why would he choose to go back? Enoch had to wonder. Why would a rebel captain—a man who was, Enoch had been told, suffering from the flu—travel behind enemy lines? There was, of course, only one explanation.[35]

Chapter 22

The Search Ends

Once he'd located and introduced himself to Colonel Charles Webb, Enoch was hit with the sobering news. Webb quickly corroborated the rumors. And so, as Enoch walked through camp and spoke to several different soldiers from Nathan's regiment, various versions of one story came out. All established that Nathan was dead. He had been hanged by the British. Everyone Enoch spoke to was certain of it. He didn't describe his feelings in his journal, but the news was the worst he could have expected.[1]

For those soldiers waiting at White Plains to do battle with Howe and his redcoats, if Nathan had indeed given his life for the cause, it was in the army's power to make sure that his life was not sacrificed for nothing. Even though the Americans had suffered great casualties at Harlem Heights and had been forced out of the City of New York, as Enoch worked his way around and learned the particulars of Nathan's final days, the morale of the troops around him was inspiring. Washington's men were confident they could win at White Plains. "Our work is now plain before us," one soldier wrote near this time, "to preserve to the end in supporting the Declaration we have made to the world."[2]

These soldiers held a "deep sense of duty." Most had not become patriots simply for "their own glory," but more so a "duty to God" first that provoked them to take up arms and make sacrifices for their country. As Nathan had displayed in taking on such a dangerous mission, "this rule of right was what motivated [him]. He had been surrounded from his birth with the doctrine that men should do right *because* it is right; and he went upon his hazardous mission just because it was right to go, not thinking what bodies would say, or expecting or caring to be called a hero." There was nothing romantic about the life Nathan Hale chose. His passionate, unconditional belief in the Lord, in addition to the piety Richard Hale had instilled in him, told Nathan that defending the colonies was what God wanted him to do. The average soldier viewed King George's men as murderers, noted one soldier fighting alongside Nathan, and "must bid adieu to America forever . . . therefore we have nothing to do but to be faithful to God and our country."[3]

Like their leader, most of Washington's men knew victory wasn't going to be achieved with one battle. In that respect, some soldiers and commanders viewed the retreat from New York not as a defeat, but as one more step toward triumph. "The price of liberty is not to be gained in a day," wrote a soldier from White Plains, "nor bought with a small price, but is the reward of long labor and unremitting exertions; and a people are commonly made to realize their dependence on Heaven for so great a favor, before they are crowned with complete success."[4]

Winning the war depended on unity. Civilians were called upon to support the cause any way they could, be it giving up their arms or supplying food and shelter to soldiers for a night or two along the trail of battle. Richard Hale had opened the Hale homestead to troops traveling through Coventry. He fed them, offered a safe place to camp for the night, and provided provisions as they went on their way. Nathan had shared what was a different viewpoint with Enoch just a few months before he left camp to spy, noting how different things were in the city as he got settled: "Facts render this too evident to admit of dispute. In this city such as refuse to sign the Association have been required to deliver up their arms. Several who have refused to comply have been sent to prison." And so it seemed that for every colonist that wanted to support the effort, scores of British sympathizers wanted nothing more than to be left alone.[5]

As Webb explained it to Enoch, he had learned of Nathan's fate from Captain John Montrésor, a British engineer, one of Howe's most trusted and close allies. Webb said Captain Montrésor had walked across enemy lines on September 23 waving a white flag, to give them the news "that one Nathaniel Hale," Enoch wrote, recounting his meeting with Webb, "was hanged for a Spy. . . . That Being suspected by his movement . . . [that] he wanted to get out of N York, was taken up & examined by the Gen & some minutes being found on him orders were immediately given that he should be hanged."[6]

All Webb could add was that Nathan went on a covert mission, carrying direct orders from General Washington. It was the last time, Webb explained, anyone had heard from Nathan. He hadn't been under Webb's command for quite some time, he explained. When Nathan left camp, he had been part of Thomas Knowlton's team of rangers.[7]

According to Webb, Montrésor had witnessed Nathan's execution. He had even befriended him as he waited to die. Montrésor hadn't made the trip across enemy lines for the sole purpose of letting Washington know that the British had fingered a spy and hanged him. Montrésor had other business. He had been sent to hand-deliver a letter from Howe to Washington, under a white flag of truce. The letter from Howe indicated a desire to make a prisoner exchange.[8]

Upon crossing enemy lines, Montrésor met with Joseph Reed, Washington's adjutant general. Alongside Reed were General Israel Putnam and Captain Alexander Hamilton. During this meeting, Montrésor casually related word that Howe had recently hung an American spy.[9]

After relaying the story of Nathan's capture and execution, Montrésor gave Washington's men a bit of a warning. The night before Nathan was taken prisoner, Montrésor said, had been extremely windy, and it was believed that a rebel soldier in the city had ignited the terrible fire. "According to Montrésor's account," Washington Irving wrote in his *Life of George Washington*, "a great part of the city had been burnt down . . . and the whole might have been so, but for the exertions of the officers and men of the British army." Montrésor blamed "American incendiaries" for the great inferno. Addressing Reed specifically, Montrésor said, "Several of [these incendiaries] were caught in the fact and instantly shot." In his letter to Washington, Howe made the "same assertion," adding that the incendiaries "were detected, and killed on the spot by the enraged troops in garrison."[10]

Nathan's good friend Captain William Hull, after hearing the rumor of Nathan's death, had decided to find out for himself what had happened. Enoch was told that Hull had, in fact, met with Montrésor and learned further details of Nathan's capture and execution. When Enoch asked where Hull was, he was told the captain was gone, probably to the front lines.

Sitting, listening to Colonel Webb, Enoch was astonished by how Nathan had been treated while waiting to die. "When at the Gallows," Webb continued, "he spoke and told that he was a Captain in the Continental army by name Nathan Hale."[11]

To Enoch, this sounded like the brother he knew. Here Nathan was about to be hanged and yet he admitted his place in Washington's army. Apparently, until his last breath Nathan had believed in the cause and his purpose in it.

As Enoch spoke to Colonel Webb, he realized his travels were not yet done. He needed to find Nathan's body and return it home. Enoch now believed that if Nathan had been executed, it was God's will. He understood that people, as he once wrote, must "seek first the kingdom and righteousness of God." Without that nucleus of divine conviction, men could not act according to the values they had been born with. "An interest in Christ, a treasure in heaven, secured by believing in him, is important more than any earthly good."

As the sun went down on Saturday, October 26, Enoch settled into Webb's camp for the night to sleep. Out in the field, Washington was becoming increasingly impatient. "The constant beating of [rebel] Drums," Washington wrote irritably that day, "on all occasions is very improper—there should be no Drum but on the parade and Main Guard."[12]

As he had studied the terrain over the past week, the general realized there was only one plausible way into camp: the road from the Bronx into White Plains, called alternatively Tarrytown Road or Old York Road.

Washington thought it "necessary to inform the officers and soldiers, that, in such a broken Country, full of Stone-Walls, there is no Enemy more to be despised, as they cannot leave the road." He encouraged several units to set up surveillance along Tarrytown Road, "by taking post in the Woods . . . where [British soldiers]," he was certain, "will not venture to follow."[13]

Encouraging men with weapons that routinely misfired to hide like snipers in the brush and pick off Howe's men as they marched by was an overly optimistic suggestion on the general's part. Some soldiers would heed his advice, while most others would sit and wait without engaging the enemy or drop arms and run. Realizing this, not to mention how vital it was that the rebels take a stand on the road, Washington upped the ante, offering an incentive many could not refuse. "As an encouragement to any brave parties, who will endeavor to surprise some of them," for every "Trooper, with his Horse and Accoutrements," captured and brought back to camp, a "100 Dollar" bounty would be paid.[14]

One hundred American dollars was a significant amount to men who were making between $6.67 and $9.00 per month (privates to sergeant majors). Thus, a onetime payment of $100 was more than a private could earn in a year's worth of service.[15]

If anyone had questioned Washington's decision to set camp at White Plains, thinking it a vulnerable tract of land, the next two days would prove what a masterly piece of strategy it had been. Washington had chosen an ideal spot. On the night Enoch arrived, for instance, an American unit "surprised a picket of [Robert] Rogers's regiment"—possibily the same brigade who had spooked Enoch a day before he arrived in camp—"of rangers . . . taking thirty-six prisoners . . . and sixty muskets," which the Americans could use. Washington surmised that Howe couldn't surprise him from the rear because the Americans had positioned themselves around a ravine and a lake. If Howe attacked, he would have to send his troops directly at Washington up that one road into town.[16]

As the general prepared for an assault, Howe and his men crossed from New Rochelle and set camp in Scarsdale, just north of the Bronx, approximately four miles from White Plains. One of Washington's generals, the peg-legged Nathanael Greene from Rhode Island, wrote to Congress, expressing his glee at what he had witnessed in White Plains, noting, "The troops were in high spirits, and in every encampment, since the retreat from New York, had given the enemy a drubbing."[17]

Still, Enoch could not have chosen a more hazardous time to visit camp. All around him were soldiers—British and American—digging in, setting up sentinels and organizing fortifications, preparing to engage. Soon he would need to return home with some sort of explanation, preferably with Nathan's body and/or belongings.

In his *History of the United States of America*, George Bancroft referred to this stage of the conflict as the "battle which was to be the crisis of the war." Bancroft argued that White Plains was the turning point for the Americans; how the Americans performed in White Plains would either lead them to victory or strike a defining blow to the rebellion.[18]

During the early-morning hours of October 28, with fog hovering at eye level amid the swamps and creeks of Westchester County, Howe began his march into White Plains. At Hart's Corner, "a small hamlet in Greenburg, situated about three miles south of White Plains," Howe's men advanced in two separate columns, driving back "a large party" of soldiers Washington had put in position to foil any stealthy attempt by the British to surprise the Americans. This defensive line acted as a warning to the rest of the troops a mile or so back.[19]

Washington, in a move that probably saved the Continental Army from total defeat, stationed the bulk of his men on the top of Chatterton Hill, "defended by an abattis and two nearly parallel lines of entrenchments, [a] right flank and rear protected by a bend in the Bronx, [with the] left resting on very broken ground too difficult to be assailed." An *abatis* was a structure designed to protect the front lines. Branches of brush and small trees were sharpened like darts and pointed toward the enemy. "Here [Washington] seemed determined," Benjamin Tallmadge, Nathan's old friend from Yale, now a major and stationed along the front lines of the assault, later wrote, "to take his stand, his lines extending from a mountain on the right [Chatterton Hill] . . . to a lake or large pond of water on his left." In the front, an "intrenchment was thrown up from right to left." Beyond the line of abatises, Tallmadge reported several men, armed with "long poles with iron pikes upon them."[20]

When the column of British soldiers made it to the end of Tarrytown Road, Tallmadge was surveying a dead area of land where no troops had been camped. Soon, Tallmadge crossed a small river that was between the American and British lines. Tallmadge was scouting, on the lookout for a possible sneak attack by the British.

Sure enough, the British charged up Tarrytown Road, and Tallmadge made a gallop for the water, hoping to cross it and take a stand with several hundred American troops waiting on Chatterton Hill to fight off any surprise attack. But as he entered the ravine, the Reverend Dr. Trumbull, the army's chaplain, came out of nowhere and "sprang up from behind . . . on [his] horse."[21]

Both men, along with Tallmadge's horse and all of his equipment, went "headlong" into the water. "This so entirely disconcerted me," Tallmadge wrote, "that by the time I reached the opposite bank of the river, the Hessian [mounting the assault with British] troops . . . considered me their prisoner."[22]

Luckily for Tallmadge, Washington's men stationed on the hill nearby rained a cannonade of fire down upon the Hessians and British. It surprised hundreds of redcoats, who soon retreated "down the hill in disorder, leaving a considerable number of corpses on the field."[23]

Tallmadge immediately "remounted his horse" and took off. About ten minutes later, having traveled a mile or so, he entered camp and explained to Washington what was taking place on Chatterton Hill.

This was it. The battle for White Plains was on.

By the time Washington heard the news, the British had regrouped and made a second attempt to take Chatterton Hill. But the Americans held their ground and "gave them a second warm reception," Tallmadge wrote. "A severe cannonade was kept up from both armies through the day, and every moment did we expect the enemy would have attempted to force us from our lines."[24]

Once Howe realized American forces were not going to back down from Chatterton Hill, he reportedly told his men, "The rebel army could not be destroyed." Only eight rebel prisoners had been taken, with total casualties on the American side not exceeding one hundred. According to historians Martha J. Lamb and Burton Harrison, "The British lost double that number."[25]

Howe and his men retreated, camping for the night nearby, waiting for the next opportunity to strike. The following morning, however, it rained heavily. While the British waited, Washington moved the bulk of his troops, including the sick and wounded, back even farther, about two miles north. The next day, as the rains continued, Howe ordered his troops south, back into the Bronx.[26]

For now, it appeared, the fighting was over.

Once again, Howe had seen the opportunity to crush what some later believed was the "American centre," the heart, essentially, of Washington's army. But the British leader failed to take advantage of his superior military force.[27]

Seen riding the front lines, encouraging soldiers to be patient and unyielding, Washington must have taken great comfort in knowing that he had thousands of men still willing to fight beside him. Even though one could argue the Americans lost the battle of White Plains, having been forced to retreat north, it was indeed a triumphant moment for the general, whose army took far fewer casualties than that of his British rival.[28]

Near the end of October, Colonel Charles Webb's regiment left camp to support a line gathering north of White Plains. Enoch mounted and rode out of camp on October 29, confident in the information he had obtained. And yet something he heard that morning began to eat at him. He was confused. "Some deserters asserted the fact," Enoch wrote before leaving, "& described his person—Lieut.—said he saw a Woman that said she was then in NY, saw—& knew him hanging, having been before acquainted with him."[29]

Who was this woman? According to Webb, she said Nathan's executioners had left him hanging for several days after his death, and that indignant British soldiers had ridiculed the captain, treating his remains with the utmost disrespect.

Leaving convicted spies hanging from their place of execution for days became a grisly tradition for the British. "It was the custom of war thus to treat spies as a terrible example and warning," George Dudley Seymour wrote. Some reports said Nathan's corpse had been spat upon by soldiers passing by, and that redcoats skewered cartoons, making fun of Washington, to Nathan's chest as if it were a bulletin board.[30]

A British officer who wrote a letter from New York on September 26, 1776, to a friend in England described Nathan's corpse as he viewed it a day after the execution: "We hung up a rebel spy the other day, and soldiers got, out of a rebel gentleman's garden, a painted soldier on a board, and hung it along with the Rebel; and wrote a poem on it—General Washington—and I saw it yesterday beyond headquarters, by the roadside."[31]

Regarding Nathan's personal belongings, Enoch noted in his journal, "They are mostly saved. His money (if he left any) plundered—& Considerable due to his under Officers, as well as 25 Dol. That belonged to Asher Wright, & 42 to another which he had in keeping." Asher Wright, Nathan's servant, had likely taken Nathan's trunk. Enoch was certain he could find Asher. If he did, perhaps Asher knew where Nathan's remains were interred.[32]

That night, Enoch rode straight through to Greenwich and spent the night once again at Titus Mead's lodge. As he settled in, accepting the notion that his closest brother had been strung up by the British, many questions began to weigh heavily on his mind. Later, E. E. Hale, Enoch's grandson, would write of this moment, "The disgrace of his being hanged rested on the whole Connecticut household from which he came. The method of his death was what they grieved for." In the years that followed, E.E. added, "My own father," who was named after Nathan, "was forbidden to speak of him to his father, because the whole was so painful."[33]

On his knees, praying before bedtime on the night of October 29, Enoch certainly began to ask, *Why had Nathan crossed enemy lines to begin with? Why had he been accused of being a spy? Was it Cousin Samuel Hale, as he had heard back home, who betrayed him? What was Nathan doing on Long Island?*

Although Enoch would make a fruitless trip to recover Nathan's belongings before heading back to Coventry, it would be years before the Hale family had answers to these questions and had those details that Consider Tiffany recorded of Nathan's journey behind enemy lines as a spy.

Chapter 23

HOME

After hearing confirmation of Nathan's execution from an authority he could trust, Enoch planned to head back to Coventry at once, having altogether given up on searching for Nathan's belongings. He was desperate to share the latest news with his family. He stopped at Titus Mead's lodge to leave a letter for "two soldiers" who could check on Nathan's belongings in the coming days and, at a later time, let him know where they were.[1]

On November 2, Enoch rode into Granville, Massachusetts, no doubt to share the news he had learned with those who had helped him along his journey. He spent four days at his friend Lyman's house. His investigation into Nathan's possible death had come full circle: A journey that had begun in Granville back in early October was now, a month later, ending there. It would have been customary for Enoch and Lyman to pray together and speak of how dignified Nathan had been at the time of his death—and yet Enoch made no reference in his diary regarding his feelings or thoughts.[2]

Enoch returned to the Coventry farm on November 6. By November 16, Fort Washington and its battalion of 250 men, located on the east side of the

North River, fell into British hands. Fort Lee, New Jersey, on the opposite side, was abruptly deserted by the rebels two days later. Near the end of November and into early December, the British swarmed northern New Jersey and took control of Newport, Rhode Island, thus cutting off New England. Meanwhile, Washington and his troops fled south into New Brunswick. On December 7, Washington crossed the Delaware River and waited there. The British stayed close behind and set up camp in Trenton. By the middle of December, Washington received reinforcements by way of Horatio Gates and John Sullivan's forces. Patient Washington then waited until Christmas night, December 25, and along with General Henry Knox and his troops crossed the Delaware again and launched a surprise attack on British and Hessian troops encamped at Trenton. The following day, with Generals Nathanael Greene and John Sullivan leading the way, the attack continued, and Washington's army, in a major victory, took Trenton.[3]

Nathan's death had no effect on Washington's efforts in November and December. No one talked of Nathan's execution, and it was of little concern, generally, to the conflicts the Americans were waging.

Not until two months after he returned home, in January 1777, did Enoch again mention Nathan in his diary. On January 25, Enoch took a trip into Hartford, then rode three miles south into Wethersfield to meet up with Major John Palsgrave Wyllys, "who has just returned from captivity at New York," Enoch wrote. Wyllys was a brigadier major from General James Wadsworth's unit. He, Enoch, and Nathan had attended Yale together. Wyllys had delivered the Latin salutatory oration in 1773 at graduation. During the retreat from Harlem Heights the British had captured Wyllys, but had recently exchanged him for a British officer.[4]

Wyllys explained how he had seen Nathan's diploma while he was in lockup. "The Provost Marshal," he told Enoch, "showed me, who also had two letters of [Nathan's], one to you, the other to his Commanding Officer, written after he was sentenced," which contradicted reports that Cunningham tore up the letters in front of Nathan.[5]

Though Enoch had chosen not to join the rebel effort militarily, his life in Coventry was gravely affected by death both in the war and on its sidelines. During the summer of 1776, as he and Nathan corresponded, Enoch had recorded in his diary one funeral after the other. "Buried a child . . . which died suddenly Friday night of the throat ail," he wrote on one day. "Wife of friend very sick, has been put to bed, her infant died this morning," he noted days later. At times, Enoch was the minister for two burials on the same day, four or five in the same week. Musket balls were killing husbands, brothers, and sons in New York. But people were dying back home at a rate few could comprehend. During all of this, it was Nathan, Enoch had noted in his diary, that he had received a letter from; this with four other brothers fighting and writing to him.[6]

Leaving Wethersfield after talking to Wyllys, Enoch rode to Southington, where he spent the next several months working toward his vocation as chaplain. On June 4, 1777, he returned to Coventry. On this afternoon, Nathan's belongings reached the Coventry farm, in what must have been a sorrowful day for the family. It had been almost nine months since Nathan's death. Life was, as much as it could be, back to normal for the Hales. Yet what was left of Nathan's life had arrived, dredging up all those feelings of loss once again. Inside Nathan's travel trunk were his uniform, army diary, receipt book, camp basket, book of muster rolls, his captain's commission, several letters, and a few other common essentials. It was as close as the family would ever get to a last word from Nathan.[7]

Two days later, Enoch sat down and "busied myself a little looking over some paper of my Brother Nathan's." Near the end of the month, June 28, the family gave away many of Nathan's personal belongings, obliging Alice Adams with Nathan's army receipt book and his little brother Billey, now a blacksmith, with his book of muster rolls. This gesture to Alice Adams might further have fueled the buzz of Nathan's love affair with Alice, but here again is a misunderstanding. Alice needed the book out of necessity: Paper was scarce during the war. Alice used the book's empty pages to write in. In that journal, in fact, Alice writes about her struggles with depression— but makes no mention of having ever loved or, for that matter, thought of Nathan Hale.[8]

That same day, in what would be his final journal entry for quite some time, Enoch bathed "in the pond [Coventry Lake]," then took an afternoon ride to his old friend the Reverend Cotton's house across town. It would be the last time Enoch Hale ever wrote about Nathan or discussed at any length the life and death of the Hale family's most celebrated military hero. Enoch would die in 1837, living to the age of eighty-four, having named his firstborn son Nathan, a name that would carry on in the Hale family up to the present day.[9]

Chapter 24

Personal Bravery

I n March 1777, richard Hale spoke out about his nephew's possible role in his son's capture. A month earlier a Massachusetts newspaper had erroneously reported that Samuel Hale, Nathan's cousin, was responsible for the rebel spy's death. The article, printed in the *Essex Journal*, had condemned Samuel, alleging, "Having nearly accomplished his designs, who should [Nathan Hale] meet but his . . . cousin Samuel, whom he attempted to shun; but Sam knew him too well . . . [and Nathan] soon found he was advertised, and so particularly described, that he could not get through Long Island."[1]

Writing to his brother a month after the article was published, Richard was a bit more tolerant and understanding than the *Essex Journal* had been. Opening the brief missive by wishing his brother "and Family . . . well," Richard, from the letter's tone and language, was clearly feeling the ill effects of Nathan's death and the war still raging around his Connecticut farm—all of which had disturbed his spirits considerably. "[The] Difficulty of the times is very so gloomy a day wee never saw before," he wrote, mentioning next how supportive Christ and God had been to the family. Prayer,

Richard explained, was helping the Hales through some of the more trying times they had experienced together. America was a difficult place to live, Richard said, before encouraging his brother to "prepare for a world of peace and Rest it is well the Calls in Providence are loud to prepare to meet our God and O that he would prepare us."

Richard continued, "You desired me to inform you about my son Nathan. You have doubtless seen the [*Essex Journal*] paper that gives the account of the Conduct of our kinsman Sam Hale toward him in York." Although the source for the article was never mentioned, it's likely that a Tory upset with Samuel had given the information to the newspaper, or the newspaper reported rumors swirling around Long Island as fact.[2]

Richard, who would die in 1802 (likely of consumption), had become ambivalent by this point; he didn't know what to believe anymore, or how to feel. The story of Samuel betraying Nathan had been reported in the newspaper; some credibility had to be given to it. But Richard was a man of God, a fair-minded Christian: He wasn't about to judge or condemn, especially his own nephew. How Nathan had been treated, or that he was likely "betrayed" by *someone,* Richard insisted, didn't really matter at this point. "A Child . . . is gone," he wrote, ". . . we are all through the Divine goodness well."

They had made it through the worst of times and were beginning to heal. Nathan had been dead for six months now. Wallowing in sorrow over his death would not bring him back, nor bring the family any comfort. Richard had no proof Samuel had turned Nathan in. The elder Samuel Hale (Richard's brother), according to William Hale, another of Samuel's sons, read the newspaper account with "great excitement" and was determined to "fully investigate the subject." This phrase, "great excitement," was a common colonial term describing extreme sadness. For William it expressed, in the most direct sense, his father's bewilderment and ambiguity over Nathan's death and young Samuel's potential role in it—and for Richard, when he realized it, well, that was good enough.[3]

In a letter dated close to the one-year anniversary of Nathan's execution, Cousin Samuel emerged to defend himself. By one account, Samuel had fled to England at some point after Nathan's death. Shortly before he left the country, addressing the one-page letter to "My dear Girl" (his wife),

Samuel struck down the *Essex Journal*'s accusation, writing, "Depend upon it there never was the least truth in that infamous newspaper publication charging me with ingratitude . . . attachment to the old Constitution of my country is my only crime with them—for which I have still the disposition of a primitive martyr."[4]

Gilbert Saltonstall had always been a great friend to Nathan. The two men had corresponded frequently throughout 1775 and 1776. There was "something" unaccountable "in the personal Bravery of some Characters that I have met within History," Saltonstall wrote to Nathan on March 10, 1776, six months before his execution, "where a Person with calmness can advance to a Post which to judge from appearances he knows is instant Death for him."[5]

Based on the foreign diplomacy of Silas Deane and Benjamin Franklin, France and the Continental Congress agreed on and signed a treaty in February 1778, which provided Washington's embattled troops with arms, ships, and supplies. This helped, but it would be another five years before British forces evacuated the City of New York and Brooklyn and headed home.

Three of Nathan's brothers died (all probably of consumption) within ten years of the war's end: Joseph (1784), Richard (1793), and Billey (1785). Nathan was the only Hale child to die in the war. For Nathan, nothing had mattered more than the colonies' freedom from England, regardless of the price. He was a well-educated, intensely religious, candidly opinionated, beloved pedagogue, who gave up what would have been a successful career in education to join the rebel effort and fight for liberation from England. But what separates Nathan from his contemporaries more than anything else is, even at a young age, he put Christian values before all else and believed man was at his best when serving his country under God's direction—which, in his short life, sustained him throughout what was the most pivotal year of the Revolutionary War and guided this American hero along a path he knew could, and likely would, end in death.

Epilogue

A SHORT DIALOGUE IN the 1962 classic western *The Man Who Shot Liberty Valance* perfectly outlines what early twenty-first century patriotic zeal has done for Nathan Hale and his legacy. At one point in this wonderfully made John Ford film, a newspaper editor laments, "When the legend becomes fact, print the legend." Nine times out of ten, the fable is more interesting—and certainly better known—than the truth. Case in point: Part of the Nathan Hale legend includes a story of Nathan meeting his military idol George Washington. Nathan was said to be at the Old John Street Theatre on or about the night of September 5, 1776, "in citizen's dress, accompanied by several ladies." The play Nathan was allegedly watching (*The American Volunteer*) fell in line with what Washington had recently summoned Thomas Knowlton to do: find a spy. As the play commenced, Knowlton, who was also there, spotted Nathan and, approaching him, supposedly said, "General Washington wishes to confer with you . . . at your earliest leisure."

When Nathan met with Washington sometime later, he was, at first, in awe of the great general. They had briefly run into each other a year before, but Nathan had never stood in front of Washington at attention, ready and willing to serve him in any capacity the general needed. Of this supposed meeting, nineteenth-century historian F. S. Bartram wrote, "Washington . . . communicated to Nathan Hale the nature of the business and asked him if he could suggest a proper person for the duty [spying]."

Upon hearing Washington's request, Bartram claims Nathan said, "I will go myself with your permission."

Washington warned Nathan how dangerous the mission could be, especially for an officer of his caliber, and, Bartram wrote, "suggested that some civilian in whom confidence could be reposed should be selected."

Nathan was never one to allow someone else to do a job he thought he could do more efficiently himself. Nathan was said to have explained to Washington that because he had superior "mechanical and scientific knowledge," which was true, compared to most of the men in his company, he was best qualified for the job.

"I urge you, sir, that I might be permitted to go," Nathan allegedly said to Washington.

It's hard to put much faith in this story, partly because Bartram made several historial errors. He called Nathan a colonel, when we know for certain Nathan had never made higher rank than captain. Perhaps more important, if we are to accept this moment, a well-documented scene in which Nathan shows up at a meeting of Knowlton's Rangers would have had no reason to occur.*

This story and that *Man Who Shot Liberty Valance* quote embody the essential characteristics of how Nathan Hale ended up on an American stamp and ultimately had thousands of schools, streets, buildings, and businesses named after him, not to mention memorial statues and monuments, toys, souvenir cups and T-shirts, parks, plaques, busts cast from every metal and stone imaginable, and, as I found on eBay while working on this book, a twelve-inch ceramic liquor flask from 1975 with an inscription that, in all

---

* See F. S. Bartram, *Retrographs: Comprising a History of New York City Prior to the Revolution* (New York: Yale Pub. Co., 1888), 150–53.

of its absurdity, is a misquote of a quote that Nathan never said to begin with: "I regret that I have but one life to give to my country."

The true man—Yale grad, schoolmaster, soldier, son, brother, devout Christian, captain, spy—led a much more simple life than the legend would lead us to believe; and yet, like any martyr for a cause, Nathan was propelled into American pop culture and politics. His name has become synonymous with patriotism, liberty, freedom, and sacrifice. A week does not go by without an op-ed writer, columnist, or blogger—Republican or Democrat—mentioning Nathan's spy mission and his "gift" to this country or using Nathan's story and his purported "I regret . . ." quote as a way to make some sort of political point.

One good example of how important the legend of Nathan became in American history is how Alice Adams's great-granddaughters foisted the story of Nathan and Alice's supposed romance on the public, going so far as to print a pamphlet in April 1927 under the title "The Correct Story of the Romance of Nathan Hale and Alice Adams." This waste of good paper dramatizes the apocryphal love affair. A note to the reader opening the leaflet claims, "This booklet is gotten out by the great-granddaughters of Alice Adams on the advice of prominent historians"—who go unnamed—"in order to refute an unwarranted attempt to break down a well-established fact of history."

There is no way to prove any of these claims. In fact, all of the available evidence points to the opposite. The Adams pamphlet is nothing more than regurgitated folklore that has followed the story of Hale for the past two hundred or more years.

Many people wanted a piece of the legend. As Nathan's fictionalized story grew and America began to embrace his image and likeness, presenting him as a symbol of patriotism, it became almost fashionable to quote Nathan or mention him in the realm of America's fight for freedom. A bust of Nathan has been standing in front of CIA headquarters in Langley, Virginia, for decades. It's meant as a reminder that Nathan never showed ambivalence. He didn't hesitate, and his courage and strength were remarkable. When the call came, he thanked God and eagerly went, which is why we (should) commemorate his memory. Not because he stood up to his captors and pledged his life for his brethren, but because his will could never be broken, no matter what he faced.

In my view, the most important memorial to Nathan is located in his hometown. In 1837 the citizens of Coventry formed the Hale Monument Association. Their purpose was simple: raise enough money for the building of a concrete monument or statue in Nathan's memory, dedicating it to the gifts the patriot had bestowed upon the army and his fellow countrymen. A plea to Congress for the money, according to Benson J. Lossing in his book *The Two Spies,* fell on deaf ears. But the committee, finally, after pleading its case, convinced the State of Connecticut to grant it $1,200 for the construction of an obelisk. Today it sits on an elevated spot in South Coventry, standing watch over the remains of Nathan's family members buried around it. This cemetery, just a few miles from the Hale Homestead on South Street, is a magnificent place. It reflects the long history of the Hale legacy in this town, and I encourage anyone who can to pay it a visit.

In 1812 a revolutionary-era fort was renamed Fort Hale, becoming the first monument of stone bearing Nathan's name. The fort is located near the entrance to New Haven harbor upon a place called Black Rock. The state capitol in Hartford, Connecticut, as well as the Wadsworth Athenaeum, just down the street, have marvelous though historically inaccurate statues of Nathan. A statue of Nathan stands at the entrance of the *Chicago Tribune.* Any place Nathan walked or stayed or ate or might have set foot in seems to have its own shrine dedicated to him.

In New York City, two places stake claim to Nathan's execution, one uptown, the other downtown. There's Nathan Hale Beach in Huntington, Long Island, where a stone plaque wrongly claims Nathan was captured on that spot. The Nathan Hale Schoolhouse in New London, Connecticut, has been moved around the city like a piece of old furniture.

On October 1, 1985, by an act of the General Assembly, persuaded by the Nathan Hale Chapter of the Sons of the American Revolution, Nathan became Connecticut's state hero.

The first mention of Nathan in literature was recorded in 1799. Hannah

Adams (no direct relation to Alice Adams), a self-taught historian, wrote a short account of Nathan's life in a book she called the *History of New England*. Adams referred to Nathan as a "young officer, animated by a sense of duty." In about five paragraphs, she outlined what has become the common Nathan Hale story: schoolteacher, soldier, spy, hero. Yet, her ending shows how significantly overlooked Nathan's story was during the decades that followed his death, as if history, or those writing it, wanted the manner of Nathan's death to be forgotten because of the possible embarrassment surrounding it. "So far," Hannah Adams wrote nearly thirty years after Nathan was executed, "Hale has remained unnoticed, and it is scarcely known such a character ever existed."

Not until the *Long Island Star* published Stephen Hempstead's remarkably detailed letter in 1827, in which he talked about Nathan's final moments, did Nathan's star begin to rise and the masses pick up on his story. This one letter spawned a series of biographies and articles, as Nathan's legacy grew in drama and unchecked facts with each passing decade.

When the British strung Nathan Hale up and hanged him, they did so to end his influence on the American effort. And yet, at the moment Nathan died on the end of that rope, the British gave birth to a national icon of liberty and patriotism. Nathan was, during his life, a captain in the American Continental Army who was willing to risk everything for the greater good of his country, a soldier who was, certainly, ill-prepared as a spy, but had a heart that led him to fulfill his duty. Sadly, death made him a martyr, a hero, an American soldier to—rightly so—celebrate and honor. Yet he was—and could have been—all those things in life, too.

ACKNOWLEDGMENTS

ONE CANNOT WRITE A book such as this without help. The two people who went above and beyond anything that was asked of them were Hale Homestead historian Lisa Sillitto, a tour guide and Hale family expert, and Hale Homestead historian Linda Pagliuco. Lisa and Linda were, from the first moment I asked, always ready and willing to help me in any capacity. Whenever I was stuck or needed to know something—those little facts you cannot find in books—in a pinch, a quick e-mail or a telephone call and I had my answer. I am forever grateful to both.

To all my friends at Hall Memorial Library, in Ellington, Connecticut, who managed to keep a seemingly never-ending flow of interlibrary-loan books passing through my waiting hands. Without these great people at Hall Memorial, who are so deeply passionate about books and have always supported my career, finding those rare texts would have seemed impossible. Additional thanks to Ann J. Arcari at the Farmington Library.

Inevitably I'll leave someone out, and I apologize for that. Thus, in no specific order, my sincere thanks go out to Mark LaFlaur, my former editor at Thomas Dunne Books; Peter Joseph, whose editing skills on this book proved invaluable; copyeditor Steve Boldt; Michaela Hamilton; Peter Miller, my incredibly determined manager; Adrienne Rosado, who is the best at what she does; Alex Young at Josephson Entertainment; Warner Bros.; Jeff Hutton; the Connecticut Historical Society; Martha Lund Smalley, research librarian and curator of the Day Mission collection at Yale University's Divinity Library; Beverly Lucas; Connecticut Landmarks (formerly Antiquarian & Landmarks Society) Executive Director Sheryl Hack; my wife and children; and publisher Thomas Dunne, for believing in my passion for this project.

NOTES

PROLOGUE: *THUNDER OF HEAVEN*

1. Edward R. Lambert, *History of the Colony of New Haven, Before and After the Union with Connecticut* (New Haven, CT: Hitchcock & Stafford, 1838), 65–68.

2. Ibid.

3. George Dudley Seymour, *Documentary Life of Nathan Hale: Comprising All Available Official and Private Documents Bearing on the Life of the Patriot* (New Haven, CT: privately printed, 1941), 510–11.

4. Allen Forbes, *Towns of New England and Old England, Ireland & Scotland* (G. P. Putnam's, 1921), 59–65; also, G. H. Hollister, *The History of Connecticut: From the First Settlement of the Colony to the Adoption of the Present Constitution* (New Haven, CT: Durrie and Peck, 1855), 95–97.

5. Charles Collard Adams, *Middletown Upper Houses* (Canaan, NH: Phoenix Publishing, 1983), 569–70.

6. Ibid., 569.

7. Daniel Lindsey Thomas, *Kentucky Superstitions* (Princeton, NJ: Princeton University Press, 1920), 90, "A mole on the neck is a sign that the person will be hanged."

8. Adams, *Middletown Upper Houses*, 569–70. I give Isaac Gridley's story a tremendous amount of credence because he was known later in life as an upstanding, respected, honest member of the Middletown, Connecticut, community in which he lived. People spoke highly of his character. In a Puritan world, where going to church on Sunday was the law, Gridley was known to stop people on the street who weren't attending service and "instead of arresting [them]," which he could

237

have under the authority of the justice-of-the-peace badge he wore, he'd "invite [them] to spend the night as his guest." Also see Seymour, *Documentary Life*, 315–18.

9. One would think the stories of Nathan Hale's mole were romanticized over the decades as Nathan's status as an American war hero rose, given how he was executed. Yet several independent sources back up these anecdotes. Although I chose to split it in half for the purpose of my narrative, the quote "I will never be drowned, I am to be hung" can be found with Isaac Gridley's story of the sailing misadventure in Adams's *Middletown Upper Houses*, 569. Additionally, in his testimony taken shortly before his death, Nathan's friend and servant, Asher Wright, discusses Nathan's mole. See Asher's testimony in Seymour, *Documentary Life*, 315–18. Further, in Betty Brook Messier and Janet Sutherland Aronson, *The Roots of Coventry, Connecticut* (Coventry, CT: 275th Anniversary Committee, 1987), and Austin Dunham, *Reminiscences* (Hartford: Case, Lockwood & Brainard, 1914), there's a story detailing the folklore attached to Nathan's mole and how, throughout the years, mothers and fathers scolded their children by using the mole story as a warning and deterrent for bad behavior.

Chapter One: *The Righteous and Patriotic Man*

1. I. W. Stuart, *Life of Captain Nathan Hale, the Martyr-Spy of the American Revolution* (Hartford, CT: F. A. Brown, 1856), 14–15; Lisa Sillitto, Hale Homestead historian, tour guide, and Hale family expert, and Homestead historian Linda Pagliuco, who has spent twenty-one years giving tours of the Hale Homestead for the Connecticut Landmarks Society, interviews conducted by the author, September/October 2006; the "church and state" quote, from Messier and Aronson, *Roots of Coventry*, 21.

2. Seymour, *Documentary Life*, xxvi.

3. Franklin Bowditch Dexter, *Biographical Sketches of the Graduates of Yale College* (New York: Holt, 1885–1912), 2:750–52.

4. Ibid.

5. Ibid.

6. Charles Swain Hall, *Benjamin Tallmadge: Revolutionary Soldier and American Businessman* (New York: Columbia University Press, 1943), 4–5; and Sillitto and Pagliuco, interviews.

7. Dexter, *Biographical Sketches*, 3:506.

8. Hall, *Benjamin Tallmadge*, 6–7.

9. Henry Sheldon, *Student Life and Customs* (New York: Arno Press, 1969), 86–87; and Seymour, *Documentary Life*, 458.

10. Henry Phelps Johnston, *Nathan Hale, 1776: Biography and Memorials* (New Haven, CT: Yale University Press, 1914), 14.

11. Ibid.; John Hale, *Modest Inquiry into the Nature of Witchcraft* (Whitefish, MT: Kessinger York Publishing Co., 2003), 116; and Augustus Alden, *Pilgrim Alden: The Story of the Life of the First John Alden in America* (Boston: Earle, 1902), 158.

12. Sillitto and Pagliuco, interviews.

13. Ibid.; and George Dudley Seymour, *Digressive History of Captain Nathan Hale and Major John Palsgrave Wyllys* (New Haven, CT: privately printed, 1933), 6–7.

14. Seymour, *Documentary Life*, 461; and Edwin Hatfield, *The Poets of the Church* (New York: A. D. F. Randolph & Co., 1884), 587.

15. Seymour, *Documentary Life*, 458.

16. Johnston, *Nathan Hale*, 14.

17. Ibid., 14–16; and Sillitto and Pagliuco, interviews.

18. Margaret Ellen Newell, *From Dependency to Independence* (Ithaca, NY: Cornell University Press, 1998), 57.

19. Seymour, *Digressive History*, 5

20. Benson Lossing, *The Two Spies: Nathan Hale and John André* (New York: D. Appleton and Co., 1886), 3–4.

21. Ibid.; and Sillitto and Pagliuco, interviews.

22. Alice Adams, diary, November 24, 1782, and March 28, 1783; and Seymour, *Documentary Life*, 585–86.

23. Ibid.

24. Ibid.

25. Sillitto and Pagliuco, interviews.

26. Letter, Richard Hale to Nathan and Enoch, December 26, 1769 (Connecticut Historical Society); also, Seymour, *Documentary Life*, 493–94.

27. Hall, *Benjamin Tallmadge*, 7.

28. Colonel R. Ernest Dupuy, *The Compact History of the Revolutionary War* (New York: Hawthorn Books, 1963), overall reading of entire text; also, letter, Deacon Richard Hale and Enoch Hale to Nathan (Connecticut Historical Society).

29. Reverend Leonard Bacon, *Sketch of the Life and Public Services of Hon. James Hill-house of New Haven* (New Haven: 1860), 5–7; also, Seymour, *Documentary Life,* 505.

30. "Minutes of the Linonian Society" (Yale University Library).

31. Dr. Jared Sparks wrote extensively about the Revolutionary War and George Washington's role as commander in chief; yet he also wrote about Nathan Hale after interviewing and talking to many of Nathan's former friends and students. This quote is from Charles Dudley Warner, *The Complete Writings of Charles Dudley Warner,* vol. 14, *As We Were Saying, As We Go, Fashions in Literature* (Hartford, CT: American Pub. Co., 1904), 341. Out of all the early Nathan Hale scholars to have studied his life in depth, I feel Sparks understood Nathan more intimately than most, simply because he put Nathan's life into the context of the world in which he lived. Dr. Sparks left a detailed offering of Nathan's early life. It's easy to glamorize someone after we know what he or she has accomplished. Or, as in Nathan's case, to see the heroism a man of his caliber displayed at the time he stared down the barrel of death. But Dr. Sparks understood that Nathan was a complex youth who grew into a man while at Yale and later became an inherently, deeply devout Christian and patriot, which went against the grain of many of his contemporaries.

32. Letters, Richard Hale to Nathan and Enoch, December 17, 1770, and August 13, 1771 (Connecticut Historical Society); also see Seymour, *Documentary Life,* 493–94.

33. Ibid.

CHAPTER TWO: *MOST INTIMATE FRIENDS*

1. Dexter, *Biographical Sketches,* 3:506; and Hall, *Benjamin Tallmadge,* 4.

2. Letter, Benjamin Tallmadge to Nathan Hale, July 9, 1773 (New York Public Library, Hale Collection).

3. Ibid.

4. Ibid.

5. Ibid.; and Hall, *Benjamin Tallmadge,* 10.

6. Ibid., 11.

7. Letter, Tallmadge to Hale.

8. Nathan Hale wrote many poems. This one to Tallmadge is excerpted in Seymour, *Documentary Life,* 90. Seymour credits the Reverend Dr. Anson Phelps Stokes, who donated the original poem to Yale University.

9. This Eneas Munson quote has been printed in many of the old texts detailing Nathan's life, but has been quoted somewhat differently depending on which text you read. I relied on James Grant Wilson and John Fiske, *Appleton's Cyclopaedia of American Biography* (Detroit: Gale Research Co., 1968), 3:30. Munson spent time with Nathan in New Haven, so I put considerable trust in his descriptions of the patriot.

10. To construct a physical description of Nathan I used letters and testimony written about him by family and friends, which provided plenty of detail regarding hair, eyes, and build. There is also a thorough description of Nathan left by Dr. Eneas Munson, who knew Nathan and, in 1780, wrote a brief essay about him found in the *American Historical Magazine and Literary Review,* January 1836 (Yale Library). The Munson quote is from Dr. Munson's essay. The scene of Munson and his son is from Johnston, *Nathan Hale,* 37.

11. Ibid.

12. Although Nathan Hale was likely not the first to teach females mathematics, writing, and the classics, he was certainly the first in Connecticut to run a structured classroom for females. See Joseph Felt, *The Annals of Salem,* vol. 1 (Salem, MA: W. & S. B. Ives, 1827). In this text, the author collects a series of diary entries from townspeople who discuss the numerous New England schools opening before, during, and after the Revolution, in which it becomes clear that schools for females in New England were tailored to fit a specific need, such as sewing, cleaning, and cooking. It wasn't until the latter part of the eighteenth century and early nineteenth century that females became part of New England classrooms. Therefore, I firmly believe that Nathan Hale can be called the first American to run a structured classroom for females at a time in America when the practice was shunned. In this sense, Nathan Hale was a pioneer.

Chapter Three: *From Boys to Men*

1. Seymour, *Documentary Life,* 154–55.

2. Ibid.

3. Letter, James Hillhouse to Nathan, July 11, 1774 (Connecticut Historical Society).

4. Seymour, *Documentary Life,* 154–55.

5. Ibid.

6. Ibid., xxvii.

7. This "calling" Nathan had to teach females was implicit in the letters and diary entries Nathan left behind, many of which George Dudley Seymour collected in

Documentary Life of Nathan Hale. Seymour later purchased the Hale farm and turned it into an American landmark and museum. Seymour's collection of the documents associated with Nathan's life is remarkable and took Seymour, who arguably became obsessed with Nathan, many years to put together. A lot of the letters I quote throughout this book were transcribed by Seymour and printed in full in his book. I also read the original letters at the Connecticut Historical Society and the New York Public Library. The Connecticut Historical Society has the same collection of Nathan Hale letters that Seymour reprinted in his book, but Seymour took a tremendous amount of time and effort to sit and transcribe over three dozen letters written by Nathan and his many friends and family members. Although Nathan's handwriting was fairly clear, it is still hard to read. In reading these letters, I sensed that Nathan held a place in his heart for the uneducated female and made it part of his life's work to make sure females of his generation had a standing chance in life. Likewise, as Nathan traveled east toward Boston during 1775 and 1776, the letters he received from friends prove that his influence on the females he taught in New London before leaving for the war was immeasurable.

8. Letter, Nathan to Major Samuel Hale, September 24, 1774 (Connecticut Historical Society).

9. Eleanor Spiller, *Hale's Location: The Story of Major Samuel Hale* (Glencliff, NH: E. V. Spiller, 1993), 5, 21.

10. Ibid.

11. Ibid.

12. Daniel Bellamy, *The Truth and Safety of the Christian Religion Deduced from Reason and Revelation* (London: Sold by J. Deighton, 1789), 239.

13. Spiller, *Hale's Location*, 5, 21; also see letter, Nathan to Major Samuel Hale.

14. Ibid.

15. Ibid. Also see Seymour, *Documentary Life*, xxvii.

CHAPTER FOUR: *SCHOOLMASTER*

1. Charles Burr Todd, *In Olde Connecticut* (New York: Grafton Press, 1906), 147; and Henry Barnard, *The American Journal of Education* (Hartford: F. C. Brownell, 1856–82), 16:333.

2. Stuart, *Life of Captain Nathan Hale*, 28–29.

3. Letter, Nathan to Thomas Mead, May 2, 1774 (Connecticut Historical Society). Also, Stuart, *Life of Captain Nathan Hale*, 28–29.

4. This paragraph was drawn from my study of the letters Nathan wrote to friends and family, along with the letters he received throughout the time he taught in New London. If nothing else, Nathan was interested in the opinions of politics and social issues his neighbors and friends had to share. He knew what he wanted—to a certain extent. I firmly believe he thought he was too good a schoolmaster, even though he had not yet taught a day, to end up in such a remote location as Moodus, which would become apparent as boredom settled upon him and he sought a tenure in New London. I might also note that several photographs of the Moodus school-house exist, as does the house itself, although it has been moved several times.

5. Jean Christie Root, *Nathan Hale* (New York: Macmillan Company, 1915), 30.

6. Dexter, *Biographical Sketches*, 3:493. Also, letter, Elihu Marvin to Nathan, December 6, 1773 (Connecticut Historical Society).

7. Letter, Marvin to Nathan.

8. Ibid.

9. Ibid.

10. Ibid.

11. Ibid.

12. Ibid.

13. Letter, Timothy Green to Nathan, December 21, 1773 (Connecticut Historical Society).

14. Seymour, *Documentary Life*, 156–57.

15. Frances Manwaring Caulkins, *History of New London, Connecticut, from the First Survey of the Coast in 1612 to 1860* (New London CT: H. D. Utley, 1895), 654–55; also, letter, Green to Nathan.

16. Letter, Green to Nathan.

17. Letter, Green to Nathan, February 4, 1774 (Connecticut Historical Society).

18. Sillitto and Pagliuco, interviews.

19. Seymour, *Documentary Life*, 90. This poem was given to Seymour by the Chicago Historical Society.

20. Ibid.

21. Ibid.

22. Ibid.

23. Letter, Green to Nathan, February 10, 1774 (Connecticut Historical Society).

24. Ibid.

25. Ibid.

26. Letters, Green to Nathan, February 4 and 10, 1774.

27. Daniel Marston, *The American Revolution, 1774–1783* (Oxford: Osprey, 2002), 83; also see *Journals of Congress from 1774 to 1778, Ed. of 1823*, 1:36–43, 46–49.

CHAPTER FIVE: *A BORN PATRIOT*

1. Caulkins, *History of New London*, 622. My descriptions of the schoolhouse are based on a drawing (circa 1774) printed in this book. The schoolhouse still stands today in downtown New London. It has however, been moved several times.

2. Ibid.

3. Ibid., 622–23.

4. Letter, Enoch to Nathan, May 10, 1774 (Connecticut Historical Society).

5. Ibid.

6. Ibid.

7. Ibid.

8. Seymour, *Documentary Life*, 161.

9. Ibid.

10. These paragraphs describing Nathan's teaching habits and the atmosphere of his classroom were constructed from several sources: "Colonel Samuel Green's Picture of Hale as a School-teacher," as given to I. A. Stuart in January 1847, which can be found in Seymour, *Documentary Life*, 158. What's interesting to me is that Green was outspoken in his admiration for Nathan and clearly in awe of his former schoolmaster. In the many letters available from this period of Nathan's life, several of his former Yale peers wrote to Nathan in search of his approval and/or acceptance for the lives they had chosen, as if Nathan were the leader of the group and, almost a year after graduation, had some sort of hold on them. These letters, as well as Sam Green's testimony, give the impression of a natural-born leader who would one day go on to do great things. Please consider that these letters—which can be found in Seymour's book and at the Connecticut Historical Society—were written before Nathan joined the rebel effort.

11. Ibid.

12. Ibid.

13. Ibid.

14. Caulkins, *History of New London*, 501.

15. *The Case of Great Britain as Laid Before the Tribunal of Arbitration, Convened at Geneva* (Millwood, NY: Kraus Reprint Co., 1978), 709.

16. Ibid.

17. George Ticknor Curtis, *History of the Origin, Formation, and Adoption of the Constitution of the United States* (New York: Harper and Bros., 1854–58), 6–7.

18. Ibid.

19. Ibid.

20. I. W. Stuart, *Life of Jonathan Trumbull* (Boston: Crocker and Brewster, 1859), 152.

21. Letter, Earl of Dartmouth to General Thomas Gage, April 9, 1774 (Richard Frothingham, *History of the Siege of Boston and of the Battles of Lexington, Concord, and Bunker Hill* [New York: Da Capo Press, 1970], 5).

22. Frothingham, *History of the Siege*, 7.

23. Ibid.

24. Ibid, 8.

25. Ibid.

26. Ibid.

27. Letter, Ebenezer Williams to Nathan, June 7, 1774 (Huntington Library, San Marino, California). My paragraphs leading up to this quote by Williams were constructed with the help of information culled from reading dozens of letters written to Nathan while he was in New London, which paint a pretty clear picture of how happy he was when he arrived in town. These letters can be found in Seymour, *Documentary Life*, 1–92.

28. Ibid.

29. Ibid.

30. Ibid. Nathan's letter to Williams did not, unfortunately, survive. If it had, we could be certain whom Williams was referring to in his return correspondence. Obviously, Nathan had expressed a desire to marry some young woman. In the next paragraph of the same letter, Williams talks about Nathan losing the woman because of his move to New London. This cannot be the woman he met in Moodus, seeing how close Moodus was to New London. Furthermore, the last two lines of the letter I quote from clearly point to an ongoing friendly discussion Williams and Nathan had

concerning young ladies—which tells us, in effect, that Nathan was continually playing the field, further proving he was not betrothed to his stepsister Alice Adams.

31. Ibid.

32. Ibid.

33. Letter, Nathan to Major Samuel Hale, September 24, 1774 (Groton School,
    Massachusetts); and letter, Nathan to Dr. Eneas Munson, November 30, 1774
    (Connecticut Historical Society).

34. Letter, Nathan to Enoch, September 8, 1774 (Connecticut Historical Society).

35. Historians I have spoken to about Nathan's desire to teach females tell me that his
    chief motivation was additional income. However, from reading Nathan's letters
    and studying his life in depth, I can say with certainty that other ideals were driv-
    ing Nathan—mainly, the death of his mother at such a young age. I firmly believe
    that he knew how much Elizabeth Strong suffered with having to cook, clean, tai-
    lor, and raise a houseful of children, not to mention giving birth to a dozen kids.
    Nathan certainly knew that for females their climb up the social ladder could begin
    in the classroom.

36. Letter, Nathan to Major Samuel Hale, September 24, 1774 (Groton School,
    Massachusetts). This is an important document concerning Nathan's time in New
    London. Nathan writes this in a different voice from that of his correspondence
    with friends and family. He seems here to almost project dread, as if he is at a loss
    regarding what to do with his life. He had achieved what he had set out to while in
    Moodus, yet, after the initial freshness of the situation in New London wore off,
    he yearned for more.

37. Ibid.

38. Ibid.

39. Ibid.

CHAPTER SIX: *TALK OF WAR*

1. Letter, Nathan to Thomas Mead, May 2, 1774 (Connecticut Historical Society).

2. Ibid.

3. Ibid. My discussion of this attitude of Nathan's is the result of reviewing and studying the letters he wrote from January through December 1774. Many of Nathan's
   peers wrote to him during this time. In these letters you'll find considerable ambivalence on Nathan's part. It's strange, really, knowing what would happen inside the

next eighteen months. I got the feeling Nathan sensed that something significant was about to occur in his life and he was somehow missing out on that opportunity.

4. Ibid.

5. Ibid.

6. Letter, Benjamin Tallmadge to Nathan, July 4, 1774 (Connecticut Historical Society).

7. Ibid.

8. Letter, James Hillhouse to Nathan, July 11, 1774 (Connecticut Historical Society).

9. Ibid.

10. Ibid.

11. Ibid.

12 Stuart, *Life of Jonathan Trumbull,* iii.

13. Ibid., 150.

14. Ibid., 151. Also, Hollister, *History of Connecticut,* 1:152.

15. Stuart, *Life of Jonathan Trumbull,* 151.

16. Stuart, *Life of Captain Nathan Hale,* 37. Here we come to a period in Nathan's life when, several of his early biographers argued, Elijah's death opened up an opportunity for Nathan to pursue Alice. I. W. Stuart wrote, "After the decease of Mr. Ripley, the match was renewed between Nathan and Alice—the latter at the time having been adopted into the family of Hale's father—and remained unbroken until Hale's death" (p. 37, footnote). This claim could not have been further from the truth. As we'll see in the letters written to Nathan during this period, he was in fact pursuing *other* females, and not once was Alice mentioned in those surviving letters. Moreover, Alice saved her journals and kept records of her life. Why, one must ask, if she and Nathan were romantically involved, does not one letter or one note or one journal entry about the relationship or love affair exist?

17. Seymour, *Documentary Life,* 568–69. In this section of his book, which Seymour titled "The Hale Romances," he goes into great detail regarding all the women in Nathan's life during the period when other biographers claimed Nathan was in love with, and planning to marry, Alice Adams. Furthermore, Ebenezer Williams writes to Nathan on January 11, 1775 (Connecticut Historical Society), "And I am apprehensive that I might be misrepresented to Miss [Betsy] Adams or some other young lady [as] an officious meddler in affairs that did not concern me." This sentence makes clear that Nathan and Williams had become entangled in a quarrel over who

it was that Nathan had romantic eyes for. That said, what's clear is that Nathan was pursuing *several* young ladies at the time, one of whom was Betsy Adams.

18. Letter, Ebenezer Williams to Nathan, January 11, 1775 (Connecticut Historical Society).

19. Ibid.

20. Letter, Richard Sill to Nathan, March 5, 1775 (Connecticut Historical Society).

21. Ibid.

22. Letter, John Hale to Nathan, March 20, 1775 (Connecticut Historical Society).

23. Ibid.

CHAPTER SEVEN: *FREE FROM THE SHADOW OF GUILE*

1. William Vincent Wells, *The Life and Public Services of Samuel Adams* (1865; repr., Freeport, NY: Books for Libraries Press, 1969); and Mark Puls, *Samuel Adams: Father of the American Revolution* (New York: Palgrave Macmillan, 2006), 169.

2. Martha J. Lamb et al., *Magazine of American History with Notes and Queries* 13 (January–June 1885) (New York: A. S. Barnes), 118; and *The Military Journals of Two Private Soldiers, 1758–1775* (Poughkeepsie: Abraham Tomlinson, 1855), 52–53.

3. Lamb et al., *Magazine of American History*, 13:118.

4. Ibid.; also see Frances Manwaring Caulkins, *History of Norwich, Connecticut* (Norwich: T. Robinson, 1845), 880–82.

5. Ibid.

6. Messier and Aronson, *Roots of Coventry*, 51.

7. Ibid.

8. Caulkins, *History of Norwich*, 881.

9. Ibid.; also see Benson John Lossing, *Harper's Encyclopedia of United States History* (New York: Harper & Brothers Publishers, 1912), 289.

10. Messier and Aronson, *Roots of Coventry*, 51.

11. Warner, *Complete Writings*, vol. 14, 337–39.

12. Ibid.

13. Ibid.

14. Caulkins, *History of New London*, 394, 513. Also see New London County Historical Society, *Records and Papers of the New London County Historical Society* (New London, CT: The Society, 1890–1912), 69.

15. Ibid.

16. Ibid.

17. Letter, Leverett W. Saltonstall to Cyrur P. Bradley, January 17, 1837, in Seymour, *Documentary Life*, 347.

18. Ibid. This quote, probably more than Nathan's famously misquoted line from the gallows ("I only regret that I have but one life to lose for my country"), is the most reprinted Hale quote. In the totality of Nathan's life, this quote is more profound than anything he said before or after, simply because at the time he said it the colonies were confused, desperately trying to form government bodies and army regiments to fight the British. Nathan's life had been going along rather smoothly. He was about to get a substantial raise, continue building his classroom for females, and also start, possibly, writing and conducting scientific experiments, something he was looking forward to. Instead, he decided to give it all up and enlist.

19. Edward Everett Hale, *The Story of Massachusetts* (Boston: D. Lathrop Company, 1891), 289.

20. Letter, Saltonstall to Bradley, in Seymour, *Documentary Life*, 347.

21. Ibid.

22. Stuart, *Life of Captain Nathan Hale*, 44–45.

23. Ibid.

24. Ibid.

Chapter Eight: *A Sense of Duty*

1. Curtis, *History of the Origin*, 33–34.

2. Ibid.

3. H. Niles, *Principles and Acts of the Revolution in America* (Baltimore: William Wiley, 1822), 350.

4. George Washington, et al., *The Writings of George Washington* (Boston: American Stationers' Company, 1837), 1:136–41.

5. Ibid., 1:142.

6. Royal R. Hinman, *A Historical Collection from Official Records, Files . . . of the Part Sustained by Connecticut, During the War of the Revolution* (Hartford: E. Gleason, 1842), 79.

7. In reading Nathan's letters during his tenure at Yale, I developed a strong sense of his plans for the future and how he reacted to the colonies' struggle for independence. Moreover, letters to Nathan from former classmates often speak of the great

worldly view Nathan had for the colonies. The quote about "politicks" is from a letter Nathan's classmate Ebenezer Williams wrote to him on April 20, 1775, which can be found in Seymour, *Documentary Life,* 35.

8. Letter, Ebenezer Williams to Nathan, April 20, 1775 (Connecticut Historical Society).

9. Letter, Ezra Selden to Nathan, June 25, 1775 (Connecticut Historical Society).

10. Ibid.

11. Letter, Benjamin Tallmadge to Nathan, July 4, 1775 (Connecticut Historical Society).

12. Ibid.

13. Letter, Nathan to the "Proprietors of the Union School," New London, July 7, 1775 (Connecticut Historical Society).

14. Ibid.

15. Ibid.

16. Letter, Lieutenant John Belcher to Nathan, July 27, 1775, in Seymour, *Documentary Life,* 40.

17. Ibid.

18. Ibid.

19. *Putnam's Monthly Magazine of American Literature, Science and Art* 7 (January–July 1856): 477.

20. Ibid. Also Richard Richmond, *New York and Its Institutions, 1609–1871: The Bright Side of New York* (New York: E. B. Treat, 1873), 80.

21. George Washington, General Orders, July 4, 1775 (Library of Congress, Manuscript Division).

22. Ibid.

23. Ibid.

24. Abraham Tomlinson, *Military Journals,* 60–62.

25. Washington, General Orders.

26. George Washington, General Orders, July 4–27, 1775 (Library of Congress, Manuscript Division).

27. Ibid.

CHAPTER NINE: *BAND OF BROTHERS*

1. From the payroll of the Seventh Connecticut Regiment (Connecticut State Library); and Seymour, *Documentary Life,* 164–65.

2. Ibid. Also see Nathan's Army Journal, September 23, 1775 (Connecticut Historical Society). These diary entries are transcribed in Seymour, *Documentary Life*, 174. For the excerpts I used, I went back and studied Seymour's transcriptions, which were done in the 1920s, against the actual entries in Nathan's book at Hartford's Connecticut Historical Society.

3. Frothingham, *History of the Siege*, 295. Also Stuart, *Life of Captain Nathan Hale*, 50–52.

4. Stuart, *Life of Captain Nathan Hale*, 50–53.

5. Ibid.

6. From the testimony of Lieutenant Elisha Bostwick in Seymour, *Documentary Life*, 321–25.

7. Ibid.

8. Ibid.

9. Maria Campbell, *Revolutionary Services and Civil Life of General William Hull* (New York: Appleton & Co., 1848), 22.

10. Ibid.

11. Nathan's Army Journal, September 23, 1775 (Connecticut Historical Society).

12. Norman M. Isham and Albert Frederic Brown, *Early Rhode Island Houses: An Historical and Architectural Study* (Providence, R.I.: Preston & Rounds, 1895), 49–53.

13. Ibid.

14. From the testimony of Lieutenant Elisha Bostwick in Seymour, *Documentary Life*, 321–25.

15. Ibid.

16. Ibid.

17. Ibid.

18. Nathan's Army Journal, September 23, 1775. Also Tomlinson, *Military Journals*, 74.

19. Ibid. Also Edward Lengel, *General George Washington: A Military Life* (New York: Random House, 2005), 93 (from which the "farmers; shopkeepers; and rich merchants; ministers and convicts" quote was excerpted). Lengel's book gives a great overview on page 93 of the tense moments around camp and how a bunch of men who would otherwise never have had reason to associate with one another were corralled in one small area waiting on the call to fight. Also James Thacher, *A Military Journal During the American Revolutionary War: From 1775 to 1783* (Boston: Cottons & Barnard, 1827), 36.

20. Nathan's Army Journal, September 29, 1775.

21. Tomlinson, *Military Journals*, 73.

22. Letter, Gilbert Saltonstall to Nathan, October 2, 1775 (Connecticut Historical Society).

23. Robert La Follette, *The Making of America* (Philadelphia, PA: John D. Morris and Company, 1906), 9:203–4.

24. Letter, Gilbert Saltonstall to Nathan, October 9, 1775 (Connecticut Historical Society).

25. Ibid.

26. Washington et al., *Writings of George Washington*, 1:158–59; and Lengel, *General George Washington*, 94–95.

27. Ibid., 159.

28. Ibid., 160.

29. Nathan's Army Journal, October 6 and 7, 1775.

30. Letter, Saltonstall to Nathan.

31. Nathan's Army Journal, October 8 through 11, 1775.

32. Letter, John Hallam to Nathan, October 9, 1775; and letter, Gilbert Saltonstall to Nathan, October 16, 1775 (Connecticut Historical Society).

33. Letter, Nathan to Betsey Christophers, October 19, 1775 (Yale University Library).

34. Ibid.

35. Ibid.

36. Ibid.

Chapter Ten: Siege and Counterplot

1. Nathan's Army Journal, October 12 through November 1, 1775 (Connecticut Historical Society). Also Washington et al., *Writings of George Washington*, 1:189–92; Stuart, *Life of Captain Nathan Hale*, 56; and Richmond, *New York and Its Institutions*, 252–55.

2. Ibid.

3. Ibid.

4. George Washington, General Orders, October 21, 1775 (Library of Congress, Manuscript Division); also Nathan's Army Journal, October 12 through November 1, 1775. I used a quote from a letter Washington wrote to Rhode Island governor

Cooke on November 15, 1775, which can be found in Richmond, *New York and Its Institutions,* 253.

5. Campbell, *Revolutionary Services,* 22–23. Also see Nathan's Army Journal, October 12 through November 1, 1775.

6. Ibid.

7. Ibid.

8. Ibid.

9. Nathan's Army Journal, October 12 through November 1, 1775; and Thomas Jones, *History of New York During the Revolutionary War* (New York Historical Society, 1879), 102 (Thomas's notes on the bottom of page).

10. John Disturnell, *The Eastern Tourist, Being a Guide Through the States of Connecticut, Massachusetts, Vermont, New Hampshire, and Maine, and Also a Dash into Canada* (privately published, 1848), 141; and James Grant Wilson and John Fiske *Appleton's Cyclopaedia of American Biography* (New York: D. Appleton and Co., 1887–1900), 4:288.

11. Ibid.

12. In creating this series of paragraphs, I relied on a variety of primary documents. Among them were William Willis, *Collections of the Maine Historical Society* (Portland, ME: The Society, 1904–6), 1:514; Moses Coit Tyler, *The Literary History of the American Revolution* (New York: F. Ungar Pub. Co., 1957), 383, 417; and Return Jonathan Meigs, *Journal of the Expedition Against Quebec* (New York: Privately printed, 1864).

13. Ibid.

14. Ibid.

15. Ibid.

16. Nathan's Army Journal, October 30, 1775.

17. Ibid.

18. Nathan's Army Journal, November 28, 1775.

19. Nathan's Army Journal, November 1 through 8, 1775; and Warner, *Complete Writings,* 338–40.

20. Washington et al., *Writings of George Washington,* 1:160.

21. George Washington, General Orders, November 1 through 5, 1775 (Library of Congress, Manuscript Division).

22. Frothingham, *History of the Siege,* 250–54.

23. Ibid., 253–54.

24. David K. Barnhart and Allan A. Metcalf, *America in So Many Words* (New York: Houghton Mifflin Company, 1997), 80.

25. Nathan's Army Journal, November 6, 1775.

26. Nathan's Army Journal, November 7 and 8, 1775.

27. Ibid.

28. Ibid.

CHAPTER ELEVEN: *OF THEE I SING*

1. Nathan's Army Journal, November 9, 1775 (Connecticut Historical Society). This entry is one of the more detailed narrative accounts of the action in the journal. Nathan writes, at times, as a reporter, giving blow-by-blow descriptions. In none of these entries, however, does he once talk about his own service or what role he played, if any, in a particular attack. In keeping with his unselfish character, it's as if he wanted his men and the soldiers around him to partake in the glory. The fighting abilities of these men, as Nathan describes them, are quite remarkable, considering their inexperience.

2. Ibid.

3. Ibid.

4. Ibid.

5. Ibid.

6. Ibid.

7. Ibid.

8. Nathan's Army Journal, November 14, 1775. That Nathan took the time to copy each of these directions—some of them were a hundred words or more—shows how eager he was to learn the rules of war. In just about every entry Nathan penned in his journal, it's clear he wanted to continue to learn what a commanding officer needed to get his men ready for battle.

9. A full list of the "Directions for the Guards" can be found in Nathan's Army Journal between the dates November 14 and 15, 1775. Also Washington, General Orders, November 12, 1775 (Manuscript Division, Library of Congress).

10. Ibid.

11. Washington, General Orders, November 12, 1775.

12. Nathan's Army Journal, November 19–20, 1775.

13. Ibid.

14. Ibid.

15. Thacher, *Military Journal,* 37–38.

16. Nathan's Army Journal, November 25–December 1, 1775.

17. Thacher, *Military Journal,* 38.

18. Nathan's Army Journal, November 25–December 1, 1775.

19. Nathan's Army Journal, November 25, 1775; Hollister, *History of Connecticut,* 1:644–45; and *Collections of the Massachusetts Historical Society,* 5th ser. (Boston: Published by the Society, 1885), 9:493–94.

20. Nathan's Army Journal, December 12, 1775.

21. Nathan's Army Journal, December 21, 1775.

22. Ibid.; and Seymour, *Documentary Life,* 519–20.

23. Nathan's Army Journal, December 23, 1775.

24. Ibid.

25. Nathan's Army Journal, December 23–29, 1775.

26. Letter, Gilbert Saltonstall to Nathan, December 18, 1775 (Connecticut Historical Society).

27. Ibid.

28. Ibid. In his biography of Nathan Hale, I. W. Stuart seems to interpret this section of Gilbert Saltonstall's letter in a much different manner from what perhaps Saltonstall intended. For one, Stuart refers to the word *compliments* as a "cold phrase," inferring patronization in the words of Nathan's former lady friends. In reviewing the letter carefully and matching it up against the temperament in Nathan's Army Journal, my only logical conclusion is that the females were former students of Nathan's, sending their regards to a schoolmaster they had adored and missed greatly. Calling Nathan "Master" was a reference to his title while in New London. For Stuart's interpretation, see Stuart, *Life of Captain Nathan Hale,* 64.

29. Nathan's Army Journal, December 24–29, 1775.

30. Nathan's Army Journal, January 24, 1776.

31. Letters, George Hurlbut to Nathan, December 28, 1775, and January 4, 1776 (Connecticut Historical Society).

32. Seymour, *Documentary Life,* 315–18.

33. Nathan's Army Journal, January 24–27, 1776; and Seymour, *Documentary Life,* 316.

34. Stuart, *Life of Captain Nathan Hale*, 63.

35. Nathan's Army Journal, January 24–27, 1776; and Seymour, *Documentary Life*, 316.

36. Nathan's Army Journal, February 14, 1776.

37. Hollister, *History of Connecticut*, 1:243.

38. Ibid. Also Sidney Lee, *Dictionary of National Biography* (New York: Macmillan and Co., 1892), 32:343–46. The quotes from Lee are derived from "The Lee Papers," which can be found in the *Collections of the New-York Historical Society for the Year 1871* (Privately printed for the Society, 1872), 234–36.

39. Ibid.

40. Ibid., 236–37.

41. Seymour, *Documentary Life*, 316.

CHAPTER TWELVE: *INDEPENDENCE DAY*

1. The quotes and information drawn in this paragraph are derived from the (Washington, DC) Public Affairs Office of the Central Intelligence Agency's privately printed text titled "Organization of Intelligence," and Congress's Committee of Secret Correspondence Resolution, both of which can be found at https://www .cia.gov/library/center-for-the-study-of-intelligence/csi-publications/books-and -monographs/intelligence/main.html.

2. Isaac Bangs, *Journal of Lieutenant Isaac Bangs* (Cambridge: J. Wilson and Son, 1890), 57.

3. Ibid.

4. Ibid.

5. Caroline Clifford Newton, *Once Upon a Time in Connecticut* (Boston: Houghton Mifflin Co., 1916), 40.

6. Bangs, *Journal*, 57.

7. W. C. Beecher and Samuel Scoville, *A Biography of Henry Ward Beecher* (New York: C. L. Webster & Co., 1888), 34.

8. Ibid.

9. Ibid.

10. Terry Crowdy, *The Enemy Within: A History of Espionage* (New York: Osprey, 2006), 94.

11. Ceane O'Hanlon-Lincoln, *County Chronicles* (Chicora, PA: Mechling Bookbindery, 2004), 47.

12. Washington Irving, *Life of George Washington* (Boston: Twayne Publishers, 1982), 4:139–43.

13. Ibid.

14. Ibid.

15. William B. Reed, *Life and Correspondence of Joseph Reed* (Philadelphia: Lindsay and Blakiston, 1847), 189.

16. Wilson and Fiske, *Appleton's Cyclopaedia*, 5:208–9.

17. Reed, *Life and Correspondence*, 189.

18. Letter, Nathan to Enoch Hale, August 20, 1776 (Connecticut Historical Society); and Johnston, *Nathan Hale*, 85–86.

19. Washington et al., *Writings of George Washington*, 1:347.

20. Letter, Thomas U. Fosdick to Nathan, December 7, 1775 (Connecticut Historical Society).

21. Ibid.

22. Letter, George Hurlbut, December 17, 1775 (Connecticut Historical Society).

23. Letter, Nathan to Enoch Hale, August 20, 1776.

24. Ibid.

25. Ibid. Also *Pennsylvania Evening Post*, August 20, 1776.

26. Ibid.

27. William P. Upham, *A Memoir of General John Glover of Marblehead* (Salem, MA: C. W. Swasey, 1863), 11; Frank Moore, *Diary of the American Revolution: From Newspapers and Original Documents* (New York: C. Scribner, 1860), 202–3; and *Pennsylvania Evening Post*, August 20, 1776.

28. Letter, Nathan to Enoch Hale, August 20, 1776.

29. Ibid.; and George Washington and Worthington Chauncey Ford, *The Writings of George Washington* (New York: Putnam, 1889), 4:356.

30. Letter, Nathan to Enoch Hale, August 20, 1776.

31. Ibid.

32. Washington, General Orders, August 20, 1776 (Library of Congress, Manuscript Division).

33. Ibid.

34. Ibid.

35. Letter, Nathan to Enoch Hale, August 20, 1776.

36. Ibid.

37. Hinman, *Historical Collection,* 81–82.

38. William Ordway Partridge, *Nathan Hale, the Ideal Patriot: A Study of Character* (New York: Funk & Wagnalls, 1902), 54–56.

39. Ibid. Also, F. S. Bartram, *Retrographs: Comprising, a History of New York Prior to the Revolution* (New York: Yale Pub. Co., 1888), 148.

40. Ibid.

41. Ibid.

42. Ibid.

43. Ibid.

44. Ibid.

45. These quotes are from a fragment of a letter written by Nathan that George Dudley Seymour received from Frederick Winthrop Allen, a Hale family friend. See Seymour, *Documentary Life,* 81–82. Although undated and unsigned, we know for certain the letter was written by Nathan (because of his unique handwriting); it can be dated somewhere in the neighborhood of June 14–21, 1776. The letter shows a different side of Nathan. He used two styles of writing: One was professional and direct, which he saved for Yale friends and those in New London he was looking to impress; the other style, which was more comforting, personal, and joyous, was reserved for the females in his life.

46. Ibid.

47. John Bakeless, *Turncoats, Traitors & Heroes: Espionage in the American Revolution* (New York: Da Capo Press, 1998), 110–11.

48. Thacher, *Military Journal,* 57–58; and Hinman, *Historical Collection,* 80–81.

49. David McCullough, *1776* (New York: Simon & Schuster, 2005), 178; and *Memoirs of the Long Island Historical Society* (hereafter: LIHS), vol. 3: *The Campaign of 1776* (Brooklyn, NY: The Society, 1867–89), 112–13.

50. Nathan Hale's Army Journal, August 21, 1776 (Connecticut Historical Society).

51. Washington et al., *Writings of George Washington,* 1:420 (letters, Washington to the President of Congress, September 19 and 20, 1776).

52. *Memoirs,* vol. 3: *Campaign of 1776,* documents section.

53. Nathan's Army Journal, August 23, 1776.

54. Washington et al., *Writings of George Washington,* 1:420 (letters, Washington to the President of Congress, September 19 and 20, 1776).

55. Ibid.

56. Ibid., 420–24.

57. Thacher, *Military Journal*, 33.

58. *Memoirs of General La Fayette, Embracing Details of His Public and Private Life* (Hartford, CT: Barber and Robinson, 1825), 67–68.

59. Letter, Nathan to Enoch Hale, June 3, 1776 (Connecticut Historical Society).

60. Ibid.

61. Thomas Wilson, *The Biography of the Principal American Military and Naval Heroes* (repr., Whitefish, MT: Kessinger, 2006), 272.

62. Ibid., 353–54; and Thacher, *Military Journal*, 56.

63. Letter, Nathan to Enoch Hale, June 3, 1776.

64. Eugene Kinkead, "Our Local Correspondents: Still Here," *New Yorker*, June 23, 1776.

65. William Dunlap, *History of the New Netherlands, Province of New York, and State of New York, to the Adoption of the Federal Constitution*, Burt Franklin Research and Source Works Series 538 (New York: B. Franklin, 1970), 197.

66. Letter, Nathan to Enoch Hale, June 3, 1776.

67. Ibid; and Washington et al., *Writings of George Washington*, 1:549.

Chapter Thirteen: *A Necessary Purpose*

1. Thomas Knowlton is one of the true heroes of the American Revolution. Much has been written about his service, mostly firsthand accounts given by soldiers fighting next to him. I read no fewer than ten volumes on Knowlton's military life, as well as his upbringing in Massachusetts and Connecticut. Of those, see Charles Coffin, *The Lives and Services of Major General John Thomas; Colonel Thomas Knowlton; Colonel Alexander Scammell; and Major General Henry Dearborn* (New York: Egbert, Hovey & King, printers, 1845). As in most of the volumes written about Knowlton, Coffin dedicates an entire section to Knowlton's life.

2. Ibid. Also Fred Pushies, *U.S. Army Special Forces* (St. Paul, MN: MBI Pub. Co., 2001), 11.

3. Nathan's Army Journal, September 23, 1775, to August 23, 1776 (Connecticut Historical Society). In his journal, Nathan speaks of his attachment to the cause and his sincere disdain for those who had taken up arms against America. For the quote "prostrated with illness," see Bartram, *Retrographs*, 151.

4. Seymour, *Documentary Life*, xxix, 527. Seymour writes, "The [*Asia*] exploit may have been a factor in [Nathan's] selection to a command in a picket regiment . . . known as 'Knowlton's Rangers.'"

5. LIHS, *Memoirs*, vol. 3: *Campaign of 1776*, 35–37.

6. Ibid., 36. Several different volumes helped me understand this critical period of the war, when Washington and his troops were basically surrounded. Reading Washington's letters between September 2 and September 15, 1776, helped me understand his point of view. Likewise, see Rick Britton's map "Manhattan: Aug. to Nov. 1776," in Lengel, *General George Washington*, 151. Also see Bakeless, *Turncoats, Traitors & Heroes*, 111–14.

7. Washington et al., *Writings of George Washington*, 1:390–400. Also Lengel, *General George Washington*, 149–53; and Bakeless, *Turncoats, Traitors & Heroes*, 111–14.

8. Ibid.

9. Bakeless, *Turncoats, Traitors & Heroes*, 112. Also Johnston, *Nathan Hale*, 92–93.

10. Ibid.

11. Seymour, *Documentary Life*, 317–18.

12. Ibid, 316. Also see Nathan's Army Journal, August 23, 1776.

13. Colonel Charles Webb, Orderly Book (Connecticut State Library). Webb clearly outlines Nathan's status during this period, detailing his ill health and involvement in Knowlton's Rangers. Also see Terry Golway, *Washington's General: Nathanael Greene and the Triumph of the American Revolution* (New York: Henry Holt, 2005), 92–93 (the letter Greene wrote to Washington was excerpted in Golway's book).

14. Ibid. Also Washington, General Orders, September 1 and 7, 1776 (Library of Congress, Manuscript Division).

15. Joseph Thompson, *Memoir of David Hale, Late Editor of the Journal of Commerce with Selections from His Miscellaneous Writings* (New York: John Wiley, 1850), 494.

16. John Austin Stevens, *Progress of New York in a Century: 1776–1876: An Address* (New York: Printed for the society, 1876), 5.

17. Henry Howe, *Adventures and Achievements of Americans: A Series of Narratives* (New York: Geo. F. Tuttle, 1860), 19. Many statements left behind by Nathan's colleagues detail this meeting. Among them, see "General Hull's Account of the Last Hours and Last Words of Hale," in Seymour, *Documentary Life*, 307–10.

18. Howe, *Adventures and Achievements*, 19.

19. Seymour, *Documentary Life*, 307–10.

20. Howe, *Adventures and Achievements*, 19.

21. Ibid. There is no question about what Nathan said at this pivotal moment in his life. His words were recalled by several officers on hand and later reported by near-ly every historian and scholar who later studied and wrote about his life. What I found confusing was the next statement attributed to Nathan, which is one of his more profound remarks. Some claim he said it at the Knowlton Rangers meeting, while others claim it was said later that day in private to his friend William Hull. For this reason, I relied on Hull's memoir, in which he records Nathan's statement as a personal discourse between two friends who sat and talked about this couragous decision Nathan was about to make.

22. Seymour, *Documentary Life*, 308.

23. Ibid.

24. Ibid.

25. Campbell, *Revolutionary Services*, 35–36.

26. Ibid.

27. Ibid.

28. Ibid., 309.

29. Ibid.

30. Ibid.

31. Ibid.

32. Ibid.

Chapter Fourteen: *Brave Resistance*

1. William Baker, *Itinerary of General Washington* (Lambertville, NJ: Hunterdon House, 1970); and Washington, General Orders, September 20, 1776 (Library of Congress, Manuscript Division).

2. Stevens, *Progress of New York*, 4.

3. Reed, *Life and Correspondence*, 238–39; and Washington, General Orders, September 22 and 23, 1776 (Library of Congress, Manuscript Division).

4. Washington, General Orders, September 22 and 23, 1776.

5. Letter, Nathan to Enoch Hale, May 30, 1776 (Connecticut Historical Society).

6. Ibid.

7. Ibid.

8. Ibid.

9. Ibid.

10. Ibid.

11. Ibid.

12. Seymour, *Documentary Life*, 315–18.

13. Letter, Nathan to Enoch Hale, August 20, 1776 (Connecticut Historical Society).

14. Ibid.

15. Seymour, *Documentary Life*, 316–17. Nathan never told Asher Wright where he was going or why he was leaving camp. Like William Hull, Asher felt that if given the opportunity, he could have talked Nathan out of the secret mission.

16. Stuart, *Life of Captain Nathan Hale*, 88.

17. Ibid.

18. Seymour, *Documentary Life*, 317.

19. Ibid., 519–20. The quote from Stephen Hempstead's sister is from a letter Anna Hempstead Branch wrote to George Dudley Seymour (Coventry, CT: Hale Homestead).

20. Stephen Hempstead, "The Capture and Execution of Capt. Hale in 1776," *Missouri Republican*, January 18, 1827.

21. Ibid.

22. Ibid.

23. Thatcher, *Military Journal*, 55–56.

24. Ibid.

25. Martha J. Lamb, *History of the City of New York: Its Origin, Rise, and Progress* (New York: A. S. Barnes, 1877), 2:122, 2:432.

26. Washington, General Orders, September 11 and 14, 1776 (Library of Congress, Manuscript Division).

27. For Private James Martin's journal entry, see LIHS *Memoirs*, vol. 3: *Campaign of 1776*, 81 (the documentary section).

28. Ibid., 82.

29. Theodore Roosevelt, *New York* (New York and London: Longman, Green and Company, 1891), 134–35.

30. Ibid., 135. Also Washington, General Orders, September 14–17, 1776 (Library of Congress, Manuscript Division).

31. For "Lieutenant Elisha Bostwick's Narrative," a detailed portrait of his time in the war, the latter part of which describes his fond memories of Nathan, see Seymour, *Documentary Life*, 319–25.

32. Seymour, *Documentary Life*, 316; and Bakeless, *Turncoats, Traitors & Heroes*, 114.

33. Washington, General Orders, July 3, 1775, through September 30, 1776 (Library of Congress, Manuscript Division); and Howe, *Adventures and Achievements*, 18.

34. Ibid. A comprehensive study of all the available documents written by Washington shows no mention of Nathan Hale's secret mission. Obviously, generals weren't going to be writing about the spy missions they sent soldiers on—especially missions that failed. Yet, nowhere in any of Washington's writings (during or after the war) does he mention Nathan Hale. Those close to him said he refused to talk about the ill-fated mission of the American captain, either out of desire to remove the terrible tragedy from his memory, or for embarrassment and/or guilt the general felt for sending Nathan.

35. While at camp in White Plains, Nathan's brother Enoch heard that Nathan had crossed the Sound in Stamford. I use Norwalk because Stephen Hempstead, who was with Nathan, remembered it that way. George Dudley Seymour also points out this inconsistency, writing that "two 'rebel' sloops were in [the Norwalk] Harbor when Hale crossed." Furthermore, Seymour says, "Hempstead should be followed as having been Hale's attendant, while Enoch got his information in camp near White Plains" (Seymour, *Documentary Life*, 312). Additionally, it has been documented that Captain Pond's sloop, *Schuyler*, was in Norwalk harbor near this date.

36. Washington et al., *Writings of George Washington*, 1:167.

37. Hempstead, "Capture and Execution of Capt. Hale."

38. Ibid.

39. Coffin, *Lives and Services*, 72–76. Also see LIHS, *Memoirs*, vol. 3: *Campaign of 1776*, 82–84.

40. Ibid. (both books).

41. Ibid., 75.

42. Johnston, *Nathan Hale*, 104–5. This date, September 15, has been the subject of debate among scholars, historians, and Hale's early biographers, some of whom claim it was the sixteenth. I chose September 15, but it may well have been September 16. That the *Halifax* reported two sloops in nearby waters is a fairly

good indication that Captain Pond's ship was in fact making its way across the Sound with the *Montgomery* by its side. I could find no documentation to support a theory that the *Halifax* spotted two different ships.

CHAPTER FIFTEEN: *THROWN INTO THE FLAMES*

1. The detail in this opening paragraph was drawn from a letter Anna Hempstead Branch wrote to George Dudley Seymour (property of Hale Homestead, Coventry, CT), as well as Hempstead, "Capture and Execution of Capt. Hale." Also see Martha Bockée Flint, *Early Long Island: A Colonial Study* (Port Washington, NY: I. J. Friedman, 1967), 436–37. In Flint's book there's a description of Huntington harbor during the period Nathan landed. I. W. Stuart depicts this scene a little differently in his *Life of Captain Nathan Hale,* 100. In Stuart's telling, Nathan handed Hempstead his watch, but then took it back, saying, "He would risk his watch where he would risk his life." The problem I had using this in the narrative was that Stuart never noted where he found the story. I relied on a primary document, a letter written to George Dudley Seymour by a Hempstead relative, Anna Hempstead Branch, who mentions this story of Nathan handing Hempstead his precious watch.

2. Hempstead, "Capture and Execution of Capt. Hale."

3. Flint, *Early Long Island,* 436. The flag story can be found in a letter written by a Huntington resident on July 23, 1776, which is preserved in the *American Archives,* 5th ser. 1972 (Northern Illinois University Libraries), 1:543.

4. Seymour, *Documentary Life,* 543.

5. Stuart, *Life of Captain Nathan Hale,* 102; and Lossing, *Two Spies,* 16.

6. Stuart, *Life of Captain Nathan Hale,* 103. Interestingly enough, Stuart claims the account of William Johnson is "on good authority." A Johnson family member was obviously an anonymous source of Stuart's. Other texts mention the Johnson story. See Howe, *Adventures and Achievements,* 20; and Lossing, *Two Spies,* 16. I believe Stuart was a thorough researcher, working with only those documents and interviews he viewed as reliable and primary. Reading Stuart's copious notes, resources, and correspondences from his time working on his Hale biography (which can be found at the Connecticut Historical Society) gave me the impression that he was totally absorbed in Nathan's life and quite picky about his sources. It's a shame, really, that Stuart died before the Consider Tiffany journal was discovered and Nathan's final movements in Long Island were unearthed. And even a further

shame, truly, that Alice Adams's ancestors conned Stuart into believing Alice and Nathan were lovers.

7. Washington, General Orders, September 16 and 17, 1776 (Library of Congress, Manuscript Division).

8. Ibid.

9. Ibid.

10. LIHS, *Memoirs*, vol. 3: *Campaign of 1776*, 45–47.

11. Ibid., 46.

12. Robert Rogers and Franklin B. Hough, *Journals of Major Robert Rogers* . . . (Albany: Joel Munsell's Sons, 1883), 8–18. For a description of Rogers, I relied on a sketch by Professor James Grafton Rogers.

13. Ibid.

14. James Hutson, "Nathan Hale Revisited: A Tory's Account of the Arrest of the First American Spy" (*Library of Congress Information Bulletin* [July/August 2003]). Hutson, according to his biography published by the Library of Congress, received his Ph.D. in history from Yale University in 1964. "He has been a member of the History Departments at Yale and William and Mary and, since 1982, has been Chief of the Library's Manuscript Division." Hutson was in charge of verifying and transcribing one of the most important Nathan Hale documents ever to surface: Consider Tiffany's manuscript history of the American Revolution, two pages of which contain the only firsthand account written of Nathan's capture. Tiffany, a Tory storekeeper from Connecticut, was "held under house arrest by local authorities for 15 months during the Revolution." His account of the Revolution is a document rich in detail that had eluded historians for centuries. The diary was discovered by a family member, G. Bradford Tiffany, the family's current representative, in 2000 and donated to the Library of Congress shortly thereafter. Some may question Tiffany's account because he was a Tory, but much of his story of Nathan's capture has been verified. In a sense, the diary is the one missing link in a chain of written histories of Nathan's time on Long Island and gives Nathan's story an ending.

15. LIHS, *Memoirs*, vol. 3: *Campaign of 1776*, 47–48. It's hard to pinpoint who wrote the exact quotes used in this paragraph, as the Society used a number of journals to write its history of Long Island. On some pages, the narrator is clearly identified, while on others, he or she is not.

16. Johnston, *Nathan Hale*, 109. Also see Seymour, *Documentary Life*, 321–25.

17. Barnet Schecter, *The Battle for New York: The City at the Heart of the American Revolution* (New York: Penguin Books, 2003), 204. Also Mark Caldwell, *New York Night: The Mystique and Its History* (New York: Scribner, 2005), 48.

18. Frederick Mackenzie, *Diary of Fredrick Mackenzie* (Cambridge: Harvard University Press, 1930); and George Scheer and Hugh Rankin, *Rebels and Redcoats: The American Revolution Through the Eyes of Those Who Fought and Lived It* (New York: Da Capo Press, 1987), 188.

19. Ibid.

20. Ibid.

21. Thacher, *Military Journal,* 59.

CHAPTER SIXTEEN: *PRETENDED FRIEND*

1. Two works helped me craft these paragraphs. See Caleb Stark and John Stark, *Memoir and Official Correspondence of General John Stark* (Boston: Gregg Press, 1972), 386–89; and Rogers and Hough, *Journals of Major Robert Rogers,* 5–8.

2. Ibid.

3. John R. Cuneo, *Robert Rogers of the Rangers* (New York: Oxford University Press, 1959), 24. Also see "Where and by Whom Was Hale Captured: An Inquiry," James Grafton Rogers, which can be found printed in full in Seymour, *Documentary Life,* 435–45.

4. Consider Tiffany Diary (Library of Congress, Manuscript Division). Also see Rogers and Hough, *Journals of Major Robert Rogers,* 17.

5. Ibid.

6. Ibid.

7. Consider Tiffany Diary.

8. Ibid. Also see William Cutter, *The Life of Israel Putnam* (New York: Derby & Jackson, 1861 [Stanford University Library]), 370–72 (the appendix of the book, which includes several letters between Rogers and his American foes). For the quote from Rogers to Washington, see Rogers and Hough, *Journals of Major Robert Rogers,* 17. Also see Rogers and Nathan's Army Accounts, January 1776 (Connecticut Historical Society), or Seymour, *Documentary Life,* 223.

9. Consider Tiffany Diary.

10. Ibid.

11. Cutter, *Life of Israel Putnam,* 372.

12. Consider Tiffany Diary.

13. Ibid.

14. Ibid.

15. Ibid.

16. Ibid

17. Seymour, *Documentary Life*, 303–304.

18. William Aitken, *Distinguished Families in America: Descended from Wilhelmus Beekman and Jan Thomasse Van Dyke* (Knickerbocker Press–G. P. Putnam's Sons, 1912), 118–19, 304–5. My descriptions of the Beekman mansion are derived from a sketch I found in Aitken's book, which is strikingly similar to a sketch made by Mrs. Beekman. There is also a sketch of the home in James Grant Wilson, *The Memorial History of the City of New York* (New York: New York History Co., 1892–3), 2:545.

19. Stephen Jenkins, *The Story of the Bronx: From the Purchase Made by the Dutch from the Indians in 1639 to the Present Day* (New York: G. P. Putnam's Sons, 1912), 135.

20. Ibid., 138–39.

21. Ibid., 135; also Sillitto and Pagliuco, interviews.

22. Stevens, John Austin, B. F. DeCosta, Henry Phelps Johnston, Martha J. Lamb, Nathan Gillet Pond, and William Abbat. *The Magazine of American History with Notes & Queries* (New York: AS Barnes & Company, 1877), 4:370.

23. Ibid.

24. *Boston Gazette*, October 7, 1776 (Boston Public Library). Also Washington et al., *Writings of George Washington*, 1:110.

25. Consider Tiffany Diary.

26. Ibid.

27. Ibid.

28. Ibid.

Chapter Seventeen: *The Will of God*

1. Consider Tiffany Diary.

2. Ibid.

3. Ibid.

4. Henry Onderdonk, *Documents and Letters* (New York: Leavitt, Trow & Co., 1846), 204.

5. Consider Tiffany Diary.

6. Ibid. Robert Rogers would eventually die a peasant's death: penniless, ridiculed, lonely, beaten down by years of heavy drinking and hard living. He was in Southwark, England, then, under the roof of John Walker, who said the loquacious former hard-line soldier would, "in his drunken frenzies," carry on about his glory days, mumbling "names and places to the bewilderment of [anyone around him]." As Rogers continued drinking like an alcoholic into his latter years, he woke one morning coughing up "bloody phlegm." The condition, whatever it was, killed him on May 18, 1795. The local Southwark newspaper, the *Morning Press,* eulogized Rogers, calling him a "man of uncommon strength" who "performed prodigious feats of valour" and yet who, at the time of his death, had been "reduced . . . to the most miserable state of wretchedness."

7. Letter, Gilbert Saltonstall to Nathan, November 27, 1775 (Connecticut Historical Society).

8. Ibid.

9. Ibid.

10. Ibid

11. I constructed this paragraph from the letters Nathan wrote to Enoch and the letters he received from his friends and peers. Through my study of these documents I concluded that Nathan viewed his role in the war with perhaps a higher sense of duty than his commanders did. Some would later call Nathan nothing more than a junior officer, one of dozens stationed in New York, who, if he had not died a martyr's death, would not have been remembered. I disagree. In Nathan's journal during his time in Boston, it's clear that he was respected and held to a much higher standard than many of his fellow captains. Nathan was intelligent, well educated, and well read—while many of the captains he served with were illiterate farmers. This alone set him apart.

12. Seymour, *Documentary Life,* xxx, xxxi. Several secondary sources claim one of the *Halifax*'s small schooners transported Nathan to the shores of the city, yet there is no official record of this. In fact, all of the diary entries supporting Nathan's trip into the city claim it was aboard Captain Quarme's *Halifax,* which seems more likely than not. Catching a spy was a major coup. To place a spy aboard a small sloop would have been a security risk.

13. Ibid.

CHAPTER EIGHTEEN: *WITHOUT CEREMONY*

1. *Confession of Captain William Cunningham, Formerly British Provost Marshal, New York City*, pamphlet (Boston: Belkap and Young, February 17, 1792). I found a copy of this document in Hezekiah Niles, *Republication of the Principles and Acts of the Revolution in America* (New York: A. S. Barnes & Co., 1876), 510–11.

2. Ibid. For a complete and comprehensive picture of prison life in New York during the period Nathan found himself imprisoned at the Beekman mansion estate, see Daniel Curry, *New-York: A Historical Sketch of the Rise and Progress of the Metropolitan City of America* (New York: Carlton & Phillips, 1853), 139–42, 187–89. Also see Danske Dandridge, *American Prisoners of the Revolution* (Charlottesville, VA: Michie Company, 1911), 33–47.

3. *Confession of Captain William Cunningham;* in Niles, *Republication*, 510–11.

4. Dandridge, *American Prisoners*, 34–36.

5. Stuart, *Life of Captain Nathan Hale*, 114.

6. "General Hull's Account of the Last Hours and Last Words of Hale," in Seymour, *Documentary Life*, 310. Also see Lossing, *Two Spies*, 20.

7. Ibid.

8. Ibid.

9. Ibid.

10. "General Hull's Account," in Seymour, *Documentary Life*, 310.

11. Ibid., xxxi.

12. Ibid., 310. Also see George Dudley Seymour, *Digressive History of Captain Nathan Hale and Major John Palsgrave Wyllys* (New Haven; CT: Privately printed 1933), 27.

13. Roosevelt, *New York*, 139. Also see Scull, G. D. et al. *Montrésor Journals* (Privately printed by the Society, 1887), 120–25.

14. Seymour, *Documentary Life*, xxxi; and Schecter, *Battle for New York*, 213.

15. Seymour, *Documentary Life*, 379.

16. Ibid. William Hull received the information about Nathan's final moments from John Montrésor, who crossed enemy lines under a white flag a few weeks later.

17. Ibid.

18. Ibid. Legend would lead us to believe that Nathan wrote three letters: one to his step-mother, a second to his brother Enoch, and a third to Alice Adams, his supposed lover (several of Nathan's biographers and even contemporary writings of the Revolutionary War, where Nathan's story is always retold, continue to feed this myth). But nothing

supports this claim. Common sense tells us that it was highly unlikely Nathan would have penned a letter to his stepmother and stepsister. It's clear he wrote to Enoch, his favorite brother, to whom he had been writing throughout the summer of 1776. The other letter, to Knowlton, was a formality, part of his duty as an officer under orders of execution. Nathan's writing to Alice Adams at the gallows is nothing more than pure romanticism ladled onto his legacy to make this final hour more dramatic.

CHAPTER NINETEEN: *SWING THE REBEL OFF*

1. Hugh McAtamney, *Cradle Days of New York* (Harvard College Library: Drew & Lewis, 1909), 190–94; and Charles Walter Brown, *Nathan Hale: The Martyr Spy, an Incident in the Revolution* (New York: J. S. Ogilvie Pub. Co., 1899), 9–10.

2. Ibid.

3. Howe, *Adventures and Achievements*, 22.

4. Lossing, *Two Spies*, 23.

5. Ibid.

6. E. E. Hale, *Tarry at Home Travels* (New York: Macmillan, 1907), 125.

7. Ibid.

8. Lossing, *Two Spies*, 24.

9. Mackenzie, *Diary* 61–62. In Mackenzie's journal we find more anecdotal evidence that Nathan wanted to make it known that he was dying under orders and not as a spy. It was his duty to die because he had been caught. Nowhere in Mackenzie's journal do we find a reference to the "I only regret . . ." quote so commonly attributed to Nathan. If Nathan had indeed said this, Mackenzie would have noted it. Furthermore, Mackenzie corroborates the often-argued place of Nathan's capture— noting that he was taken prisoner on Long Island. Mackenzie, who was simply acting as a reporter, had no reason to downplay the moment or to make things up. Reading Mackenzie's account, one gets the idea that he respected Nathan.

10. Stuart, *Life of Captain Nathan Hale*, 137.

11. The location of Nathan's grave is my own calculation based on the documents, journal and diary entries, and oral narratives I've studied. Also see Seymour, *Documentary Life*, 302.

Chapter Twenty: *A Brother's Search*

1. Enoch Hale, Diary entry, September 23, 1776 (New Haven, Yale Divinity School Library).

2. Letter, Nathan to Enoch Hale, August 20, 1776 (Connecticut Historical Society).

3. Enoch Hale, Diary entry, August 15, 1776, and September 23, 1776. The Nathan Hale quote is from a letter Nathan wrote to Enoch on August 20, 1776. Both of these sources can be found in Seymour, *Documentary Life*, 1–30.

4. Ibid.

5. Ibid.; Enoch Hale, Diary entry, August 15, 1776, and September 23, 1776.

6. Dexter, *Biographical Sketches*, 2:481; letter, Nathan to Enoch, June 3, 1776 (see second paragraph); and letter, Enoch to Nathan, May 1776 (Connecticut Historical Society).

7. Seymour, *Digressive History*, 15.

8. Enoch Hale's diary, from which much of the information in these paragraphs was derived, is rich with subtle and common, everyday detail of life at the Hale farm in Coventry during those days when rumors spread that Nathan had possibly met his fate at the hands of the British. Enoch's complete collection of diaries, along with hundreds of pages of his sermons, can be found at the Yale Divinity School Library, New Haven, CT.

9. Ibid.

10. Enoch Hale, Diary entry, September 30, 1776.

11. From the "recollections" of the Reverend Dr. Dorus Clarke, reprinted in Dexter, *Biographical Sketches*, 2:483–84.

12. Ibid.

13. Enoch Hale, Diary entry, October 2, 1776.

14. Dexter, *Biographical Sketches*, 2:483–84.

15. Enoch Hale, Diary entry, October 16, 1776.

16. Sillitto and Pagliuco, interviews.

17. Enoch Hale, Diary entries, October 14, 15, 16, 17, 18, and 19, 1776; and Seymour, *Documentary Life*, 298.

18. Enoch Hale, Diary entries, October 14, 15, 16, 17, 18, and 19, 1776.

19. Ibid.

20. Enoch Hale, Sermon, May 17, 1776 (New Haven, Yale Divinity School Library).

21. Enoch Hale, Diary entries, October 14, 15, 16, 17, 18, and 19, 1776.

22. Sydney George Fisher, *The True History of the American Revolution* (Philadelphia and London: J. B. Lippincott Co., 1902), 156.

23. Curtis, *History of the Origin*, 66.

24. Enoch Hale, Diary entries, October 14, 15, 16, 17, 18, and 19, 1776.

CHAPTER TWENTY-ONE: *GLOOMY DEJECTED HOPE*

1. Enoch Hale, Diary entries, April 17, 1776, to August 1, 1776 (New Haven, Yale Divinity School Library).

2. Enoch Hale, Diary entry, October 19, 1776.

3. Enoch Hale, Diary entries, May 9, 1776, to August 1, 1776.

4. Washington, General Orders, October 15, 1776 (Library of Congress, Manuscript Division); and Lamb, *History of the City of New York*, 2:137–42.

5. George Washington, *Letters to Washington, and Accompanying Papers* (Boston: Houghton, Mifflin, 1898), 11–12.

6. Enoch Hale, Diary entries, May 9, 1776, to October 19, 1776.

7. Enoch Hale, Diary entries, August 20, 1776, to October 21, 1776.

8. Washington, *Letters to Washington*, 11–12.

9. Ibid.

10. Washington, General Orders, October 17–21, 1776 (Library of Congress, Manuscript Division).

11. Ibid.

12. Ibid.

13. Baker, *Itinerary of General Washington*, 54.

14. Ibid.

15. Ibid.

16. Colonel Charles Webb, Orderly Book, March 1776 to December 1776 (Connecticut Historical Society).

17. Ibid., October 4, 1776.

18. Ibid.; also see Scheer and Rankin, *Rebels and Redcoats*, 193; LIHS, *Memoirs*, vol. 3: *Campaign of 1776*, 129–32; and Enoch Hale, Diary entries, October 21–23, 1776.

19. Robert Bolton, *A History of the County of Westchester from Its First Settlement to the Present Time* (New York: Alexander Gould, 1848), 370–71.

20. Enoch Hale, Diary entry, October 24, 1776.

21. Ibid.

22. LIHS, *Memoirs*, vol. 3: *Campaign of 1776*, 265.

23. Enoch Hale, Diary entry, October 24, 1776. In his diary, Enoch barely mentions, beyond their names, Joseph and Richard. He writes, "Ride to Camp to see some friends Jos. & Rich." One can only conclude that the three of them were so distraught over the rumors surrounding Nathan's possible demise, not to mention caught up in the tension of the war around them, that writing in a journal about what was said might have seemed inappropriate, especially without knowing for sure what had happened. If Enoch had heard any news from Joseph or Richard, he would certainly have noted it in his diary.

24. LIHS, *Memoirs*, vol. 3: *Campaign of 1776*, 265–67.

25. Ibid.

26. Ibid., 268.

27. Ibid.

28. Ibid.

29. Ibid.

30. Ibid.

31. Enoch Hale, Diary entries, October 25–26, 1776.

32. Cuneo, *Robert Rogers*, 270.

33. Enoch Hale, Diary entry, October 26, 1776.

34. Ibid.

35. Ibid.

CHAPTER TWENTY-TWO: *THE SEARCH ENDS*

1. Enoch Hale, Diary entry, October 26, 1776 (New Haven, Yale Divinity School Library).

2. Frank Moore, *Diary of the American Revolution* (New York: Washington Square Press, 1967), 1:328.

3. "The American Spy," *Journal of Commerce*, July 10, [1890?]; also see Moore, *Diary*, 1:328.

4. Ibid.

5. Letter, Nathan to Enoch Hale, May 30, 1776 (Connecticut Historical Society).

6. Enoch Hale, Diary entry, October 26, 1776.

7. Ibid.

8. Irving, *Life of George Washington*, 4:342.

9. Ibid.

10. Ibid.

11. Enoch Hale, Diary entry, October 26, 1776.

12. Washington, General Orders, October 26, 1776 (Library of Congress, Manuscript Division).

13. Washington, General Orders, October 28, 1776 (Library of Congress, Manuscript Division).

14. Ibid.

15. Ibid. Also Thacher, *Military Journal*, 61.

16. Ibid.

17. George Bancroft, *History of the United States of America: From the Discovery of the Continent* (New York: D. Appleton and Company, 1885), 5:72–76.

18. Ibid.

19. Ibid.

20. LIHS, *Memoirs*, vol. 3: *Campaign of 1776*, 77–81. For a more detailed account of this pivotal battle from Tallmadge's point of view, see Benjamin Tallmadge, *Memoir of Col. Benjamin Tallmadge* (New York: T. Holman, 1858).

21. Ibid.

22. Ibid.

23. Ibid.

24. Ibid.

25. Lamb, *History of the City of New York*, 2:141.

26. Ibid. 2:142.

27. Ibid, 2:73–74.

28. Ibid.

29. Enoch Hale, Diary entries, October 26–29, 1776.

30. For a reference to the grisly "custom," see Seymour, *Documentary Life*, 301–2; and I. N. Phelps Stokes, *The Iconography of Manhattan Island* (New York: Arno Press, 1967), 1025.

31. Ibid.

32. Enoch Hale, Diary entries, October 26–29, 1776.

33. Hale, *Tarry at Home Travels*, 125.

CHAPTER TWENTY-THREE: *HOME*

1. Enoch Hale, Diary entry, October 29, 1776 (New Haven, Yale Divinity School Library).

2. Seymour, *Documentary Life*, 297.

3. Washington, General Orders, October 28, 1776–January 1777 (Library of Congress, Manuscript Division).

4. Enoch Hale, Diary entry, January 25, 1777. Also Dexter, *Biographical Sketches*, 2:511.

5. Enoch Hale, Diary entry, January 25, 1777.

6. Enoch Hale, Diary entry, January 1, 1776–September 11, 1776.

7. Ibid.

8. Ibid.; also see Seymour, *Documentary Life*, 560–61.

9. Ibid.

CHAPTER TWENTY-FOUR: *PERSONAL BRAVERY*

1. "Account of Hale," *Essex Journal* (Newburyport, MA), February 13, 1777.

2. Letter, Richard Hale to Samuel Hale, March 28, 1777 (Property of the Rhode Island Historical Society).

3. Ibid. Also letter, William Hale to Cyrus Bradley, September 21, 1836 (republished in Seymour, *Documentary Life*, 344–45).

4. Letter, Samuel Hale to his wife, September 10, 1777 (republished in Seymour, *Documentary Life*, 305–6).

5. Letter, Gilbert Saltonstall to Nathan, March 10, 1776 (Beinecke Library, Yale University).

BIBLIOGRAPHY

Beyond all of the available Nathan Hale letters, in addition to letters written by immediate Hale family members and friends, here is a partial list of the documents I found most helpful during my research: books, essays, testimony (interviews), newspaper articles, speeches, and other texts. For a complete list of the Nathan Hale letters, refer to the table of contents in George Dudley Seymour's *Documentary Life of Nathan Hale, Comprising All Available Official and Private Documents Bearing on the Life of the Patriot.* The Seymour book, which is a collection of primary documents (as of 1933) connected to Nathan Hale, is an important text. (Most of the original Hale letters can be found in Hartford at the Connecticut Historical Society.) Without Seymour's book, I would have spent an additional year or more compiling all of the available documents associated with Hale's life. As it was, I spent a lot of time comparing Seymour's transcriptions of letters to the originals, I am indebted to the late Mr. Seymour for his research passion, and dedication to making Nathan Hale a national hero and the Hale home a museum.

Adams, Charles Collard. *Middletown Upper Houses.* Canaan, NH: Phoenix Publishing, 1983.

Aitken, William. *Distinguished Families in America: Descended from Wilhelmus Beekman and Jan Thomasse Van Dyke.* New York: Knickerbocker Press–G. P. Putnam's Sons, 1912.

Alden, Augustus Ephraim. *Pilgrim Alden; The Story of the Life of the First John Alden in America with the Interwoven Story of the Life and Doings of the Pilgrim Colony and Some Account of Later Aldens.* Boston: Earle, 1902.

Allyn, Charles. *Groton Heights Centennial. A Report of the Memorial Services, September 6 and 7, in New London and on Groton Heights, in Honor of Their Brave Defenders. One Hundredth Anniversary of the Attack on and Destruction of New London, the Battle of Groton Heights, and the Massacre in Fort Griswold, September 6, 1781.* New London, CT: Allyn, 1881.

Bacon, Leonard. *Sketch of the Life and Public Services of Hon. James Hillhouse of New Haven; With a Notice of His Son, Augustus Lucas Hillhouse.* New Haven, 1860.

Bakeless, John. *Turncoats, Traitors & Heroes: Espionage in the American Revolution.* New York: De Capo Press, 1998.

Baker, William Spohn. *Itinerary of General Washington from June 15, 1775, to December 23, 1783.* Lambertville, NJ: Hunterdon House, 1970.

Bancroft, George. *History of the United States of America: From the Discovery of the Continent.* New York: Appleton, 1883–1885.

Bangs, Isaac. *Journal of Lieutenant Isaac Bangs.* Edited by Edward Bangs. Cambridge, MA: John Wilson & Son, 1890.

Barnhart, David K., and Allan A. Metcalf. *America in So Many Words: Words That Have Shaped America.* Boston: Houghton Mifflin, 1997.

Bartram, F. S. *Retrographs: Comprising a History of New York City Prior to the Revolution; Biographies of George Washington, Alexander Hamilton, Nathan Hale; Sketches of John André and Beverly Robinson; Schemes of Aaron Burr and Benedict Arnold . . . Embodying More Than a Hundred Letters and*

Signatures of Famous Persons, Many of Which Have Not Previously Been Published: Including a Fac-Simile of an Original Official Map of the City of New York, Made in 1728, Representing All the Streets, Blocks, Wards, Keys and Docks Then Existing. New York: Yale Pub. Co., 1888.

Beecher, William Constantine, and Samuel Scoville. *A Biography of Rev. Henry Ward Beecher.* New York: C. L. Webster & Co., 1888.

Bellamy, D. *The Truth and Safety of the Christian Religion Deduced from Reason and Revelation. A Series of Sermons Preached at Kew and Petersham in the Years 1773 and 1774.* London: Sold by J. Deighton, 1789.

Birkenhead, Frederick Edwin Smith, and James Wylie. *International Law.* Boston: Little Brown & Co., 1911.

Bolton, Robert. *A History of the County of Westchester from Its First Settlement to the Present Time.* New York: Printed by Alexander S. Gould, 1848.

Bowers, Frank. *A History of the Order of Knights of Pythias in Indiana with the Story of Damon and Pythias.* Indianapolis: Carlon & Hollenbeck, 1885.

Brown, Charles Walter. *Nathan Hale, the Martyr Spy. An Incident of the Revolution.* (New York: J. S. Ogilvie Pub. Co., 1899).

Burr, George Lincoln. *Narratives of the Witchcraft Cases, 1648–1706.* New York: C. Scribner's Sons, 1914.

Caldwell, Mark. *New York Night: The Mystique and Its History,* New York: Scribner, 2005.

Campbell, Maria, and James Freeman Clarke. *Revolutionary Services and Civil Life of General William Hull Prepared from His Manuscripts.* New York: D. Appleton & Co., 1848.

Cates, William L. R. *A Dictionary of General Biography; With a Classified and Chronological Index of the Principal Names.* London: Longmans, 1867.

Caulkins, Frances Manwaring. *History of New London, Connecticut: From the First Survey of the Coast in 1612 to 1852.* New London CT: H. D. Uttey, 1895.

————. *History of Norwich, Connecticut: From Its Settlement in 1660 to January 1845.* Norwich: T. Robinson, 1845.

Clinton, Henry. *The American Rebellion: Sir Henry Clinton's Narrative of His Campaigns, 1775–1782, with an Appendix of Original Documents.* Yale Historical Publications 21. New Haven: Yale University Press, 1954.

Coffin, Charles. *The Lives and Services of Major General John Thomas, Colonel Thomas Knowlton, Colonel Alexander Scammel, Major General Henry Dearborn.* New York: Egbert, Hovey & King, printers, 1845.

Crowdy, Terry. *The Enemy Within: A History of Espionage.* Oxford, England: Osprey Publishing, 2006.

Cuneo, John R. *Robert Rogers of the Rangers.* New York: Oxford University Press, 1959.

Curry, Daniel. *New York: A Historical Sketch of the Rise and Progress of the Metropolitan City of America.* New York: Carlton & Phillips, 1853.

Curtis, George Ticknor. *History of the Origin, Formation, and Adoption of the Constitution of the United States: With Notices of Its Principal Framers.* New York: Harper and Bros., 1854.

Cutter, William. *The Life of Israel Putnam.* New York: Derby & Jackson, 1861 (Stanford University Library).

Dandridge, Danske. *American Prisoners of the Revolution.* Charlottesville, VA: Michie Company, printers, 1911.

Dexter, Franklin Bowditch. *Biographical Sketches of the Graduates of Yale College with Annals of the College History.* New York: H. Holt and Company, 1885–1912.

Drake, Francis Samuel. *Dictionary of American Biography Including Men of the Time; Containing Nearly Ten Thousand Notices of Persons . . . Who Have Been Remarkable, or Prominently Connected with the Arts, Sciences, Literature, Politics, or History, of the American Continent.* Boston: Houghton, Osgood & Company, 1879.

Dunham, Austin. *Reminiscences.* Hartford, CT: Case, Lockwood, & Brainard, 1914.

Dunlap, William. *History of the New Netherlands, Province of New York, and State of New York, to the Adoption of the Federal Constitution.* Burt Franklin Research and Source Works series 538. New York: B. Franklin, 1970.

Dupuy, R. Ernest, and Trevor Nevitt Dupuy. *The Compact History of the Revolutionary War.* New York: Hawthorn Books, 1963.

Felt, Joseph B. *The Annals of Salem from Its First Settlement.* Salem, MA: W. & S. B. Ives, 1827.

Fisher, Sydney George. *The True History of the American Revolution.* Philadelphia: J. B. Lippincott Co., 1902.

Flint, Martha Bockée. *Early Long Island: A Colonial Study.* New York: G. P. Putnam's Sons, 1896.

Forbes, Allen. *Towns of New England and Old England, Ireland & Scotland* (Part I). New York: G. P. Putnam's Sons, 1921.

Frothingham, Richard. *History of the Siege of Boston and of the Battles of Lexington, Concord, and Bunker Hill*. New York: Da Capo Press, 1970.

Golway, Terry. *Washington's General: Nathanael Greene and the Triumph of the American Revolution*. New York: H. Holt, 2005.

Hale, Edward Everett. *The Story of Massachusetts*. Boston: D. Lothrop Co., 1891.

———. *Tarry at Home Travels*. New York: Macmillan, 1906.

Hale, John. *Modest Inquiry into the Nature of Witchcraft*. Whitefish, MT: Kessinger Publishing, 2003.

Hall, Charles Swain. *Benjamin Tallmadge: Revolutionary Soldier and American Businessman*. New York: Columbia University Press, 1943.

Hatfield, Edwin F. *The Poets of the Church. A Series of Biographical Sketches of Hymn-Writers with Notes on Their Hymns*. New York: A. D. F. Randolph & Company, 1884.

Hinman, Royal R. *A Historical Collection from Official Records, Files, & C., of the Part Sustained by Connecticut, During the War of the Revolution: With an Appendix, Containing Important Letters, Depositions, & C., Written During the War*. Hartford: Printed by E. Gleason, 1842.

Hollister, G. H. *The History of Connecticut from the First Settlement of the Colony to the Adoption of the Present Constitution*. New Haven: Durrie and Peck, 1855.

Holloway, Charlotte Molyneux. *Nathan Hale: The Martyr-Hero of the Revolution, with a Hale Genealogy and Hale's Diary*. New York: Perkins Book Company, 1902.

Howe, Henry. *Adventures and Achievements of Americans: A Series of Narratives Illustrating Their Heroism, Self-Reliance, Genius and Enterprise.* New York: Geo. F. Tuttle, 1860.

Irving, Washington. *Life of George Washington.* Edited by Allen Guttmann and James A. Sappenfield. Boston: Twayne Publishers, 1982.

Isham, Norman Morrison, and Albert F. Brown. *Early Rhode Island Houses: An Historical and Architectural Study.* Providence, RI: Preston & Rounds, 1895.

Jenkins, Stephen. *The Story of the Bronx: From the Purchase Made by the Dutch from the Indians in 1639 to the Present Day.* New York: G. P. Putnam's Sons, 1912.

Johnston, Henry Phelps. *The Campaign of 1776 Around New York and Brooklyn.* Brooklyn, NY: Long Island Historical Society, 1878.

———. *Nathan Hale, 1776: Biography and Memorials.* New Haven: Yale University Press, 1914.

———. *Yale and Her Honor-Roll in the American Revolution, 1775–1783: Including Original Letters, Records of Service, and Biographical Sketches.* New York: Privately printed by G. P. Putnam's Sons, 1888.

Jones, Thomas, and Edward F. De Lancey. *History of New York During the Revolutionary War: Eyewitness Accounts of the American Revolution.* New York: New York Historical Society, 1879.

La Follette, Robert M., William Matthews Handy, and Charles Higgins. *The Making of America.* Chicago: Making of America Co., 1906.

La Fayette, Gilbert du Motier, marquis de, *Memoirs of General La Fayette, Embracing Details of His Public and Private Life, Sketches of the American*

Revolution, the French Revolution, the Downfall of Bonaparte, and the Restoration of the Bourbons. Hartford, CT: Barber and Robinson, 1825.

Lamb, Martha J. *History of the City of New York: Its Origin, Rise, and Progress.* New York: A. S. Barnes, 1877.

Lambert, Edward R. *History of the Colony of New Haven, Before and After the Union with Connecticut.* New Haven: Hitchcock & Stafford, 1838.

Lee, Henry, and Charles Carter Lee. *Observations on the Writings of Thomas Jefferson: With Particular Reference to the Attack They Contain on the Memory of the Late Gen. Henry Lee; in a Series of Letters.* Philadelphia: J. Dobson, 1839.

Lengel, Edward G. *General George Washington: A Military Life.* New York: Random House, 2005.

Lossing, Benson John, and Anna Seward. *The Two Spies: Nathan Hale and John André.* New York: D. Appleton and Co., 1886.

Lossing, Benson John, and Woodrow Wilson. *Harper's Encyclopedia of United States History from 458 A.D. to 1915.* New York and London: Harper Bros., 1912.

Mackenzie, Frederick. *Diary of Fredrick Mackenzie.* Cambridge, MA: Harvard University Press, 1930.

McAtamney, Hugh. *Cradle Days of New York.* New York: Drew & Lewis, 1909.

Marston, Daniel. *The American Revolution, 1774–1783.* Oxford: Osprey, 2002.

McCullough, David G. *1776.* New York: Simon & Schuster, 2005.

Meigs, Return Jonathan. *Journal of the Expedition Against Quebec.* New York: Privately printed, 1864.

Messier, Betty Brook, and Janet Sutherland Aronson. *The Roots of Coventry.* Coventry, CT: 275th Anniversary Committee, 1987.

Moore, Frank. *Diary of the American Revolution: From Newspapers and Original Documents.* New York: Washington Square Press, 1967.

Nelson, William. *William Burnet, Governor of New York and New Jersey, 1720–1728: A Sketch of His Administration in New York.* New York: 1892.

Newell, Margaret Ellen. *From Dependency to Independence: Economic Revolution in Colonial New England.* Ithaca, NY: Cornell University Press, 1998.

Newton, Caroline Clifford. *Once Upon a Time in Connecticut.* Boston: Houghton Mifflin Co., 1916.

Niles, Hezekiah. *Republication of the Principles and Acts of the Revolution in America: or, An Attempt to Collect and Preserve Some of the Speeches, Orations, & Proceedings, with Sketches and Remarks on Men and Things, and Other Fugitive or Neglected Pieces, Belonging to the Men of the Revolutionary Period in the United States.* New York: A. S. Barnes, 1876.

Underdonk, Henry. *Documents and Letters.* New York: Leavitt, Trow & Co., 1846.

———. *Revolutionary Incidents of Suffolk and Kings Counties; With an Account of the Battle of Long Island and the British Prisons and Prison-Ships at New York.* Empire State Historical Publications Series 75. Port Washington, NY: I. J. Friedman Division, Kennikat Press, 1970.

O'Hanlon-Lincoln, Ceane, *County Chronicles.* Chicova, PA: Mechling Bookbindery, 2004.

Partridge, William Ordway. *Nathan Hale, the Ideal Patriot: A Study of Character*. New York: Funk & Wagnalls, 1902.

Puls, Mark. *Samuel Adams: Father of the American Revolution*. New York: Palgrave Macmillan, 2006.

Pushies, Fred. *U.S. Army Special Forces*. St. Paul, MN: MBI Pub. Co., 2001.

Reed, William B. *Life and Correspondence of Joseph Reed: Military Secretary of Washington, at Cambridge, Adjutant-General of the Continental Army, Member of the Congress of the United States, and President of the Executive Council of the State of Pennsylvania*. Philadelphia: Lindsay and Blakiston, 1847.

Richmond, Richard. *New York and Its Institutions, 1609–1871*. New York: E. B. Treat, 1871.

Robinson, Edward. *Memoir of the Rev. William Robinson, Formerly Pastor of the Congregational Church in Southington, Ct., with Some Account of His Ancestors in This Country*. New York: John F. Trow, 1859.

Rogers, Robert, and Franklin Benjamin Hough. *Journals of Major Robert Rogers: Containing an Account of the Several Excursions He Made Under the Generals Who Commanded upon the Continent of North America During the Late War*. Albany, NY: Joel Munsell's Sons, 1883.

Rogers, Robert, and Timothy J. Todish. *The Annotated and Illustrated Journals of Major Robert Rogers*. Fleischmanns, NY: Purple Mountain Press, 2002.

Roosevelt, Theodore. *New York*. New York and London: Longmans, Green, 1891.

Root, Jean Christie. *Nathan Hale*. New York: Macmillan, 1915.

Sabine, Lorenzo. *Biographical Sketches of Loyalists of the American Revolution.* Port Washington, NY: Kennikat Press, 1966.

Schecter, Barnet. *The Battle for New York: The City at the Heart of the American Revolution.* New York: Penguin Books, 2003.

Scheer, George F., and Hugh F. Rankin. *Rebels and Redcoats: The American Revolution Through the Eyes of Those Who Fought and Lived It.* New York: Da Capo Press, 1987.

Seymour, George Dudley. *Digressive History of Captain Nathan Hale and Major John Palsgrave Wyllys.* Coventry, CT: Privately printed, 1933.

———. *Documentary Life of Nathan Hale, Comprising All Available Official and Private Documents Bearing on the Life of the Patriot, Together with an Appendix, Showing the Background of His Life.* New Haven, CT: Privately printed, 1941.

Sheldon, Henry Davidson. *Student Life and Customs.* New York: Arno Press, 1969.

Smith, George, and Sidney Lee. *The Dictionary of National Biography.* London: Oxford University Press, 1953.

Spiller, Eleanor V. *Hale's Location: The Story of Major Samuel Hale.* Glencliff, NH: E. V. Spiller, 1993.

Stark, Caleb, and John Stark. *Memoir and Official Correspondence of Gen. John Stark, with Notices of Several Other Officers of the Revolution. Also a Biography of Capt. Phine[h]as Stevens and of Col. Robert Rogers, with an Account of His Services in America During the "Seven Years' War."* Boston: Gregg Press, 1972.

Stevens, John Austin. *Progress of New York in a Century, 1776–1876. An Address Delivered Before the New York Historical Society, December 7, 1875.* New York: Printed for the society, 1876.

Stokes, I. N. Phelps. *The Iconography of Manhattan Island, 1498–1909*. New York: Arno Press, 1967.

Stuart, I. W. *Life of Jonathan Trumbull, Sen., Governor of Connecticut*. Boston: Crocker and Brewster, 1859.

Stuart, I. W., and Edward Everett Hale. *Life of Captain Nathan Hale, the Martyr-Spy of the American Revolution*. Hartford, CT: F. A. Brown, 1856.

Tallmadge, Benjamin. *Memoir of Col. Benjamin Tallmadge*. New York: T. Holman, 1858.

Thacher, James. *A Military Journal During the American Revolutionary War, from 1775 to 1883*. Boston: Cottons & Barnard, 1827.

Thomas, Daniel Lindsey. *Kentucky Superstitions*. Princeton, NJ: Princeton University Press, 1920.

Thompson, Joseph Parrish. *Memoir of David Hale, Late Editor of the Journal of Commerce, with Selections from His Miscellaneous Writings*. New York: J. Wiley, 1850.

Todd, Charles Burr. *In Olde Connecticut; Being a Record of Quaint, Curious and Romantic Happenings There in Colonial Times and Later*. New York: Grafton Press, 1906.

Tomlinson, Abraham, Lemuel Lyon, and Samuel Haws. *The Military Journals of Two Private Soldiers, 1758–1775: With Numerous Illustrative Notes* [by B. J. Lossing] *to Which Is Added a Supplement, Containing Official Papers on the Skirmishes at Lexington and Concord*. Poughkeepsie, NY: A. Tomlinson, 1855.

Tyler, Moses Coit. *The Literary History of the American Revolution*. New York: F. Ungar Pub. Co., 1957.

United States et al. *Journals of the Continental Congress, 1774–1789*. Washington, DC: U.S. Government Printing Office, 1904.

Upham, William Phineas. *A Memoir of General John Glover of Marblehead*. Salem, MA: Printed by C. W. Swasey, 1863.

Warner, Charles Dudley, and Thomas Raynesford Lounsbury. *The Complete Writings of Charles Dudley Warner*. Hartford, CT: American Pub. Co., 1904.

Washington, George, et al. *The Writings of George Washington: Being His Correspondence, Addresses, Messages, and Other Papers, Official and Private*. Boston: American Stationers' Co., John B. Russell, 1837.

Washington, George, and Worthington Chauncey Ford. *The Writings of George Washington Collected and Edited by Worthington Chauncey Ford*. New York: Putnam, 1889.

Washington, George, and Stanislaus Murray Hamilton. *Letters to Washington, and Accompanying Papers: Published by the Society of the Colonial Dames of America*. Boston: Houghton, Mifflin and Co., 1898.

Wells, William V. *The Life and Public Services of Samuel Adams: Being a Narrative of His Acts and Opinions, and of His Agency in Producing and Forwarding the American Revolution: with Extracts from His Correspondence, State Papers, and Political Essays*. Boston: Little, Brown, 1865; Freeport, NY: Books for Libraries Press, 1969.

Willis, William, ed. *Collections of the Maine Historical Society*. Vol. 1. Portland, ME: Privately printed by the society, 1904–1906.

Wilson, James Grant. *The Memorial History of the City of New York*. New York: New York History Co., 1892–93.

Wilson, James Grant, and John Fiske. *Appleton's Cyclopaedia of American Biography*. Detroit: Gale Research Co., 1968.

Wilson, Thomas. *The Biography of the Principal American Military and Naval Heroes; Comprehending Details of Their Achievements During the Revolutionary and Late Wars. Interspersed with Authentic Anecdotes Not Found in Any Other Work*. New York: J. Low, 1821.

ADDITIONAL SOURCES

Adams, Alice. Diary, November 24, 1782, and March 28, 1783. Published in George Dudley Seymour, *Documentary Life of Nathan Hale, Comprising All Available Official and Private Documents Bearing on the Life of the Patriot*. New Haven, CT: Privately printed, 1941.

American Historical Magazine and Literary Review, January 1836.

"The American Spy," *Journal of Commerce*, July 10, late 1800s.

Army and Navy Journal. Washington, DC: Army and Navy Journal Inc., 1924.

Armstrong, Reverend Robert. "Nathan Hale—a Word Portrait," speech, June 6, 1955. Connecticut Historical Society, Hartford.

Baker, Mary E. "The Past Belongs to the Living: Nathan Hale and the Making and Breaking of an American Icon," Ph.D. diss., Department of History, University of Connecticut, Richard D. Brown, adviser, January 1998.

Barnard, Henry. *The American Journal of Education* Hartford, CT: F. C. Branell, 1856–82.

———. *The Connecticut Common School Journal and Annals of Education*. Hartford, CT: Connecticut State Teachers' Association, 1854.

Boston Gazette, October 7, 1776.

Carpenter, Edward. "The History of Damon and Pythias from *De Amicitiae Vinculo* (early first century CE)," essay. Fordham University.

Clarke, Reverend Dr. Dorus. "Recollections." In the *Biographical Sketches of the Graduates of Yale College with Annals of the College History,* by Franklin Bowditch Dexter, vol. 3: May 1763–July 1778.

Cuneo, John R. Extensive Notes for Rogers of the Rangers, Containing Much Unpublished Information. (William L. Clements Library, University of Michigan at Ann Arbor: s. n., 1959).

Cunningham, Captain William. *Confession of Captain William Cunningham Formerly British Provost Marshal, New York City* (pamphlet). Boston: Belknap and Young, February 17, 1792.

The Cyclopedia of American Biography. New enlarged edition of *Appleton's Cyclopedia of American Biography*. New York: Press Association Compilers, 1915.

Disturnell, John. *The Eastern Tourist: Being a Guide Through the States of Connecticut, Rhode Island, Massachusetts, Vermont, New Hampshire, and Maine: Also, a Dash into Canada, Giving a Brief Description of Montreal, Quebec, Etc*. New York: J. Disturnell, 1848.

Essex (NH) *Journal*, February 13, 1777.

Fithian, Philip Vickers, and Hunter Dickinson Farish. *Journal & Letters of Philip Vickers Fithian, 1773–1774: A Plantation Tutor of the Old Dominion*. Williamsburg, VA: Colonial Williamsburg Inc., 1943.

Great Britain. *The Case of Great Britain as Laid Before the Tribunal of Arbitration, Convened at Geneva Under the Provisions of the Treaty between the United States of America and Her Majesty the Queen of Great Britain, Concluded at Washington, May 8, 1871*. Millwood NY: Kraus Reprint Co., 1978.

Green, Colonel Samuel. "Picture of Hale as a School-teacher." As given to I. A. Stuart in January 1847, published in *Life of Captain Nathan Hale, the Martyr-Spy of the American Revolution*. Hartford, CT: F. A. Brown, 1856.

———. Testimony. Taken in 1847 by I. W. Stuart, published in *Life of Captain Nathan Hale, the Martyr-Spy of the American Revolution*. Hartford, CT: F. A. Brown, 1856.

Hempstead, Stephen. "The Capture and Execution of Capt. Hale in 1776," letter. *Missouri Republican,* January 18, 1827.

Hull, William. "General Hull's Account of the Last Hours and Last Words of Hale." In *Documentary Life of Nathan Hale, Comprising All Available Official and Private Documents Bearing on the Life of the Patriot,* by George Dudley Seymour.

Hutson, James. "Nathan Hale Revisited: A Tory's Account of the Arrest of the First American Spy," *Library of Congress Information Bulletin.* (July–August 2003).

Independent Chronicle, May 17, 1781.

Kinkead, Eugene. "Our Local Correspondents: Still Here," *New Yorker,* June 23, 1776.

Long Island Historical Society. *Memoirs of the Long Island Historical Society.* Brooklyn: 1867–1889.

Martha J. Lamb et al. *Magazine of American History with Notes and Queries* 13 (January–June 1885).

Massachusetts Historical Society. *Collections of the Massachusetts Historical Society.* 5th series, vol. 9. Boston: The Society, 1885.

New London County Historical Society. *Records and Papers of the New London County Historical Society*. New London, CT: The Society, 1890–1912.

Pagliuco, Linda, Hale Homestead historian. Interviews by the author.

Pennsylvania Evening Post, August 20, 1776.

Public Affairs Office of the Central Intelligence Agency. "Organization of Intelligence," essay. Washington, DC: Privately printed.

Putnam's Monthly Magazine of American Literature, Science and Art 7 (January to July 1856).

Rogers, James Grafton. "Where and by Whom Was Hale Captured: An Inquiry," essay. [The essay can be found in *Documentary Life of Nathan Hale*, ed. by George Dudley Seymour reprinted by Kessinger Publishing, White fish, MT]

Saffell, William Thomas Roberts, et al. *Records of the Revolutionary War: Containing the Military and Financial Correspondence of Distinguished Officers; Names of the Officers and Privates of Regiments, Companies, and Corps, with the Dates of Their Commissions and Enlistments; General Orders of Washington, Lee, and Greene, at Germantown and Valley Forge; with a List of Distinguished Prisoners of War; the Time of Their Capture, Exchange, Etc. To Which Is Added the Half-Pay Acts of the Continental Congress; the Revolutionary Pension Laws; and a List of the Officers of the Continental Army Who Acquired the Right to Half-Pay, Commutation, and Lands*. New York: Pudney & Russell, 1858.

Scull, G. D., John Montrésor, and James Gabriel Montrésor. *The Montrésor Journals*. Collections of the New York Historical Society for the Year 1881, vol. 14. New York: Printed for the society, 1882.

Sheldon, Alicia. Testimony. In *Documentary Life of Nathan Hale, Comprising*

All Available Official and Private Documents Bearing on the Life of the Patriot, by George Dudley Seymour.

Sillitto, Lisa, Hale Homestead historian. Interviews by the author.

Sparks, Jared. *The Diplomatic Correspondence of the American Revolution: Being the Letters of Benjamin Franklin, Silas Deane, John Adams, John Jay, Arthur Lee, William Lee, Ralph Izard, Francis Dana, William Carmichael, Henry Laurens, John Laurens, M. De Lafayette, M. Dumas, and Others, Concerning the Foreign Relations of the United States During the Whole Revolution: Together with the Letters in Reply from the Secret Committee of Congress, and the Secretary of Foreign Affairs: Also, the Entire Correspondence of the French Ministers, Gerard and Luzerne, with Congress: Published Under the Direction of the President of the United States, from the Original Manuscripts in the Department of State, Conformably to a Resolution of Congress, of March 27th, 1818.* Boston: N. Hale and Gray & Bowen, 1829.

Tiffany, Consider. Unpublished diary, two pages containing the only personal account of Nathan Hale's capture. Library of Congress, Washington, DC.

Wright, Asher. "Testimony." In *Documentary Life of Nathan Hale, Comprising All Available Official and Private Documents Bearing on the Life of the Patriot*, by George Dudley Seymour.

INDEX